A
HOUSEHOLDER'S
GUIDE
TO THE
UNIVERSE

A HOUSEHOLDER'S GUIDE TO THE UNIVERSE

A CALENDAR OF BASICS FOR THE HOME AND BEYOND

BY HARRIET FASENFEST

Tin House Books

Portland, Oregon & New York, New York

Published by Tin House Books, Portland, Oregon, and New York, New York
Distributed to the trade by Publishers Group West, 1700 Fourth St., Berkeley, CA 94710, www.pgw.com

Library of Congress Cataloging-in-Publication Data

Fasenfest, Harriet.
 A householder's guide to the universe / Harriet Fasenfest. -- 1st U.S. ed.
   p. cm.
 ISBN 978-0-9825691-5-3
 1. Home economics--Anecdotes. 2. Kitchen gardens. 3. Vegetables--Preservation. 4. Fruit--Preservation. I. Title.
 TX295.F37 2010
 640--dc22
                          2010028602

First U.S. edition 2010
Printed in the U.S.A.

Illustrations on pages 69, 71, 88, 89, 101, 109, 115, 120, 121, 143, 145, 147, 148, 188, 246, 253, 265, 267, 274, 291, 301, 302, 317, 328, 335, 351, 361, 382, 384, 386 © 2010 Wyatt Lazar Reed (aka Elephant Smiley)
Interior design by Janet Parker
www.tinhouse.com

The canning yields chart on page 105 is reprinted by permission of Utah State University Extension.

The publisher is grateful for permission to reproduce excerpts of Wendell Berry's work. Copyright © 2003 by Wendell Berry from *A Continuous Harmony: Essays Cultural and Agricultural*. Reprinted by permission of Counterpoint.

The recipe on page 277 for Pickled Plums with Red Wine is from *The Joy of Pickling*, by Linda Ziedrich. © 2009. Reprinted by permission of The Harvard Common Press.

The recipe on page 383–84 for Light Old-Fashioned Fruitcake is from *The King Arthur Flour 200th Anniversary Cookbook*, copyright © 1991 by Brinna Sands. It is reprinted here with permission of the publisher, The Countryman Press/W. W. Norton & Company, Inc., www.countrymanpress.com.

To the memory of my paternal grandmother,
the Hocher (Tall) Channa.
Oh, what you could have taught me!

CONTENTS

APRIL

MAY

JUNE

JULY

AUGUST

SEPTEMBER

INTRODUCTION

Welcome to *A Householder's Guide to the Universe*. This is a how-to book, a cookbook, a getting-back-to-basics-in-the-city book. It is a book on home economics and systems analysis, physics, linguistics, and housekeeping. It is part gardening journal and part food-preservation guide. It is part protest and part celebration. It is domestic in its expression and global in its reach. It follows the seasons. It follows the soul. It follows the unfolding of a life.

If today I call myself a householder, it is with the hope that you might do the same. With all the obstacles currently facing our planet, householding has given me a way to understand—and challenge—the quagmire of contemporary society. It has turned my frustration into action and my problems into solutions. Perhaps it will do the same for you.

My idea of householding emerged over time and through a number of significant events in my life. To know what came first is difficult for me to figure out, but these events rocked the foundation of a life that had previously been aligned with business as usual. It is remarkable how these things happen, although I believe all change has its roots in discomfort. That was certainly true for me. After many years as a small-business owner on Main Street, I had grown increasingly dismayed with the way conditions were changing in line with the logic of "market forces." Small businesses, once friendly and cooperative, had begun to apply a new ethic to their efforts—a business ethic of branding, logos, market shares, identity, and roll-out plans. I had started my first business in the early 1980s, and this shift in tone annoyed me. Not that us old-timers did not care about success, but we were less savvy or self-assured about it. We were more interested in a lifestyle than a business model, and went about our work with a certain degree of innocence. Were we naive, or just stuck in an earlier time that had allowed such freedom? My sense is that it had been an easier, less competitive time, but it wasn't simply the tone of these new business models that confused me; it was the change occurring on Main Street itself.

During the years I was in business, I noticed a shift in the "colonization," if you will, of local neighbor-hoods. By 2000, communities had been gentrified, local cultures had been upended, and reasonable rents had vanished. I understood that there was nothing remark-able in such a story of displacement, but now it seemed to be happening in overdrive. My first café existed in a semi-industrial area for years without any invasion from the boutique shops. If I was fortunate enough that folks came to my shop, it was due to my efforts, not the result of colorful shopping maps distributed to tour-ists. In the span of two decades, life on Main Street was transformed from the simple domain of shopkeepers supplying the surrounding community with goods and services to the hoo-ha of street fairs and destination shopping, if only as a way to stand up to the relentless, constantly growing competition. Right on the heels of this evolving culture came the replacement of mom-and-pop stores by chains and the transformation of affordable housing stock into fancy, high-design living quarters at fancy, high-design prices. And as the pace of development changed on Main Street, the pulse and tenor of the wider world was changing, too.

In 1999, I went to a symposium sponsored by the International Forum on Globalization. Held during the larger protests against the World Trade Organization

> With all the obstacles currently facing our planet, householding has given me a way to understand— and challenge— the quagmire of contemporary society.

(WTO) conference in Seattle, this symposium introduced me to an unfamiliar world. It was a revelation of sorts. Learning about U.S. global development policies caused a fissure in the way I saw the world. Perhaps I was misguided, but I used to trust, or simply accept, the fundamentals of our economic policy. I take no pride in saying so, but for most of my adult life you could not take me for a radical girl—odd and alternative, certainly, but radical? Not so much. In fact, as the daughter of a sample tailor in a high-fashion designer salon in New York City, I'd had a clear moment of grief when the possibility of visiting a Paris salon to buy my spring, fall, or winter wardrobe faded from view. Fantasizing about the world of Paris fashion felt entirely discordant with what I was hearing at the symposium. Which is why I cannot overstate the importance of that moment. It offered me an entirely new lens through which to look at my world. Over the years that followed, I became more and more unsettled by the way in which the world of Main Street was developing, and this was due in large part to the things I was learning. By 2004 my participation in the ongoing displacement of local communities was making me more uncomfortable than I could bear, so I left the business world and started hacking up my backyard.

It was while working in my garden that I received my second revelation (though *revelation* is maybe too strong a word), in the form of a huge, old pear tree that for years had simply been a nuisance—dropping too many pears into the yard, attracting too many fruit flies. Now it was as if a pear had fallen on my head to wake me up (I call it my "Newton moment"): If food in the form of pears was a resource, an original "asset," so to speak, how had I come to take them for granted and leave them to rot? What had turned them into valueless objects? What had happened to my understanding of supply and demand, surplus, resources, stewardship, labor, value, time, and equity? I wondered how the rotting pears in my backyard were connected to the dead-earth systems of mountain-top removal, or the disheartening consequences of global trade, or the workings of agribusiness—because somewhere, somehow, each is connected in its own way to an economic logic that favors industry's worldwide systems of resource management over the values and systems of a local and natural economy. Each, in its own way, suggests that someone else should supply our needs, design our systems, steward the earth, and define the models of efficiency that govern our economy. I was still unsure of the deeper connection, but it was that unsettling moment (not some country-comfort ethic) that encouraged me to take my pears to heart.

Over the next few years I became a backyard food grower, gleaner, forager, and preserver. I began to teach others. Slowly I traded in the store-bought for the homegrown, and in the process I found myself living more in the natural world than the industrial one. As it turned out, the more I sidestepped that industrial world the happier I became, not only because of my changed shopping habits (though not having to go into grocery stores made me very happy indeed), but also as a result of my baptism into the illuminating, complex, and humbling systems of the natural world. What my hands-in-the-soil adventure provided was the no-kidding truth that it is the natural world, not market forces, that really calls the shots. Ask anyone who grows food, farms the land, watches the sky, listens to the wind, and feels the soil, and he or she will tell you what we city slickers refuse to understand: if the earth is sick, we all will be sick, and no amount of market manipulation will change that. If this foray into backyard gardening was inciting a revolution in my mind and soul, it was a mark of how far I had strayed. Born and raised in the Bronx, I was a city girl, to be sure. What did I really know of natural cycles? Not much, I can assure you. So while I am not saying we all need to get our hands in the soil, it sure helps. It helps shift our understanding

> What my hands-in-the-soil adventure provided was the no-kidding truth that it is the natural world, not market forces, that really calls the shots.

of our place and purpose in the world, which, given the circumstances, can be a big deal right about now.

According to those who research such matters, we are at a wholly new place in history. We are in an environmental and social endgame, although there are still a few hopeful scenarios for change if we act quickly. This makes the matter of getting your hands dirty in a garden a little more relevant. Still, I am not sure which came first for me—the call to action I was feeling from the world around me or the epiphanies of the soil. But taken together, they called on me to make a shift in my life from the intellectual to the pragmatic. It was in that swirl of discovery that I received my final revelation, from the guy most of us city slickers get it from—good old Mr. Wendell.

I first encountered the term "householding" in a book of essays by Wendell Berry entitled *A Continuous Harmony: Essays Cultural and Agricultural.* I was no newcomer to Wendell (please forgive the first-name usage, but we are old bedside-table friends). In fact, I think most of us have been looking to him for answers for some time. But at that moment the word *householding* resonated in a particular way. It brought together my wild and divergent thoughts, thoughts that had been percolating during my time on Main Street, in the symposiums, in my garden, under the pear tree, in my classes, and in my home. Slowly, I began to understand not only what I was reaching for, but also how I might get there—not as a singular act but as a lifestyle, not just as it related to me but as a way of challenging the system at large.

As I would learn, the concept of householding is hardly new. Though modern society has reduced its meaning to little more than property ownership, there are references to householding in the Anguttara Nikaya, a text consisting of several thousand discourses ascribed to the Buddha and his chief disciples that describes an ethic of responsibility within one's household. For the early Greeks, householding was the original meaning behind the concept of an economy. The Greek word *oikonomos*, from which our word "economy" is derived, translates literally as "one who manages a household," and is composed of the words *oikos* (household) and *nemein* (to manage). That was a remarkable discovery for me. Do true economies, original economies, exist most honestly within our land, our homes, and our households? Are we all perhaps members of an "Earth Household" and a "web of life," as suggested by Fritjof Capra, the author of *The Tao of Physics*? Is our participation in the earth household vital for any meaningful approach to ecological sustainability? Capra's position is clear: "[W]hat needs to be sustained is not competitive advantage, corporate profits, or economic growth. What needs to be sustained are the patterns of relationships in the web of life." So how have we strayed so far from that fundamental truth? What has hijacked our imagination?

I began to wonder if we had all been fooled—if we had all embraced, by choice or circumstance, some uppercase notion of an economy rooted more in large-scale global systems than the ones in our soil and our homes. Had we all been born into some wildly mismanaged system whose entrenched history had captured our minds? It sounds dramatic, I know, but it is not wholly unlikely. At times it feels as if there can be no other explanation for what we are witnessing in the world at large. Would a healthy and truly functional economic system really look like the one we have? Have we all engaged in some collective abdication of personal responsibility, and would a return to these early, scaled-down definitions of householding and resource management offer an opportunity for change? Could I, in my everyday efforts at household management—in my home, my garden, and my community—help shift the logic of modern-day global economic systems? If so, then how, exactly? Looking deeper into the most basic element of economic systems offered me a clue.

Regardless of their apparent complexity, economic systems are designed to manage the production, distribution, and consumption of resources. That's it. Quite apart from political motives, theories, and application, economics is a system of resource management. When it is designed with the noblest of intentions, an economic system concerns itself with the equitable distribution of limited resources among unlimited wants—each want being considered, each resource being respected. At the other end of the spectrum is a system designed to manage, control, hoard, and profit from limited resources to the advantage of the few over the many. So where are we along that continuum? Well, in my eyes, we're exactly where the system has designed us to be. Today's expanding income gap between the haves and the have-nots, and the dire condition of our environment, are not so much an aberration in an otherwise well-designed system, but the goal of a poorly designed system. We should not underestimate the difference.

Believing that our economy is a well-designed system allows one to hope that while mistakes are made, a well-intentioned tweak here or there can set things straight. It permits those ridiculous debates in Washington and across the United States as we try to confront global warming through market forces alone (nothing else is seen as practical). It fans the faux-distinctions between the states, as if God and libertarians would prefer the continual plundering of the world's assets for the privileged few. It takes away our capacity to envision the type of solutions we must all embrace, lest they be seen as "socialist." It causes me no end of grief when I think how willing politicians are (as representatives of the fat cats) to sell their constituency down the river, if only because they know that voters do not understand what is really being said or done in their name. I'm sorry, but I am more inclined to think of our system as having been specifically designed to be exactly what it is—an economic system designed to give the most to a chosen few. When it was founded, it may not have been with this goal in mind, and perhaps this is not the way its ordinary citizens have sought to live their lives, but the overriding reality is of such a system—a system that has met its final hour. At least, that is the starting point of this conversation.

Remember, I did not come to this position overnight, or as a result of some desire to run willy-nilly into a nostalgic world of urban gardens, backyard chickens, and stocked pantries. (Which is not to say that the householding life has no beauty and enchantment, for surely it does. Lots of it.) I simply want to locate my commitment to householding within the context of a global economic system run amok, because, if nothing else, householding defies the logic, the premise, and the status quo of that system. Householding promotes the revival of a personal system of resource management, founded on principles of equity, thrift, and stewardship. Householding attacks and reenvisions the systems that have betrayed us and replaces them with something that is reasoned and in scale with the world. Householding is in form and function the foundation for a home-based economy because it is in our homes, gardens, and communities that the work needs to be done. It is a move away from industry and the marketplace and a return to our homes and neighborhoods. It is a move away from a consumer culture and toward a culture of producers. It is a reclaiming of skills that were once common among people who lived off the land. It is a way to reimagine our lives in the city, to take much of what we love in our urban lives and rescale it in line with rural wisdom. It is a way to take back the production, distribution, and consumption of goods from industry's economic system into our own. It is a system that seeks to close the gap between the producer and the consumer, between the land, the farmer, and our table. In the most general terms, it is an effort to regain our labor, skills, trades, dignity, time, resources, home, community, culture, and reverence for the natural world.

Householding is in form and function the foundation for a home-based economy because it is in our homes, gardens, and communities that the work needs to be done.

In its most developed form, house-holding becomes a model for the world at large.

But it goes beyond that. In order to be a truly effective system, householding requires the reevaluation of needs and wants, of our stuff and our lifestyles, because bound up with our current economic model are the complicated commitments, obligations, and expectations that keep us tethered to it. Certainly we can all start in small ways, and I advocate just that, but at its heart, householding implies stepping away from the modern American lifestyle that has all but defined us. And that might well be the most difficult task before us. But in its most developed form, householding becomes a model for the world at large. It shows that we care, that we are willing, that we know better, that solutions are to be found not only in the marketplace but also in our own hands, hearts, homes, gardens, and communities.

And just when I am wondering if I am no more than a cockeyed optimist, Wendell's words return to me:

"You are tilting at windmills," I will be told. "It is a hard world, hostile to the values that you stand for. You will never enlist enough people to bring about such a change." People who talk that way are eager to despair, knowing how easy despair is. They want to give up all proper disciples and all effort, and stand like cattle in a slaughterhouse, waiting their turn. The change I am talking about appeals to me precisely because it need not wait upon "other people." Anybody who wants to can begin it in himself and in his household as soon as he is ready—by becoming answerable to at least some of his own needs, by acquiring skills and tools, by learning what his real needs are, by refusing the merely glamorous and frivolous. When a person learns to act on his best hopes he enfranchises and validates them as no government or public policy ever will. And by his action the possibility that other people will do the same is made a likelihood.

So in our own homes and then beyond, let us begin.

A YEAR

~ *of* ~

HOUSEHOLDING

JANUARY

JANUARY

The Home

Personal Inventories • Hair Shirts •
Bathrobes • Clay Ashtrays

So, here we are at the beginning of the journey: the start of a new lifestyle. It is good that January is a time for reflection, because you will need it—not only because you need to think about the skills and tasks ahead, but also because you need to reflect on the emotional and spiritual reasons why you are setting out on this path. This life will be harder before it will be easier. Swimming upstream in a system designed to promote convenience and leisure is more than an intellectual challenge. There is a reason why folks do not grow and store all their own food: industry has stripped away the logic and the need to do so. Plus, it is hard work. So be prepared: there will be times when canning tomatoes in one-hundred-degree heat will appear insane, given the siren call of modernity. That is why I suggest you start with a personal inventory, which will help you explore your reasons for taking this on. And there is no better time to do this than January, with its long-standing tradition of resolutions.

Creating a personal inventory will help keep you from abandoning your goal once you understand the reality of what's involved. I know how disjointed and out-of-kilter life can feel at times. Modernity offers many lures and distractions—trips to faraway places, the urge to move and reinvent your life, home, and career. Fast and convenient foods have grown into a huge industry, because they serve us. Forgoing these services will not be easy unless you can recognize why you need them and accept the trade-offs involved in doing without them. You must be honest with yourself, because these are the issues that will sabotage your efforts. The biggest challenges to householding are the commitments modernity requires of us and the expectations it allows us.

KNOW YOUR LEVEL OF COMMITMENT

How committed are you to getting off the teat of technology and fancy living? Now, that sounds a bit harsh, particularly as there is an endless, resounding call within our culture for all things to be faster, cooler, and more artfully designed. It is not helpful to deny the call of the hip; or at least it was not helpful for me, because I was a cool-design baby. I love fashion—or rather, I love to express my aesthetic self. It's a plain fact that silk feels better on the skin than burlap, so there is no point in denying the obvious delights of a fine meal, or clothing, or art, or whatever your aesthetic self longs for. Still, I believe we have forgotten that, at least historically, such expression has been only a small part of a life more generally defined by utility and hard work. So that, too, is a

Swimming upstream in a system designed to promote convenience and leisure is more than an intellectual challenge.

place you can start. What is your commitment to a life more defined by hard work and simplicity than by conveniences and fine fancies? I make no judgment either way; I merely caution you that if you are not honest with yourself, it will get you in the end. I'm not saying you must give it all up, but if you are to take on the work of a householding life, some conveniences will have to be traded in. So add that to your personal inventory list: what can I do without? Be realistic, because martyrs make strange bedfellows and nobody is suggesting you don a hair shirt. Just think about what it will take. And while you're at it, you might take on the mamma jamma of reality checks—namely, how you think you should stack up in the world.

FACING OFF WITH EGO

Perhaps you are a selfless soul, free of the ego that drives many of us. Me, well, I'm a little smitten with myself, so spending the majority of my days working in the garden, kitchen, or home can be a bit deflating. Yes, householding is important in a million different ways, but in the end it is a quiet and somewhat invisible life. Not to the people, soil, or universe you have taken to your heart, but it's a behind-the-scenes affair, nevertheless. Can you handle that?

There are no right or wrong positions, really—except to say that we are used to pegging our personal horizons to the world at large. Certainly there can be an honesty to that equation, but also a grueling comparison when you set your worth against the accomplishments of your peers. So be forewarned: until we grow a like-minded movement of our peers, it can get pretty lonely and freaky at times. You might find yourself asking things like, "I went to law school to make cookies?" Or something like that. I can't tell you how many people tell me they want my life, but they don't have a clue.

Through most of history, the human population has lived a rural lifestyle, dependent on agriculture and hunting for survival. In 1800, only 3 percent of the world's population lived in urban areas. By 1900, almost 14 percent were urbanites. By 1950, 30 percent of the world's population resided in urban centers and the number of cities with over one million residents had grown to 83.

SOURCE: POPULATION REFERENCE BUREAU

At times like that, I wish I had a picture to hand them of me in my bathrobe mopping up the pasture-raised chicken broth I spilled on the floor. (How did it get in the dining room?) That would slow their roll. So while I'm not saying it won't have its significant returns, I am suggesting that trading in a life out there for one in here can seem a tad more glamorous in theory than it is in practice. And that can be a major stumbling block to active householding, because much of the work required will be done in the confines of your home and garden. This brings me to another important point: before you embrace the ethic of householding, consider how you feel about being at home. To be sure, being home is a notion that has received very short shrift recently.

WHAT HOME MEANS TO YOU

Being home to make a home was not always seen as a form of internment, the way it is today. It was not always the place of second choices or no choices at all. Home, for much of our history (for both men and women), was the center of our cultural, emotional, environmental, and physical well-being. It was the engine of our home economy, the place to practice our skills and trades. Being home meant being in place, living on the land you were to care for, surrounded by the resources you needed. But the farther we have moved from the land, the more the arts and trades required to manage a home have lost their significance. If householding is an attempt to bring the wisdom and the systems of the natural world back into the urban environment, we need to reevaluate what being home means. Taking the time to consider our position will liberate us from the honest but somewhat intractable position that staying home, especially as it relates to women, is a trap, or a surefire road to gender subjugation. I will not belittle the concerns of the feminist movement (indeed, early

> If householding is an attempt to bring the wisdom and the systems of the natural world back into the urban environment, we need to reevaluate what being home means.

home economists were advocates of it), since a life of no choice is no life at all. No one, on either side of the fence, should feel obliged to live a life for which he or she is not suited. At the same time, I support unapologetically the opportunity that staying home to make a home offers—not just for women but for everyone. In fact, householding requires many hands and many skills— and, as a life, offers the means for a social, political, economic, and environmental transformation. Which is to say: home is not the place where lazy minds go to die, but rather where the active mind, heart, and soul can find their resurrection. That we can practice much of householding in our bathrobes is an added plus.

ENJOYING THE WINTER'S SILENCE

With the festivities of the harvest and holidays behind us, January is a perfect time to go deep and internal, to go underground before reemerging in spring. These are the true rhythms of a life. To sit within January's silence is to witness the natural world around us. Just as the natural world is fast and furious during the season of sowing and stowing, so is it peaceful when things lie dormant. We should follow its lead; I am quite sure our bodies would appreciate a similar cycle. Modern living requires us to accept a 24/7 existence, irrespective of our natural rhythms and seasons; I believe such non-stop motion affects our spirit and our health. Other than the greatly coveted two-week vacation (if you're lucky) and all-too-brief weekends, when do we have the time to unwind? So I cling to January. I want it to go slowly. I don't get bored shifting quietly from room to room, because it is the pleasure of the season. I enjoy the privilege because I have earned it. And as a result of this free time, it is quite possible you will discover the world of arts and crafts. Not as high art or as a specta-tor, but as a producer once more. Self-reliant societies

> To sit within January's silence is to witness the natural world around us.

have a long history of creating art during the quiet times of the year. As both embellishment and tool, such work shows off the human instinct to express oneself through art. It's funny how much collectors will pay for folk and "outsider" work when it is no different than something we might produce ourselves. So, consider this a bonus for your efforts. Get quiet and make art. Besides, who doesn't love a clay ashtray?

So that is householding at home in January: silence, self-reflection, napping, and art. It is the time to become internal, regenerative, and personal. It is a gift of the season. It is ours to enjoy. Besides, it's only a moment in time. The rest of the year's work will soon be upon us.

A 2001 study at the Chicago Medical Institute suggested that sleep deprivation may be linked to more serious diseases, such as heart disease and mental illnesses including psychosis and bipolar disorder.

SOURCE: GOES FS, ZANDI PP, MIAO K, ET AL. "MOOD INCONGRUENT PSYCHOTIC FEATURES IN BIPOLAR DISORDERS." *AMERICAN JOURNAL OF PSYCHIATRY* 164 (2007).

JANUARY

The Garden

Walking the Yard • Making Maps •
Side-Dish Gardening • Moderation

Somewhere amid all of January's resolutions, naps, and artistic endeavors, the January garden offers time to sit and imagine what it is you will be doing out there in the year ahead. Those of us already in the swing of things might lie low a little longer and continue to make our folk art; but for those of you just starting out on your journey, January is the time for imagining gardens, big or small.

The first thing I did when I put in my vegetable garden was to spend a lot of time simply imagining. I sort of knew what I wanted, but not exactly. I looked at a lot of pictures and read a lot of books, but in the end I think the best thing I did was to walk around my yard. I knew that I was completely unaware of the most basic information about the natural world. Things like: Where in my yard does the sun rise and fall? How high will the sun be in the sky in summer as opposed to spring? How will the summer leaves on that now bare tree affect the sunlight I receive in my garden later in the year? What will city animals (cats in particular) do to my nicely turned garden beds? How many strawberries does one small city lot need and are they a good use of my limited space?

Even though, despite your best efforts, you will make mistakes (you should expect to do so), the best way to begin gardening is to observe where you live. Think of your backyard as a microclimate and a region. Stand out there on a cold winter's day and notice how the winds blow. Are you set down at the bottom of a hill, surrounded by other homes? Where, in your yard, is it warmer or colder? Even a degree or two can make a difference to a garden. I plant my beets before my neighbor up and over the hill does because I am at a slightly lower elevation and in the "valley," so to speak. I also plant on the south side of the house, which is protected from the last of the late-winter chills by fences and a large, heat-reflecting house. I'm not saying you will understand this immediately, but don't think of your yard as any yard. Think of it as your little plot of land and walk it. Imagine opportunities, embrace visions, jot down observations and/or keep them all in mind when you start the next part of January's garden effort: drawing your map.

> Where in my yard does the sun rise and fall? How high will the sun be in the sky in summer as opposed to spring?

MAPPING YOUR YARD

I'm not sure why I feel it is so necessary to do this, but I do. I have drawn many, many maps and game plans for my garden. This has helped me fashion a garden that works within the limitations of the space I have and has also given me a recorded history of what I planted and when I planted it—the yield, the victories, and the defeats. Mostly, it has been a practical teaching tool, sending me back to the gardening books over and over

Continued on page 32

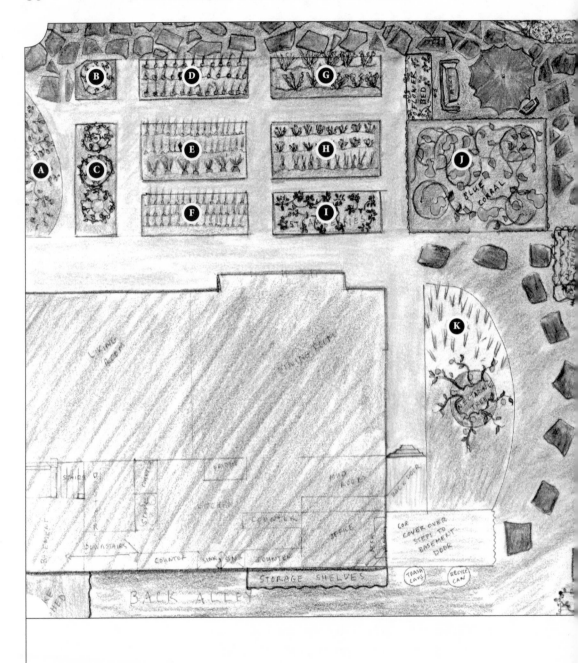

Kuddoo

My Garden in Its Second Planting *Start slow with your garden plans.*
Though today my little plot of land has been transformed into the vegetable
kingdom, it took at least five years to get there. You'll make many garden
maps to help you along your way.

For key and full chart of plantings, see pages 58–63.

to move the information from the pages of someone else's book into my own. I have also kept journals for all those things that did not fit into my map. My journal pages are the place for my revelations, my inquiries, my imaginings, and my hopes. In tandem with my journals, these maps chronicle the evolution of the person I am today. I love going back to review them. It is not such a long history, but you'd be amazed by the amount of information and writing I have crammed into them. Although, as you have probably already realized, I can get a little too thoughtful about this stuff.

Get out a large piece of paper and draw a map of your yard to scale. To do this well, you should measure out your space accurately. Of course, gardens are also magical places, so you may want to do a separate series of free-flowing drawings that offer the imaginative look and feel you long for. But do not abandon the formal and concrete, particularly in the early years. Start with walking your yard, measuring your space, and transposing it correctly onto your map. Besides the surveying of available gardening space, walking your yard allows you to consider how else the space is used. If you have a family or housemates, it is important that your household is on board for the transition, at least to some extent.

IS EVERYONE ON BOARD?

I must admit, my own family put up a fair amount of resistance to the loss of Frisbee-playing space, but they have since been won over, or maybe they've just become resigned. I did not disregard their concerns entirely, though. When plotting the garden, I left room for picnic blankets, bike paths, and the occasional, albeit convoluted, croquet course. Actually, I think it was my husband who was most annoyed. For whatever reason, he was attached to the notion of a lawn. I have come to consider this as some survival of a 1950s sensibility, with its nod to good living. Be that as it may, it is nice to have a little lounging space around the vegetable beds. I have been known to roll around on our small patch of grass with my cat, each of us preening in the late summer sun.

Drawing a map also allows you to consider seasons; what to plant in spring and what may follow it in summer. It will give you an opportunity to consider how much you can grow in the space you have and whether, considering space and seasonal requirements, you really want to grow a jack-o'-lantern pumpkin. A big, happy, carving pumpkin is a sprawling plant and will not only invade the better part of your garden but also work its way into your kitchen if you let it. So be forewarned. Know what makes sense if space is at a premium. And do your homework. I hate to tell you how many times I have overheard well-intentioned garden clerks suggest totally inappropriate vegetable starts to customers. More and more garden stores are bringing in clerks who know their stuff, but not all. Besides, who other than you knows what you will eat and what you want to grow?

Only 1 to 2 percent of all food consumed in the United States in 2009 was locally produced.

SOURCE: PETER DIZIKES, "GOOD FOOD NATION." MASSACHUSETTS INSTITUTE OF TECHNOLOGY NEWS, NOVEMBER 2009.

WHAT WILL YOUR GARDEN GROW?

After drawing out your plot, it is time to look to the seed catalogs and gardening books. Oh, the joy when the new seed catalogs start coming in. Admittedly, we gardeners are a fairly nerdy bunch. But there is so much good information in those catalogs, and so many lovely things to grow, that it makes the heart leap. Of course, by harvest time you will think (as most farmers do, backyard or otherwise) that you will never grow food again, so maddening is the season. But believe me, you will forget. Each year you will approach the season with renewed energy and a tendency to go overboard. Who can blame you?

Browsing the catalogs that come in January and February will tempt you with visions of bounty. You

There are things I always grow: Romano green beans, shelling peas, potatoes, paste tomatoes, pickling cucumbers, storage onions, garlic, and winter squash.

will be so filled with reckless enthusiasm that you will want to defy the logic and prudence beginners must employ. Let me caution you to dream big but act small. I can safely say that you could cut your seed or start order in half and you will still have more than you can handle.

GROW WHAT YOU'LL EAT

Ask yourself what sort of garden you want. I have come to call myself a side-dish gardener, or preserving gardener, because much of what I grow is destined for the root cellar, jar, or freezer, to serve me through the winter. Of course, there is always seasonal eating, but I make my choices with an emphasis toward foods that will go the distance. There are things I always grow: Romano green beans, shelling peas, potatoes, paste tomatoes, pickling cucumbers, storage onions, garlic, and winter squash. Others are seasonal favorites like spinach and lettuce, things I enjoy only fresh. There are certain crops that offer me greens throughout the winter months, like collards and kale, but the real attention is given to my preserving beauties. I will say more about them later, but I do think a lot about my preserving season when I plan my garden.

I have also, over the years, planted my fair share of berries (raspberries, strawberries, and blueberries), fruit trees (apple, pear, and nectarine), currants, grapes, and rhubarb. These perennial wonders yield so much for my pantry that I rarely go to the farmers market or farm stands. That was my intention when I planted them, but keep in mind that they will take some time to bear the quantity of fruit you may desire. Be patient and follow the rules related to their individual planting, growing, and pruning requirements. This may be challenging, since the information specific to each variety and species of fruit can be daunting. Go slow and keep that journal. Make a page for each new plant you buy and put in the information you gain over the years. Certainly, keep the name of the variety and anything else the nursery owner can tell you.

YOUR COMMUNITY NURSERY

This brings to mind an important matter. Develop a relationship with the nurseries in your community. Look for the ones that concentrate on the type of gardening that interests you. If, for example, you are mostly interested in an organic and edible landscape, then seek out nurseries that share this interest. My own neighborhood has four nurseries in close proximity to one another and each has a slightly different focus. Look for staff who are willing to answer your questions, since you will have lots of them in the beginning. But remember, even the staff can be new to the craft, so ask whoever is helping you if they are a vegetable gardener and for how long. It takes at least five years to really get up to speed, and even then you are still a near beginner. I know, I'm still there—a near beginner. I have enough knowledge not to be completely dumbfounded, but not enough to consider myself an expert in any way. Perhaps that is why I think I have something to offer. I remember how nutty it can be, trying to learn all this stuff. And that is also why I keep encouraging you to make that map and keep that journal. It will force you to put some order into your process, which you will definitely need.

Now that you've spent the month walking around your yard, jotting down your notes, drawing up your garden, poring over catalogs, and picking out your precious choices, it is time to go to the kitchen. This is where I spend most of my time in the quiet months of winter.

JANUARY

The Kitchen

Creating Your Stores • True Costs • Harvest Times •
Meet the Farmers • The Value of Home Cooking

We're all familiar with the squirrel, that frisky creature that darts about in summer and fall setting aside its nuts for the winter. It's odd to imagine it, but I have become a squirrel in some small way—putting up my harvest for winter dining. Of course, there is nothing new about this practice; our ancestors did it for centuries, if only because they had to—which makes my effort appear a little less relevant, given the easy access we have now to food of every sort. Certainly, those of the sustainable mind-set can easily shop for organic, locally grown, grass-fed, and pasture-raised foods in grocery stores and farmers markets all across the country, and this is a very good thing. Without a doubt, the availability of good food grown by good people can only be a plus. So why be a squirrel when you can shop sustainably? Well, all I can do is tell you why I do it.

Plainly, I am in awe of food, soil, and the web of life. I'm in awe of systems that respect those things, and I feel obliged to live within them. But more romantically, I am in love with picking berries on sun-filled mornings and harvesting peaches under a startling blue sky. I love meeting my walnut farmer every year in November and my blueberry farmer in July. I love the first of the spring cream and the last of the autumn quince. I love the traditions of the seasons—the apple-cider pressing and backyard fruitcake. I love taking what is growing in abundance and putting it up with the reverence that is its due. I am in awe of the sowing, growing, and stowing of my squirrel world and have taken it to heart. But more importantly, I hate grocery shopping. I can't stand pushing that cart around, going up and down grocery aisles staring at the mind-numbing array of overpackaged products on the shelves. I can't stand the scale, the marketing, or the hype. I can't stand the slap-happy jingles—the holiest, friendliest, most-sustainable-store-in-town intention of it all. The fact is, I have a dislike for grocery stores that ranges from the mild to the severe. Sorry, but that's me. I'll take putting up my own stores over their stores any day.

SHOPPING YOUR "STORES"

Now when I say "stores," I am referring to all the items I have put up—canned, cellared, frozen, or dried during the harvest—to use throughout the winter. Putting up my stores is a way to participate in the web of life. It is a way to show my support for small-scale agriculture and production loops and to sidestep all the intermediary stops food generally makes between the soil and the grocery shelves—and there are many.

We have all come to understand some of these stops as the "true cost" of food; we realize that there is a real cost to the environment, and to workers and farmers,

> I am in love with picking berries on sun-filled mornings and harvesting peaches under a startling blue sky.

The average meal in the United States travels 1,200 miles from farm to table.

SOURCE: LEOPOLD CENTER FOR SUSTAINABLE AGRICULTURE, IOWA STATE UNIVERSITY. JULY 2003

when food is shipped and processed according to traditional agri-industrial models. On its normal trajectory (and this is also true for much of the organic produce and "natural" processed foods out there), there is the trip from farm to processing plant, from processing and packaging plant to distributor, from distributor to your grocery store, and from grocery store to your home. In a global system these distances and inherent energy costs can be astounding, but even on a national level this model of food production and distribution involves using an amazing amount of fossil fuels just to get your food to the table. Those within the environmental movement are already discussing the carbon footprints of our food-distribution systems, along with the notion of food scarcity. These are all very real issues that will only become more significant over time. What better way to respond to these true costs than by redesigning your personal system of production, distribution, and consumption—by putting up your stores? It is their system or your own. Honestly, I see few ways around it.

When thinking about "stores," I realized that is how grocery stores came to have that name. That was another aha moment for me. Grocery stores do for us what we used to do for ourselves—stock provisions and provide nourishment for our family throughout the year. That the food is coming off their shelves rather than ours offers a clue into how we have structured our systems and prioritized our world. Sure, grocery stores are convenient—even indispensable for that last-minute or otherwise unavailable ingredient you might need—but in general terms they are a service born of urban America's distance from rural resources and wisdom. Were this simply a missed opportunity, a lost occasion for picking just-ripe berries in the early-morning sunlight, it would be sad but not fatal. And I suppose *fatal* is a strong word, but it is nevertheless true that many of our industrial food systems, from growing practices to delivery to consumption, are killing us and the planet. So it is no small matter to consider the alternatives and to learn the skills needed to create (and use) a fully stocked pantry.

But (and here is the real work) figuring out what to grow, pick, or buy from a farmer, in what season and in what quantity, has been an ongoing education for me. Without a doubt, preserving the harvest and using it in meals throughout the year is anything but a simple process. Sure, after time and a huge learning curve, I am figuring it out, but undoing the dumbing down of my modern consumer mind hasn't been easy. I imagine I'm not alone. In fact, I remember speaking to an otherwise brilliant young friend who admitted to a near epiphany when she realized that mashed potatoes need not come from flakes in a box. So there you have it: we have all been had. We are a culture that knows not only very little about how food grows but (most happily for industrial food producers) almost less about cooking. We have been completely stripped of its logic and importance. Who isn't able to feed him- or herself on the run, in a car, or by an office desk without doing the slightest amount of cooking? Industry has made cooking extremely easy to avoid. So be forewarned: walking into the web of life will also require walking into the kitchen.

So be forewarned: walking into the web of life will also require walking into the kitchen.

YOU'RE ONLY AS HOT AS YOUR KITCHEN

After thinking for so long that the objective of our modern lives was to get out of the kitchen, it does seem a bit ironic to write about being in it again. I think much of our negative association with being in the kitchen has to do with our disassociation from nature. Isn't it just like us to make such a fuss about contemporary victory gardens (originally, gardens planted during World War I and World War II to relieve pressure on the public food supply) without mentioning what goes along

Having a stigma about "rattling those pots and pans" is something we cannot afford anymore.

with them? Growing food or supporting local farmers during the harvest is nothing but a concept if it is severed from the work we must do in the kitchen. Having a stigma about "rattling those pots and pans" is something we cannot afford anymore. Householding suggests—even requires—a return to the kitchen not only to put up our stores, but also to cook our meals. Not just occasionally, but on a regular basis. That is where we put the bounty to good use.

I have always been a cook. I have owned and cooked in restaurants over the years, and since the earliest days of Julia Child I have been teaching myself the tricks of the trade. I know my way around a kitchen. So it was surprising to me how much I needed to learn about running a householding kitchen—not so much about technique (although food preservation required a huge amount of new knowledge), but about meal planning and its relationship to the seasons. Yes, on one level it is about squirrel consciousness, stewardship, and side-stepping industry, but it is also about the remarkable variety with which nature expresses itself, and how sun, soil, and water all play a part in what's for dinner. Over time you begin to understand why plum tomatoes are used to make sauce and slicing tomatoes are eaten fresh. Why spring's cream is preferable to winter's. Why to eat grass-fed over grain-fed beef—what breed and what forage. You will discover a love for one berry jam over another and why applesauce is king. Over time you will learn how much is needed to get you through the year, what your family and friends like to eat, and what menu planning was meant to be. You will stop clipping out recipes you will never make or cutting coupons for foods you probably should not eat. You will discover a new logic, system, and appreciation for cooking that you could in no way have anticipated. Honestly, at times it feels like holy ground. For now, I'm making the point that, taken together, these things become the miracle and joy of a householding kitchen, particularly in January, when it is time to put all your hard work and stores to good use.

JANUARY'S SLOW SIMMER

Maybe it is because I am willing to stay in a nice warm kitchen, and the notion of bread baking and a pot simmering on the back of the stove speaks of comfort the way few things can, but one thing is certain—winter is my time for invention. Putting food to good use is the fun of it all. How can I use my applesauce? What can I turn this milk into? (We'll talk about dairy fermentation later.) How do I use up all those dried herbs in innovative ways to transform stew into STEW? By cooking from your stores and using the ingredients of the region, you will discover, in a sort of anthropological way, the spirit of great regional cooking. Not as it has come down through cookbooks or as the domain of gourmands, but as it is in spirit and purpose. Without a doubt, great cooks are born of need and invention, as something plain is turned into something divine.

Throughout this book I hope to offer you some of the inspiration you'll need for your own creative cooking, but be forewarned that my recipes (if I can call them that) are neither fancy nor unique. Rather, they speak to just the sort of wisdom I am encouraging—homespun and personal, more guide than exact recipe. The recipes and systems you come up with will suit your own needs, tastes, gardens, seasons, and pantry stores, which is exactly as it should be. This is all part of a system, your system, a householding system. If I really knew all that it could be, I would tell you; but my garden, region, likes, time, and commitment are specific to my world. You will have to sort out your own.

So these are the things to do, think about, and enjoy in January's kitchen. Consider the "true costs" hanging

Ninety percent of American food is processed.

SOURCE: PETER DIZIKES, "GOOD FOOD NATION." MASSACHUSETTS INSTITUTE OF TECHNOLOGY NEWS, NOVEMBER 2009.

out in your cupboards. Reconsider your definition of efficiency. Create a system that supports it. If you've been preserving for a few years, check out your pantry. Take an inventory of your goods. Notice where the gaps are. Make a list of what to add and, finally, ultimately, get to cooking what you have. Put to good use what is humans' strongest suit, the genius of utility and invention. Enjoy the meals of your labor. And while that pot simmers on the back of the stove, take a nap. After all, it is winter.

FEBRUARY

FEBRUARY

The Home

The Family System

With so much written today about the changing face of the family, it is hard to approach the notion of a working family system without caution. What constitutes a family today, and how should it operate? Are there really any rules left? And yet, regardless of the words you use to define it, or how the concept has changed over the past fifty years, the notion of family still means something.

My idealized vision of family comes from the stories and experiences of rural farm families I have met in Oregon, whose lives are defined by the needs and cycles of the land and whose members each play a valuable role in maintaining the farm. The adage that many hands make light work must surely have found its roots on the farm. It is precisely this collectivism, this shared purpose and function, that I believe can keep us intact in the face of modernity's credo of individualism. Whether we choose to set up our households within an urban or a rural environment does not matter. Nor does it matter whether our families are biological ones, or have come together from disparate and distant places. What does matter is that we are joined in purpose and function. But do we understand what working together as a family really means? Do we know what staying in place, year in and year out, to do the chores of a household requires? Is it even in our DNA anymore?

FAMILY DISTRACTIONS

My householding effort, this late in life, is not so much an exact return to a farm family system as an effort to emulate it. To a certain extent this has happened naturally. I am only one person, and I must ask for help sometimes. I must send my kids out to do what I cannot summon up the energy to do alone. But more importantly, I must summon up the energy to confront any objections they might have, because they have many. I would like to say they have all donned their overalls happily, but that would be far from the truth. They feel they have better things to do, involving the Internet, DVDs, and video games. I am undoubtedly not alone in confronting these ridiculous distractions (for surely they are distractions). Of course, there are those among my friends who think it does not help to hammer the next generation with the impending consequences of modernity's folly; they will figure it out on their own, just as we did. Certainly, contemporary assumptions about leisure and distraction are not unlike those of my generation, in that they are born of a certain myth.

CHALLENGING THE MYTH

Maybe the next generation will not listen to the story of American privilege (in fact, they rarely do), but they might—if they are very, very lucky—discover at some moment in a garden how a breeze or a raindrop,

Maybe the next generation will … discover at some moment in a garden how a breeze or a raindrop, a harvest or a sowing, can awaken the wonders of the natural world in a deep, soul-stirring way.

a harvest or a sowing, can awaken the wonders of the natural world in a deep, soul-stirring way. And maybe, just maybe, if we stand up to their resistance long enough, they will feel, at the dinner table and in the pantry, that they are a part of something different from what they normally see around them. That is what my farm friends tell me. Parents and children alike tell me that they feel a part of something. That each one has his or her own job to do, a garden to grow, an animal to raise. I will write more about the brilliant opportunity our rural 4-H programs afford, and how we might implement them in the city, but my point here is that I have seen how this family farm system has worked in my own householding life, both as a reality and in the form of hope.

The changes in my family's lifestyle during the past five years have been both dramatic and subtle. On one level, everyone saw Mom go crazy; they watched as I went from someone who shopped like a "normal person" to one at odds with everything in a package. At times, my family had to sneak things into the house or take a stand about why they deserved whatever it was they assumed they deserved (from canned soup to disposable razors). In its extreme forms, this made everyone uncomfortable. Where the shifts were more subtle, they could go somewhat unnoticed, which everyone preferred. Yet slowly, and in time, this new life offered a tangible distinction between this year's bountiful apple harvest and the one three years before, when the apple tree was still young; between our granola and the stuff in a box; between this type of onion and another; between the applesauce from our apples and that from a neighbor's; between raspberries, marionberries, and wild blackberries, which Mom took another unexpected roadside detour to pick ("Again?"). It infused in them an understanding that we live with the seasons, and that they are expected to help accordingly, so that when Thanksgiving comes we can celebrate it within the context of the original Thanksgiving feast. Which is not to say that they have been won over completely—far from it. In fact, it is precisely because my children have been so close to going under in their lives that I fight as hard as I do. That is what I mean by hope.

MY SON/MYSELF

I had wondered when, and if, I would weave the story of my eldest son's battle with heroin addiction into this account. The more I thought about it, the more I realized there is no book without it. He was another reason for my decision to create a home that fosters the resilience of purpose a strong householding system can offer. Because what is householding other than a stab at recovery? Are we not all seeking to recover a better way to live and to untangle the odd legacy of our cultural inheritance? Yes, his story is specific, but it is also familiar in its relationship to the cultural mystique of fame and success.

THE MADNESS

I do not for one minute want to downplay the specific madness of what either he or I have been through these long years. It was a trip to hell and back. Where had he gone wrong? What part did I play? What guides one person's safe passage through life versus another's descent into the abyss? It is every parent's nightmare to be faced with questions such as these. And while I neither can nor want to list accurately the range of opinions on the matter, I do know that something particular to our modern culture was added to the mix as the idolization of popular culture reached a near-deafening pitch.

Our fascination with fame and success is not new to our culture. It is part of a long narrative and, as part of our national identity, it pits the ideals of individuation against the responsibility of the collective—staying put versus moving on, living humbly versus striking it rich. This is the story behind America's promise of manifest destiny and our immigrant hopes for opportunity, if not streets paved with gold. It is a story that suggests we can be anything we want to be if only we try hard enough. In fact, if anything has defined America, it is our capacity to redefine ourselves, to remake ourselves in the image of our own design. Flash forward a few centuries or decades, and put into a modern context, this promise of self-determination fueled a particular gusto in my son.

At first, it was his fascination with media darlings, the trumped-up idols of the time. Everything from Will Vinton's California Raisins to Mr. T, from Michael Jackson to the Notorious B.I.G. and Tupac Shakur. Each in its own way was a cultural signpost, a marker of his maturity. It would be wrong to say that I was paying attention or was aware of the threat. Some things I encouraged—the art, the music, the short stories and scripts that seemed to lean ever closer to the dark side. Was Stephen King a viable cultural spokesperson of our time or someone who had, himself, found his greatest comfort in the dark? Was the glorification of gang life and gold chains an expression of the rightful claims of an otherwise marginalized group in society, or an indicator of how low we had stooped in an effort to turn anything and anyone into fodder for record sales? Who, in the end, would make the call? Who dared? Certainly one person's sexist stereotype was another person's expression of liberation. One person's sad display of cultural self-hatred was another person's dream factory. Over and over, the heroes and heroines rose and fell on the sword of our culture's fame-making machine.

But that is the surrounding story; the immediate one is that my son could not handle what he perceived as his failure within that system. Without a doubt he wanted fame, or at least to be recognized. I do believe it drove him. So much so that by age twenty-three, with a few art installations, CDs, and a bevy of movie scripts under his belt, he let it all go to something much easier, at least in the beginning.

FREE FALL

Just at the time I stepped away from my last café and entered the world of the backyard garden, my son started his final descent. And as I filled my journals with my impressions of a global economy run amok, I thought and wrote about the world in which he was lost. I tried all the responses—anger, fear, denial, and then, ultimately, the acceptance of unconditional love. And each time I picked him up from the world of his confusion, I offered him a meal and I welcomed him into the garden. I would like to say he wanted to be there, but he didn't. When, some years later, he finally came to live with us again, he resided quite determinedly in his basement room. Slowly, I learned that I had no real power to effect change other than in my own life. If, as I believed, there was strength and truth in the cycle of the seasons and the good and constant earth, I could do no more than hold my ground. Year after year, one garden's harvest after another, one meal after another, I held my stride. And year after year, I watched him struggle—with a few stops, here and there, in the garden. He would work for money (though I suspected why), turning over the compost or transplanting this or that perennial as instructed, but never really taking much longer than was required. I would offer him a bowl of freshly picked raspberries with thick cream and hope that somewhere those flavors would revive even the faintest memory of another way of being in the world. Silly, I know, to think raspberries can stand up to the scourge of addiction, but it helped me. Year after year, worry over worry, I kept working in the garden, hoping he would eventually find his way back to an easier life.

Believe me, I have not offered all this without a reason. In fact, bits and pieces of the how, why, and when of his recovery will be sprinkled throughout this book, since it is part of my universe, after all. Moreover, I see it as a parable of our time; his journey is part of the larger one I am writing about. It is a story about finding your place in the universe. Not just the one out there, but the one in your home, your family, your community, and your world. By no small measure, my son's story (and in large part each of our stories) reflects how, when untethered from a larger familial purpose, we can become dangerously unmoored, floating precipitously from one external referent to another in search of self. Will householding hold our feet to the fire? I do not know. And while I cannot say exactly why it has happened, or how long it will last, today he seems better or, more importantly, more hopeful. Was it the garden, the support, the meals, the adherence to natural seasons, or the strength of the family system? Who knows for sure?

What I do know is that the very first thing he did when he brought his new girlfriend to *our* home was to show her *our* garden. And that's when I thought it might not simply have been conjecture on my part. That what I was witnessing was, in part, his understanding of why family matters and the recognition that he was a part of a family. That all the meals, harvests, and love had translated into a pride of sorts. And when he and his girlfriend worked together in the garden and, afterward, took me on a tour of their efforts, I was sure that somewhere along the line the logic of the family farm system had taken hold. Not as an exact emulation, but in the spirit of a shared purpose. I do not know for sure whether (or if) we quieted the relentless beast of his addiction by means of all our family gatherings and joined hands in the soil. I only know that today he is still the creative, brilliant, inventive spirit he has always been, only a little less driven by fame. Today, and on and off at other times, I think, he actually believes me when I say we have all been fooled by false gods, and that it is the health of the soil, the earnestness of our labor, and the simple and ultimate purpose of coming together as a family in an effort to bring in the harvest that makes for a good life. Of course, if someone offered him a record contract he probably wouldn't turn them down, but I think, or hope, he'd remember that self-reliant societies have a long history of creating art, not as a career, but as a personal expression; not as a life separate from the land, but one woven into it.

Perhaps you have your own story of breakdown and redemption, or of how the struggle to invite the intangible essence of the family farm into your lives shows up in the oddest of patchwork-quilt formations. We are all just getting by on hope and vapors. We know where we are going, but we don't always know how to get there. We are attempting a transformation and a recovery. That is the hope of the householder. Or, to make it personal, that is my hope, and what, in the end, keeps my nose to the grindstone—one season, one garden, one pantry, one meal, and one batch of cookies after another.

> We are all just getting by on hope and vapors. We know where we are going, but we don't always know how to get there. ... That is the hope of the householder.

The Garden

Making Your Plan • Harriet's Hit List

The ground still sleeps. Sure, you can pick the collards and kale that have withstood the winter season, or the remaining carrots, parsnips, beets, or turnips nestled in the ground. You can walk around and rightfully admire the shallots and garlic that will burst forth at the first sign of spring, like many of the brassicas you planted in late summer, but generally speaking, the true bounty is yet a dream. Honestly, I like it like that. I need the downtime. I need to sleep, to dream, even if what I am generally dreaming about is the garden and what I will plant that year.

Over the years I have developed my tried-and-true varieties, things I refer to as items for my "Side-Dish Garden." Side-dish gardening is just a way of thinking about how you cook and what you like to serve. And since I'm inclined to put up a lot of my food and create my stores—well, I want my stores to have good stuff. I certainly have my preferences, and I have learned how best to use my backyard space and how to balance what I grow with what I buy.

ONE CITY LOT

I have become convinced that you can grow a significant amount of food in a small space. I want you all to know that I garden on one city lot, house included. And in addition to making room for my vegetable garden, I have given over a large portion of my backyard to my other weakness, blooming and fragrant perennials—roses, jasmine, lavender, mint, akebia, passion flower, daphne, climbing hydrangeas, and oh, so much more. All of this on one lot, along with my teaching space, a tree house, stone-paved walkways, and a backyard kitchen.

And how did I do this? Well, just like you will. Remember my suggestion for January? Draw a map of your backyard to scale and design your space. Make some whimsical maps to develop a feel, and others more exact, so you will be sure to get what is important to you about the design. You can do this yourself. In the few years I have been working at this, I have very rarely worked with a designer. Certainly, they can help. I have occasionally asked for advice on a particular species that might be their specialty. For example, a given variety of rose or shrub will often be more suited to one particular space than another. But generally speaking, I have learned by trial and error, and so will you. That is a better approach, in any case, because then you will be the one who holds the knowledge.

Remember, you cannot simply order up this lifestyle. Sure, you can hire someone to design you an "edible garden," but it sure won't feel like something that has evolved based on your knowledge and needs. Householding is not a design concept—nor is food gardening, for that matter. That cheapens the heart of it. You must personally deconstruct your modern urban life so you can exist fully and comfortably in your new semirural world. Asking someone else to do it misses the point. But even if you do your homework, you will occasionally make mistakes.

HARRIET'S HIT LIST

Here are the things that generally show up in my garden, and notes on how I tend to preserve them, along with a list of a few things I buy.

Things I Grow

PLUM TOMATOES—Canned (diced, pureed, sauce, paste), ketchup, and dried.

GARLIC—Dried, braided, and hung in my "storage shed." I grow as much as I can.

ONIONS—Storage variety, generally Copras. As many as I can grow. I use tons over the winter. Walla Walla sweet onions, leeks, or green onions planted late in summer can be eaten fresh in winter or early spring.

HERBS—Annuals and perennials I can dry or use fresh.

SWEET SHELLING PEAS—For eating fresh and for freezing.

PICKLING CUCUMBERS—For pickles, of course.

WINTER SQUASH—Butternuts, particularly. Stores well in root cellar.

SUGAR PIE PUMPKINS—Small and sweet for making pie. Stores fairly well in root cellar.

POTATOES—Russets and new potato varieties.

CARROTS—Summer and winter varieties. For eating fresh and stored in the ground over winter.

BEETS—Mostly for eating fresh, sometimes for pickling. Beet greens eaten fresh, too.

HARDY GREENS—Sometimes for freezing but mostly for eating fresh. Kale, collards, and chard grow all winter.

BEANS—Romano variety (Italian flat green bean). For eating fresh and freezing.

PEARS—Bartlett. I have an old pear tree. I can them whole and in slices, make sauce and butter, and dry them for baking and snacking. I also make chutney.

STRAWBERRIES—Shuckson and some Benton. Enough for eating fresh, sometimes a jar or two of jam.

CURRANTS—Black and red. Enough to make syrup. We mix it with soda water for a nice drink. Also jam for eating and baking.

APPLES—Cox's Orange Pippin and Hubbardson, two young trees, just for eating fresh.

NECTARINES—For eating fresh or making fruit leather.

RASPBERRIES—Canby variety. Enough for eating fresh throughout the season and for a few jars of jam.

BLUEBERRIES—Bluecrop and one wild variety. Enough for eating fresh.

SALAD GREENS—One of the joys of summer.

RHUBARB—Victoria. Great perennial. For making pies and sauces.

SORREL—French and Devil's Tongue. Good early in the season.

RAMPS—Wild garlic. Just getting that patch going. Looking forward to eating in the spring.

GRAPES—Venus variety. For eating fresh and dried for raisins.

Things I Buy to Preserve

CORN—Shuck, parboil, and freeze off the cob. Holds up well.

PEACHES—Veterans. Canned to show up in lots of cobblers through the year.

LOGANBERRIES—Good for jam.

BLUEBERRIES—Big winner. Freeze them on trays and then bag them. Great for snacking, in smoothies, pies, muffins, pancakes.

MORE TOMATOES—If I need them.

Things I Glean or Am Given

QUINCES—I make quince liqueur, paste, and pectin.

APPLES—Sauce, sauce, sauce, and lots of dried apples.

ITALIAN PLUMS—Eaten fresh or used fresh in a lovely plum tart. Also dried.

WILD BLACKBERRIES—Be still, my perfumed heart.

FUNCTION OVER FORM

When I first started out I thought I should get a rain barrel, so I could store rainwater and reuse it in the garden. Except that here in the Pacific Northwest, it rains so much that one good downpour in winter can fill my barrel in about twenty minutes. Then it starts overflowing onto the cement right by the foundation. Get the picture? I've had to mop up more than one flooded basement. So now I have a hose attached to the rain barrel that goes out into the garden and serves as a conduit for the water. I'm not saving water as much as I am redirecting it; this keeps my basement from flooding, but does little more than that. The only way to make effective use of rain barrels is to install the five-hundred-gallon babies (and a couple of them), with an overflow hose that feeds the garden. The other option is to sink some really large tanks in the ground and use the stored water for household needs—flushing toilets, washing clothes, etc. That requires a greater commitment than I am capable of at the moment. The point is: everyone sees rain barrels and wants one without thinking it through. Had I thought about it a little, and sat out in the rain and considered actual rainfall amounts, I could have figured out that one small barrel would not provide a functional water storage system.

Another example of form over function is the current backyard chicken movement. Now, I love the sound of chickens and having fresh eggs, but chickens lay eggs for only a couple of years, so after that, unless you just want them as pets, there better be a pot in the kitchen with their name on it. So are you up for butchering? It is important that you think about it. My friend tried her hand at butchering without having a good understanding of the art, and I guess it wasn't a pretty picture. I'm glad I wasn't there. I am heartened by the latest series of classes on raising chickens—backyard butchering. We need such practicality to fend off the stench of urban farming preciousness. Recently, I heard backyard chickens referred to as the new iPod, the latest and greatest thing everyone needs to have. Our culture can quickly turn concepts into trends without considering the motives behind them. That's the reason why I go slow. Otherwise one is apt to design a life that is not in keeping with reality. Personally, I don't want to be responsible, even tangentially, for one abandoned vegetable bed when the reality of backyard farming hits home. So do the work and plan your garden yourself. And, while you do, I want you to consider perennials.

ONCE AND FOREVER

Planting perennials is an exercise in thrift and stewardship, because over time they will produce reliable supplies of food without annual seeding. They may need years to take hold, but once they do they will reward you. Then the moment comes in spring when the asparagus finally pops its head up, as do the sorrel and the chives from which you will make the first spring omelet topped with the crème fraîche you've made from the earliest spring cream. You will also discover the rhubarb bursting forth. In a few short years it has become a full and furious plant, and its stalks will be ready to pick for a pie, which you will eat beside the flowering Cameo quince bush, with its proud yet subtle coral hue. The quince's petals will fall, in a few short days, alongside the gentle white pear blossoms that spread like snow on the garden path, and you will seize this beauty in a moment both fleeting and divine, with nothing to record it but your memory and words of fancy. And that, too, is gardening in February. It grants you the opportunity to set your spirit and soul to imagining, while the natural world still sleeps. Enjoy it while you can. The season of our undoing is fast approaching.

Gardening in February... grants you the opportunity to set your spirit and soul to imagining while the natural world still sleeps.

SIDE-DISH GARDEN
A GUIDE

BED	CROP	VARIETY	APPROX. PLANTING DATE	
A	**POTATOES**	Russet Burbank	March 15	
A	**POTATOES**	Red Gold	March 15	
B	**LETTUCE**	Black Seeded Simpson	April 15	
C	**SHELLING PEAS**	Green Arrow	March 15	
D	**SPINACH**	Space	March 15	
D	**ARUGULA**	Rouquette	March 15	
E	**CARROTS**	Yaya	April – May two-week intervals	
E	**BEETS**	Early Wonder Top	April – May two-week intervals	
F	**OVERWINTERED GARLIC**	Soft Neck	Previous Fall	
G	**ONIONS**	Copra	April 1 – 15	
H	**ONIONS**	Copra	April 1 – 15	
I	**STRAWBERRIES**	Benton, Shuckson, and Tri-Star	PERENNIAL	
J	**WINTER SQUASH**	Butternut and Delicata	May 15 – June 1	
K	**CUCUMBERS**	Homemade Pickles	May – June	
L	**LETTUCE**	Crisp Mint	May – June	
M	**PEAS**	Oregon Giant	March 15	
N	**LETTUCE**	Butter Crunch	April 1 – 15	
O	**OVERWINTERED GARLIC**	← Previous Fall →		
P	**COVER CROP**	Crimson Clover	Previous Fall	

FIRST PLANTING
TO SUCCESSION

SEED OR TRANSPLANT	AMOUNT	APPROX. MATURATION DATE	APPROX. YIELD
Seed	10	September	
Seed	5	September	
Seed	Fill Bed	May 15 – June 15	12 heads
Seed	Fill Bed	June 15	5 lbs.
Seed	Half Bed	May 15	3 lbs.
Seed	Half Bed	May 15	2 lbs.
Seed	Half Bed	June – July	8 lbs.
Seed	Half Bed	June – July	8 lbs.
Cloves		June – July	7 lbs.
Transplant	Fill Bed	July – Aug.	
Transplant	Fill Bed	July – Aug.	
		June – July	5 lbs.
Seed	Hill	Aug. – Sept.	
Seed	Hill	Aug. – Sept.	7 lbs.
Transplant	Fill Bed	June 1	20 heads
Seed	Fill Bed	June 1	4 lbs.
Seed and Transplant	Fill Bed	June 1 – 15	20 heads
→		June – July	7 – 10 lbs.
Seed	Fill Bed	June 1	

SIDE-DISH GARDEN
A GUIDE

BED	CROP	VARIETY	APPROX. PLANTING DATE	
A	POTATOES	Russets		
A	POTATOES	Red Gold		
B	BEANS	Roma II	June 1	
C	TOMATOES	Amish Paste	June 1	
D	ONIONS	Copra	May	
E	CARROTS	Yaya	June – July	
E	BEETS	Detroit Red	June – July	
F	CARROTS	Yaya	July – August two week intervals	
G	CHARD	Bright Lights	August	
H	RAAB	Quarantina	August	
I	STRAWBERRIES	Benton, Shuckson, and Tri-Star	PERENNIAL	
J	WINTER SQUASH	Butternut	STILL	
K	SOFT-NECK GARLIC	Oregon Blue	September	
L	TOMATOES	Amish Paste	June 1	
M	TOMATOES	Brandywine	June 1	
N	TOMATOES	Brandywine	June 1	
O	CARROTS	Yaya	July	
P	BASIL	Genovese	June 1	

SECOND PLANTING
TO SUCCESSION

	SEED OR TRANSPLANT	AMOUNT	APPROX. MATURATION DATE	APPROX. YIELD
			September	30 lbs.
			September	15 lbs.
	Seed	Fill Bed	Sept. – Oct.	7–10 lbs.
	Transplant	Three Plants	Sept. – Oct.	30 lbs.
	Transplant	Half Bed	Aug. – Sept.	7–10 lbs.
	Seed	Half Bed	Aug. – Sept.	5 lbs.
	Seed	Half Bed	Aug. – Sept.	5 lbs.
	Seed	Fill Bed	Sept. – Oct.	10 lbs.
	Seed and Transplant	One Row Each	Oct. – Nov.	20 heads
	Seed and Transplant	One Row Each	Oct. – Nov.	3 lbs.
		PERENNIAL		
	GROWING		Sept. – Oct.	50 lbs.
	Clove	Fill Bed	Overwinter	
	Transplant	One Plant	Sept. – Oct.	10 lbs.
	Transplant	One Plant	Sept. – Oct.	10 lbs.
	Transplant	One Plant	Sept. – Oct.	10 lbs.
	Seed	Fill Bed	September	10 lbs.
	Transplant	Four Plants	Aug. – Sept.	2 lbs.

SIDE-DISH GARDEN
A GUIDE

BED	CROP	VARIETY	APPROX. PLANTING DATE	
A	SOFT-NECK GARLIC	Italian Late	September	
B	COVER CROP	Clover and Field Peas	Sept. – Oct.	
C	COVER CROP	Clover and Field Peas	Sept. – Oct.	
D	KALE	Rainbow Lacinato	September	
D	COLLARD	Cascade Glaze	September	
E	CARROTS	Yaya	Sept. – Oct.	
E	BEETS	Detroit Red	Sept. – Oct.	
F	CARROTS	Yaya	September	
G	COVER CROP	Clover and Field Peas	Sept. – Oct.	
H	COVER CROP	Clover and Field Peas	Sept. – Oct.	
I	STRAWBERRIES	Benton, Shuckson, and Tri-Star	PERENNIAL	
J	COVER CROP	Clover and Field Peas	Sept. – Oct.	
K	SOFT-NECK GARLIC	Oregon Blue	September	
L	MUSTARD	Chinese Thick Stem	September	
M	SHALLOTS	Grey French	September	
N	COVER CROP	Clover and Field Peas	Sept. – Oct.	
O	CARROTS	Yaya	Aug. – Sept.	
P	COVER CROP	Clover and Field Peas	Sept. – Oct.	

THIRD PLANTING
TO SUCCESSION

	SEED OR TRANSPLANT	AMOUNT	APPROX. MATURATION DATE	APPROX. YIELD
	Clove		Overwinter	5 lbs.
	Seed	Fill Bed	Overwinter	
	Seed	Fill Bed	Overwinter	
	Transplant	Half Bed	Overwinter	10 bunches
	Transplant	Half Bed	Overwinter	10 bunches
	Seed	Half Bed	Oct. – Nov. some will overwinter	5 lbs.
	Seed	Half Bed	Oct. – Nov. some will overwinter	5 lbs.
	Seed	Fill Bed	November some will overwinter	10 lbs.
	Seed	Fill Bed	Spring	
	Seed	Fill Bed	Spring	
		PERENNIAL		
	Seed	Fill Bed	Spring	
	Clove		Overwinter	5 – 10 lbs.
	Seed	Fill Bed	Overwinter	
	Clove	Fill Bed	Overwinter	5 – 10 lbs.
	Seed	Fill Bed	Spring	10 – 15 lbs.
	Seed	Fill bed	November some will overwinter	10 lbs.
	Seed	Fill Bed	Spring	

The Kitchen

Calculating and Creating Storage Space

Creating stores and cooking from them requires new types of storage. If you are going to put up the amount of food necessary to have serious stores for the year (or even some small portion thereof), you will need to think about creating new storage space. Most modern kitchens and small apartments do not have much space, and with the advent of heated and remodeled basements, even the cool storage areas once available in older homes are gone. Like most folks, I have a heated basement, but I have found a few dark, cool spots that work well for storing my canned foods. My guess is that anyone living in an older home that has not yet been torn apart for renovations will find those spaces as well. Remember, householding systems hark back to a not-too-distant past, and many homes will have some architectural remnants of the householding lifestyle. Happily, I have a few of those remnants, along with sufficient space for a deep chest freezer (two, actually). I suggest you walk around and think about where you will put things. In fact, February is a great time to do that, since the harvest and preserving seasons are still in the future.

CLEANING CUPBOARDS

Most of what you will design is dependent on where you live and the level of your commitment to the householding life. In the beginning, your cupboards may suit you fine. Just emptying them of the stuff you used to buy and replacing it with your own stores will go a long way toward creating the space you need. These days, I look at every packaged item in my cupboard as a personal challenge. I ask myself: What is taking up dead space, and can I replace it? I want you to open your cupboards right now and count the number of boxes of cereal and crackers and bags of pasta you've got in there. It will take some doing, but all of that can be discarded in favor of more practical—and economical—systems. Learning how to make granola, crackers, and pasta might sound daunting, but it is actually pretty easy. Cutting down the varieties of things you buy (five different cereals?) to just one or two makes a huge difference. You may feel like you are denying yourself in the beginning, but you'll get over it. You cannot usher in change if you do not make change.

> These days, I look at every packaged item in my cupboard as a personal challenge.

TAKE STOCK OF THE FRIDGE

Another great and simple source of storage space is the refrigerator. Used properly, the refrigerator holds the raw ingredients for the meals you will make during the week. Used properly, it will still have plenty of space in it to store what you add throughout the week (refrigerators are good at holding stored goods for a week or two). But here's the thing: if you don't use those stores, if you do not have a menu system, if you do not cook from the raw ingredients you buy, then your fridge will not be your storage friend. I suspect it will be a hodgepodge of accumulated items—take-out leftovers, spoiled milk, ancient and dried-up cheese, little yogurt containers (with fruit on the bottom), and lots and lots of condiments. Look inside if you dare. You will learn a whole lot about yourself by taking stock of what's in your fridge. I bet you have at least ten to twenty bottles of condiments you can get rid of. I'm not just talking about the crusty bottle of barbecue sauce, but all the other condiments you've bought for the occasional foray into exotic cuisines. One of the problems with our eating patterns today is that we eat food from all over the globe. I'm not saying other cuisines are not delicious, but stocking your pantries and fridge with the stuff it takes to cook them will, in the end, create the clusterf**k you are looking at right now.

THE SUNDAY POT ROAST

Our fascination with other cuisines is utterly divorced from the logic of regional cooking. There is only so much storage space in your fridge, and if you want to use it well, I suggest you streamline your systems. The logic of a householding kitchen is that you do more with less. It teaches you how a few basic ingredients can become everything you would ever dream of eating. This is not a value born of stewardship alone; it is the result of creating some sort of system in the kitchen that is less random and far-reaching than the way we generally eat today. This is the world of our grandparents. The world of Sunday's pot roast (stored overnight in the fridge) becoming Tuesday's sliced beef over toast with gravy or Wednesday's roast beef hash. This is the world in which Sunday's raw milk becomes Monday's yogurt, buttermilk, and crème fraîche, their reusable containers being refilled and replacing the supply from the week before. This is the world in which canned tomatoes are used in soups, stews, and sauces so they do not languish on dusty shelves. These are the systems our parents understood, and though we might not find the repetition particularly exciting, we will discover the good, simple logic of creating a menu for the week. Before you go too deeply into the system of food preservation, I would advise you to consider how well you are using what you already have. Only then should you go forward to the more advanced aspects of the craft.

THE DEEP FREEZE

It would make absolutely no sense to have a freezer full of local grass-fed beef or pork if I did not intend to cook it throughout the year, or if I did not understand how to cook in the first place. What I am touching on now is something I alluded to before. In trying to make the best use of the foods I store, I have become a better cook. I have learned which foods are appropriate for what purpose. I do not look for sauces and marinades to flavor indistinguishable cuts of meat bought from the store; I have discovered what cuts are suited to what recipes. I have learned which cuts of meats can be cured, brined, grilled, stewed, or roasted and how those things become other things. I do not rely, over and over, on anonymous packages of ground beef to make burgers or meatloaf (or Hamburger Helper, if one is completely lost). But freezers, like refrigerators, are not places to hold foods indefinitely. Knowing how to prepare foods for the freezer, and for how long they can be stored, is an important part of householding.

A 2004 study from the *American Journal of Clinical Nutrition* found that $1 could buy 1,200 calories of potato chips and 875 calories of soda, but only 250 calories of vegetables and 170 calories of fresh fruit.

SOURCE: DREWNOWSKI A, SPECTER SE. "POVERTY AND OBESITY." *AMERICAN JOURNAL OF CLINICAL NUTRITION* 79 (2004).

Freezers are not places to hold foods indefinitely. Knowing how to prepare foods for the freezer, and for how long they can be stored, is an important part of householding.

Before you turn to more sophisticated forms of food preservation, I suggest you look in your freezer. Do you have stuff left over from two years ago with a nice patina of ice crystals on it? Do you have big cartons of ice cream, pot stickers, and frozen waffles vying for space with the chicken you hope to defrost one day? Convenience foods may appeal to you, but they can be a costly and inappropriate use of your freezer. Before you run out to buy canning jars, you should try to manage your cupboards, freezers, and fridges. That should be enough work in the beginning.

For big-city dwellers, the notion of making space for an additional freezer may be simply ridiculous. I can relate; I know what New York City apartments look like. Why put a freezer in a space that would better serve as a bedroom (and it can be an either/or situation)? Those who are greatly limited for space might want to look at other systems—drying is appropriate in a limited space, for example. If you are an apartment dweller who has access to a basement storage space, you might also consider putting a freezer down there, or go in with your neighbors and buy a couple of freezers to share. Having the extra freezer space certainly helps when planning for the year. I'm confident that folks will see the wisdom of collaborating in this way, since working together will be both practical and enjoyable.

INVEST IN CONTAINERS

Another important step is to begin investing in containers that provide dry and safe storage. By virtue of my years in the restaurant industry, I have collected lots of them. I'm not always convinced I like these large "food-grade" plastic containers, but for dry foods they work well. I have them in various sizes on the shelves in my upstairs pantry, but find the half-gallon, gallon, and five-gallon containers serve me best. I generally buy twenty-five to fifty-pound bags of flour (white and wheat) for all my baking and pasta-making, and smaller quantities of what they call specialty flours—semolina, buckwheat, and the like. Since I go through the larger quantities quickly, buying in bulk makes sense. Certain flours will go rancid fairly quickly—particularly whole-grain flours—so don't buy them in large quantities until you know you will use them up quickly (within two months). Then go for it. Other grains I buy for storage include ground corn (from polenta to flour), wheat berries, brown rice, and buckwheat groats—but only in quantities I will use. And even with all my experience, I still have certain grains go to waste.

Beans, on the other hand, can easily be bought in large quantities and stored without concern for spoilage. I usually buy my supply at the end of the harvest season, in October and November. I buy them from a farmer whom I trust not to offload the previous year's harvest on me. This is something you should bear in mind: sometimes, when you buy beans on sale at the grocery store, you are actually buying last year's supply. Suppliers have to sell off last year's beans before bringing in the new ones, so they will try to entice you with a sale. The same is true for nuts and dried fruit—and, in fact, for much of what you buy in the bulk or packaged section of the grocery store. When buying bulk beans, look to see if they are shriveled or chipped. Even though they are dried, they will still get drier and older with time. Freshly dried beans will look oddly fresh. They will have a sheen to their coating and very few chips. Even if I buy them in huge quantities, I know they will generally be better than what I get at the store, and certainly no worse. And as you may already know, older beans take longer to cook. They will not be as lusciously moist and creamy as newly dried beans. Of course, nothing beats the flavor of shelling beans cooked fresh out of the pod, simmered with a clove of garlic and a little sage. A bowl of white beans, topped with a layer of good olive oil and some coarse finishing salt, can be

If you fill a six-foot-long shelf with jam, you will be set for the year, with plenty to offer as gifts.

something worth eating on its own as a meal. Beans are great for storing and, in combination with other foods (*Diet for a Small Planet*, anyone?), they create a very reliable source of protein for a small amount of money.

In addition to beans and grains, every year I buy a fifty-pound bag of walnuts. My family shells the walnuts to remove the meat, then we bag them in small quantities for the freezer. My friend just leaves hers in the shell and cracks them as she needs them, but since I do a lot of baking, I don't want to fuss with the shelling every time. Shelling them, however, leaves them vulnerable to going rancid, particularly when you buy them in quantity to last the year. That is why I freeze them; I cannot use them fast enough. Shelf storage will suffice for two to three months, but no more—it's better to store them in the fridge or freezer for the freshest flavor, or leave them in their shells in a cool storage space. Having a bowl of nuts in their shells with a nutcracker close at hand offers healthy and nutritious snacking for the family. And with so much nutrition in such a small package, nuts deserve to be eaten prudently. Throwing handfuls down your gullet isn't an option that nutcrackers support—it's too much work for so greedy a practice.

Nuts also add a lot of interest to a meal when used judiciously to garnish salads and casseroles. Many folks use them for the base of certain vegetarian dishes, like garden burgers and lentil loaves. They also make a good substitute for some flours if they are ground fine and added to a crust. In fact, nuts fulfill many dietary needs.

A PLACE FOR EVERYTHING AND EVERYTHING IN ITS PLACE

Depending on your degree of commitment, putting up your stores will, in its more advanced stages, require plenty of space. More than a large space, you will need a well-designed space for canned goods. I recommend shelving at least six feet wide and high and deep enough to hold at least two quart jars, maybe three (see illustration, below). As for the distance between shelves, think about what you like to can and in what size jar. For starters, I would suggest that at least one of the shelves be no higher than seven inches, to suit your small jars of jam and fruit butters. I rarely put my jam in anything larger than eight-ounce jars (and often in four-ounce jars, for gifts), so why put them on a tall shelf? And stacking jars is not always easy. If you fill a six-foot-long shelf with jam, you will be set for the year, with plenty to offer as gifts. For me, twelve eight-ounce jars of my husband's favorite loganberry jam, a few pint jars of strawberry preserves for the kids, a half dozen wild blackberry jams, and another half dozen eight-ounce fruit butters is enough to fill the sweet-spread stores for the year.

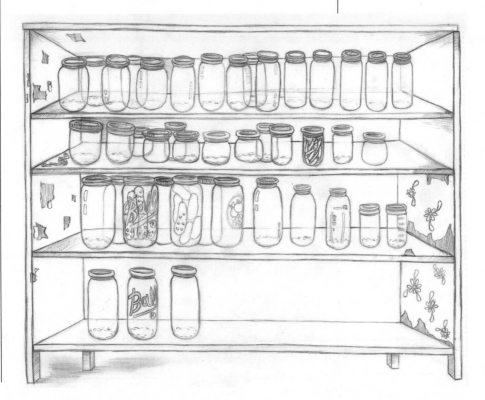

KNOW WHAT YOU WANT
AND DESIGN ACCORDINGLY

It may be a little hard to know exactly what you will need at first, but it is not impossible to figure out, particularly if you take the time to consider March's Preserving Game Plan. Designed to be a guide rather than a set of marching papers, the plan will, at the very least, give you an idea of what you are taking on. Planning, commitment, shelf building, and food-grade buckets aside, this will be hard work, and I want you to take it slow. It would be better for you to read on before deciding how large a pantry space to build. Besides, it's still February and you've got the time. Turn down the heat on the stew, cuddle up with a blanket, and do some reading. Maybe take a nap. With all the work ahead of you, I suggest you take advantage of the downtime.

MARCH

MARCH

The Home

Creating a Budget—From Kids to Boomers

I suppose I should have started this book with a chapter on budgets. It is, after all, what everyone wants to know. How will all this householding translate into the real world? But I hate budgets. Not because I am frivolous, but because I never know exactly how to do them. As commonly understood, budgets imply an equation entirely too constricted for me. They include neither the true costs involved in the production, distribution, and consumption of goods nor an honest assessment of the embodied energies found in all products. Everything created by nature, man, or machine has taken something from the natural world to come into being. Whether we call it energy or matter, all products have real resources embedded in them. Though you may not see them, they are there. All things come with a cost. Our failure to engage in an honest accounting of the true cost, along with our ridiculous criteria for justifying the transformation of one thing into another (water into soda, for example), is more than intellectually offensive to me (though it is at least that). If I do not like making budgets, it is because they cannot capture the transcendent relationship with the energy flow of the universe that I am after. They do not accurately account for the spiritual relationship with the thing (God? Energy? Tao?) that all things come from. And how exactly would one conceive of such a thing, particularly on paper? I am not trying to be obtuse or precious. I am not purposefully talking pie in the sky or, if I am, not without an honest prayer that we come up with a system of accounting a little more inclusive of the natural world—and fast. Unfortunately, all I ever hear anyone talking about is free markets and their ability to save the world. Really?

FREE-MARKET FOLLY

Though they keep working at it, free-market economists are not getting any better at factoring the worth, the wonder, and the workings of the universe into the bottom line. In fact, they are making things worse. Hopelessly tied to the party line, free-market economists claim that only the marketplace can save us. I understand that there is a deep ideological foundation to that thinking that cannot, and should not, be dismissed out of hand. At their roots, many of our founding democratic principles were attached to the individual freedoms and opportunities that free markets allowed. Which is why folks have a knee-jerk reaction when any alternative is suggested. They imagine someone is stealing their rights. Unfortunately the small-scale systems of our early democracies are gone, both economically and environmentally. We must

NATURAL CAPITAL
The term "natural capital" was first coined by E. F. Shumacher in his book *Small is Beautiful* (published in 1973). As originally defined, it suggested the need to place finite and irreplaceable resources (i.e., fossil fuels, water, minerals, etc.) into a special "natural capital" fund to be used exclusively for the production of patterns of living that do not further exploit those resources. The term has since been altered, expanded, and popularized (and corrupted) to support new systems of manufacturing and industry.

recognize the plundering and mismanagement that has taken place, and how it conflicts with our highest goals. Marching forward without concern for the effects that continued growth and an ever-expanding marketplace put on the planet and its people will be our final undoing. Such indifferent plundering should be anathema to a true democracy, lest our last remaining right become the right to despair. And while some, like today's natural capitalists, think you can save the institution of the free-market economy by tweaking the workings of nature to fit the assembly line, I don't believe that. I think nature and capitalism (the wind behind free-market ideology) have always been unhappy bedfellows, despite our tendency to link them together in a language of industry's design.

PATTERN LANGUAGE

First coined by Christopher Alexander in *A Pattern Language: Towns, Buildings, Construction*, the term "pattern language" offered the field of architecture a new, unifying way of considering the criteria of effective design. It was Alexander's position that only fully inclusive pattern languages could create fully functional and holistic designs. Though initially restricted to architecture, the concept of pattern languages has since been applied to many other fields. Not unlike linguistics, pattern languages observe how thoughts and cultural norms affect design. How, if unchallenged, those cultural norms can create a sort of self-perpetuating status quo. A case in point would be the long-standing dominance of "snout houses"—homes built with the garage in front. Once design shifted back to valuing community over cars, porches returned to the front of the home.

What does that have to do with creating a budget? It goes back to the notion of true costs, ecosystems, and the universe. It goes back to the realization that the ecosystem and the universe are sick and that this may have something to do with our pattern language. Creating a budget based on the same thoughts and cultural norms we have held on to for centuries will only keep us where we are. Continuing to objectify the elements of labor, resources, and time (in a language of industry's design), or to untether these elements from their origin in a world of self-reliance, will not get us closer to a solution. Unfortunately, when push comes to shove, this is the thinking and language we use, both for the larger economy, in a quest for market-based solutions, and for ourselves. Asking if householding pays off (which is what everyone wants to know) is part of that language. Asking if householding is worth our time is part of that language. Do we expect the web of life—and our stewardship of the same—to march to the beat of industry's standards and language? If so, there is a reason.

THE LEGACY OF ECONOMIC-SPEAK

Though we imagine our country was born from the principles of democratic freedoms, it would be better to accept its founding history as the result of explorers searching for trade routes, riches, and land on behalf of crowns and countries far away. It would be better to understand that the exploitation of humans and resources was vital to that effort and in so many ways is the foundation and legacy of our economic-speak. We can distance ourselves from this history (though it is not honest to do so) but we should, at the very least, realize how it has affected not only our planet, but also our self-perception. Generally, it is industry's language that we use to calibrate our decisions, not the language of human sovereignty and resource integrity. It is industry's language that has determined how we calculate our personal worth. What is worth our time? What pays us our worth? By what standard do we set

> Nature and capitalism (the wind behind free-market ideology) have always been unhappy bedfellows.

To live in one world and dream in another can cause only discomfort. Rebalancing our language and agenda in hopes of bringing about a better world is what we are after.

our horizons? This is not a mere theoretical point. I believe no new thinking can occur without a new language. Our failure to challenge industry's language and value systems, (both for the world at large and in our own lives), will have deep emotional and environmental consequences.

Granted, we all live in an industrial world, but we must not rely on it to save us. Continuing to do so, given the environmental and social dilemmas we are witnessing, is creating the emotional logjam in our lives. Without doubt, we are at a crossroad. We are all reading the papers, watching the news. There is a breakdown unfolding that no amount of denial will dispel. And even though, to a large extent, we are still required to live in a world defined by industry's language, we do have the ability to reclaim some of our time, labor, sovereignty, resources, hearts, minds, and spirit in, and by, the language and systems of the universe. Even though we still live by, and submit to, the linear, global, wasteful, and objectifying pattern language of industry, we can reach for that lovely circular, small-loop, cradle-to-grave pattern language of the natural world. We *must* do this, because to live in one world and dream in another can cause only discomfort. Rebalancing our language and agenda in hopes of bringing about a better world is what we are after.

Before launching into this game plan (in lieu of a strict budget), I must acknowledge that my life and family finances have provided me with privileges others do not have. I could wade into the subject of social conditions that have benefited some over others here, but suffice it to say that equity has never been uppermost on our political and economic system's agenda, for surely society would function differently if it had been. Furthermore, my generation as a whole has benefited from a cost of living that at one time worked to the advantage of the middle class. The educations we got, the homes we bought, even the jobs we found, allowed us to live a life largely without debt. Which is not to say we understood the larger backdrop to the system we were part of; we did not—or, at least, I did not. The same sort of economic thinking that stymies solutions today was also in force when I was growing up; it was just a little easier on the pocketbook back then. Yet when I say that we, the boomer generation, had economic advantages that many young people today do not, it is not with nostalgia for what we have lost but in recognition of what we unwittingly participated in and our responsibility to set things right. That, at least, is the spirit behind this game plan, and behind a householding life in the first place.

A HOUSEHOLDING BUDGET GAME PLAN

Save, and Understand, Your Nuts

Given the financial mess many of us find ourselves in today, some of the suggestions I make will seem out of reach. And some readers will simply be unwilling to do what I propose. Some of us have choices; many do not. But while income matters, values matter more, and frugality is definitely a mind-set. My husband has been a prudent saver all his life; I, on the other hand, took longer to get on board because I never really understood what money was. I used to think it was just there to buy stuff with; it was not until I saw it as a sort of stunt double for natural resources that I understood the importance of prudence.

It has been a very long time since cash was backed by tangible assets or understood as a replacement economy for natural resources, which is why I'm advocating a little reverence for its true value. At least that's how I see it, and that's why I am frugal. My husband—well, he just likes having money in the bank. Regardless of our varying motives, we've got nuts saved for the winter, which I think is important. As the saying goes, do not cast your nuts before swine unless you are making prosciutto (hmmm, I think I made that up). Save whatever you can, so you can make a deposit back into the soil we have all been recklessly withdrawing from.

Pay Off Your Mortgage If You Own Your House

My husband's habit of saving has allowed us to pay off most of our mortgage. We had the good luck not to need to refinance, and so we didn't get caught in that cycle. In fact, our reaction to that debacle was to pay off more. Paying off your mortgage will save you a very significant sum in interest, since for the first ten years of your mortgage (or longer) that is mostly what you are paying.

Refuse Debt

In addition to a reduced mortgage payment, we have no credit card debt, and no loans or car payments. We do have ancillary car and health insurance expenses, but we have not been faced with any major health expense, which, as we all know, could turn everything upside down. We have no debt because we refuse it. If we cannot afford to pay cash for something, we do not buy it. That used to be the rule of thumb for my generation's parents. I think they were on to something. Eliminating debt, or refusing it in the first place, is the surest way to get off the hook of the mainstream economic system.

Value What You Buy

My approach is to put my capital where I believe it will do the most good. Which is to say, I value what I buy, or I don't buy it. This goes for everything from socks to freezers, from seasonal produce to hair clips. I try to buy quality items and then take good care of them.

The 1:4 Housing Ratio

Back when I got my first apartment in the early 1970s, the rule of thumb was that your rent should be no more than one quarter of your income. Fiscal management was part of the social conversation. I doubt you can find anyone out there today encouraging you to be fiscally prudent (well, maybe now that the horse is out of the barn and the credit cards are maxed out). But the truth is, the financial industries pray that you never start living within your means. With 70 percent of GDP (gross domestic product) coming from the interest, fees, and penalties accrued on debt, why would they? This is probably why you never hear about that ratio anymore. So what should it be, given today's high cost of rent and mortgages? Well, just the same as it ever was. How the hell? you ask.

Here are my "back-of-the-envelope" calculations and assumptions. They may seem extreme, so I'll leave the tweaking to you. Still, I do know folks who are doing just what I suggest—living collectively, living cheap, and working together to create new householding families.

- You want your rent to be no more than one quarter of your monthly salary.
- You are working a minimum-wage job (hopefully with tips).
- You work only twenty hours a week because you are a householder and put in a lot of time inside the home.

Add those three factors together and the 1:4 ratio suggests you should pay no more than $200 per month in rent, $300 tops. If you make more, or want to work more outside the home, then you can do the math to revise that figure, but if I were a single person just starting out in the householding life, I would work no more than twenty hours a week outside the home and I'd look to pay no more than $200 per month in rent. But what can one rent for $200 per month? Good question. Here are some ideas:

Move In with the Folks (or Someone's Folks)

If you are a kid, I understand that moving back in with your folks is probably the least cool thing you can do, but then again, given a little spin, it could be about the

After thirty years of payments, a homeowner with a $240,000 mortgage (assuming a 6 percent interest and $600 for annual mortgage insurance) will have paid $536,400 over the lifetime of the loan.

coolest thing you can do. Some of that will depend on your parents—or, from your parents' perspective, on the type of kid you are. In the best of scenarios, moving in will allow you to reduce your time "out there" in the workforce, it will lower living expenses for everyone (since sharing the expenses of a household means a little less weight on each person), it will not use up any additional land or redundant resources (utilities, furniture, etc.), and it will allow for time to work on a basic householding operation for the family home. If your family is interested in starting a garden, then start one. If they are interested in increasing the family stores, then work to that end. Generally speaking, young backs are stronger than older ones, so, as I know from personal experience, they are appreciated.

From a parental perspective, if you don't see your children as adults, don't invite them back in. If you are set in your ways and not interested in householding, don't invite them back in. This will be an odd learning curve, so it is very important to understand why you are doing it (back to the personal inventory again). And set action plans, so you can all evaluate whether you are truly incorporating the systems you are interested in. If you are charging some rent or establishing a work-trade situation, then be clear and specific. My own experience is that it works well half the time, so don't expect perfection.

Live Collectively

For those interested in living collectively outside the family home, I guess the same basics apply. Know what sort of household you want and what sort of tasks it takes to maintain it and work together.

Move to a Cheap Town

If I were younger, I would move to a town that is not on everyone's list of places to go. We have so many young "cultural creatives" in Portland, Oregon, where I live, that it has produced an unemployment dilemma.

Not only are there fewer jobs, but living in a place that everyone else wants to live in translates to a high cost of living. If you are serious about being a householder, you might try moving somewhere cheap.

Stop Buying Stuff

Goes without saying.

College? Maybe Not

With so much of everyone's income going to pay off college loans (or just the interest that has accrued on them), I find it hard to imagine a solution for those on the treadmill of repayment. I can't see how it pencils out. With tuition costs now so ridiculously high, you've got to wonder if it makes sense to go to college at all.

I know what the statistics show. I have read the figures. A college education can give you an extra $25,000 a year in wages over someone with just a high school diploma. But I don't know how reliable those figures are, since I know lots of college graduates working in the service industry and living off tips. So take those statistics with a grain of salt. And given that most college students come out with debt well in excess of $30,000 before interest (and, as with a home mortgage, interest will be much of what you will paying in the beginning), it is hard to know if the trade-off is worth it.

Besides, the real point is this: what sort of work really needs to be done in our world today? I often tell my younger son that I'm sending him to pig-farming school—not just because the tuition will cost less, but because he might learn a skill he can actually use. The only thing I can think to do is to stop the madness before it starts. Admittedly, I'm coming at this from my old codger perspective, but I don't think going to college—or rather, going into such deep debt to do so—makes sense anymore. Perhaps learning a trade makes more sense, and helps with those tasks required within a householding community. I tell you what, just

Studies show that the average cost of a four-year university has increased by 76 percent since 2000.

SOURCE: *THE MIDDLE CLASS SQUEEZE.* A REPORT PREPARED BY THE UNITED STATES HOUSE OF REPRESENTATIVES COMMITTEE ON GOVERNMENT REFORM – MINORITY STAFF SPECIAL INVESTIGATIONS DIVISION, SEPTEMBER 2006, FOR DEMOCRATIC LEADER NANCY PELOSI AND REP. HENRY A. WAXMAN.

write me and I'll send you a couple of blue books so you can feel like you're in college but for a whole lot cheaper. Besides, I'll grade on a curve.

Grow Food, Preserve, and Cook

On the matter of food, well, you know what I think. Grow food and put up your stores. The costs to do that will vary from year to year and will continually diminish the longer you are at it. Like all things, there are start-up costs involved that, depending on your particular goals and design expectations, can amount to very little or be way over the top. My own initial investment was something like $5,000 over the first three years—but that involved putting in hardscaping (raised beds, trellis, arbors, stone path, garden house, and backyard kitchen) along with the trees, shrubs, herbs, perennials, canes, and vines that are dotted throughout the yard. Now that the beds are in place, my expenses come in the form of an occasional vegetable start, seed packet, or amendment. I spend anywhere from $20 (for seeds) to $300 per year depending on what I do, grow, construct, or repair. Sometimes, when I want to add a full load of soil amendment or need a major pruning operation, it can run higher, but really, once you have an established garden, costs can be very reasonable—particularly when you consider how much it would cost to replace all you grow by buying at a farmers market.

Keeping track of all the produce I grow and comparing to the cost of buying it at the farmers market, I figure I generally save well over $3,000. And that's not counting the "value added" calculations. By turning my backyard berries into jam and my apples into applesauce (to give just a couple of examples), I can save another $1,500 over what it would cost to buy all those items at the grocery store.

In addition to what I either grow or put up, I spend a fair amount on other raw ingredients to use throughout the year—dairy, meat, and the produce I do not grow.

> But one thing is for sure—none of this would make sense if I was not willing to turn all of what I buy in bulk or farmer-direct into the millions of other things we use as a family.

But one thing is for sure—none of this would make sense if I was not willing to turn all of what I buy in bulk or farmer-direct into the millions of other things we use as a family. Besides the grown and processed food I make, I cook most of our meals at home.

Here is a list of what I buy over the year along with the cost of each item.

BUDGET:

$1,300	raw milk
240	organic eggs
1,258	244-lb. half steer (paid $6.75 per pound, cut and wrapped, including kill fee)
999	234-lb. pig ($760 pig + $103 butchering+ $45 kill fee + $91 curing)
400	chickens
75	ocean-caught albacore tuna (for canning)
300	produce or fruit I do not grow
100	honey
200	olive oil from a friend who imports it
500	flours, grains, sugar, leavening agents
2,000	miscellaneous (special meals, dry goods, and sundries)
500	paper goods, toiletries, cleaning products
200	seeds, starts, and miscellaneous canning needs

$8,072   TOTAL FOOD AND MISCELLANEOUS HOUSEHOLD COSTS

Rounding up, that works out to $673 per month on food and other miscellaneous household goods, or $169 per week. That seems pretty good. It could certainly be less. Cutting out raw milk, for example, would shave a lot from my budget.

Money spent on food away from home increased about seventeen-fold in the United States from 1960 to 2005.

SOURCE: PETER DIZIKES, "GOOD FOOD NATION." MASSACHUSETTS INSTITUTE OF TECHNOLOGY NEWS, NOVEMBER 2009.

MARCH

The Garden

On Sowing the Seeds of Potatoes, Peas, and Prudence

I'm not exactly sure why one gets so impatient in March, but it seems to be the case. We hopeless gardeners get almost breathless as the planting season approaches, even though we were slaphappy from work just a few short months ago. Fall can be the final showdown, a race against the frost to put up the last of the harvest and put the garden beds to rest. It is true, I think, that one lets out a huge sigh of relief when the last of the tomato plants have been cut down and composted and the cages stored for winter, and when the canning pot is set back on the top shelf. We are ever so proud and content when our tools have been cleaned and oiled (if we are good) and the winter beds mulched against the freeze. In fact, it is fall, with its firestorm of obligations, that makes the winter months so sweet. But, like I said, we seem to forget all that very quickly and long to start the madness again. And that is most true in March, when we challenge the hand of fate.

I have a friend who keeps a good eye on the weather and knows, in general terms, what to expect of March. He advises that doing in March what might well be done in April is nothing more than folly, since most everything you plant (and I am speaking of early spring varieties) will do little until the soil has warmed up. Just because you plant early does not mean you will get a head start on others who have been patient. In fact, planting too early can be a problem, given how wet and cold the season is. But there you have it. Every year I push the envelope and ignore all sense. Of course, some things need to be started in advance—indeed, they require that you get on the stick. I am speaking of sowing seeds indoors, which is a right and proper thing to do in March.

STARTING INDOORS

It is good counsel to plant seeds indoors if you love tomatoes. I mention tomatoes specifically because they are one of the few vegetables I do start indoors. That is not the case with more serious vegetable gardeners, and maybe I will change my ways in time. But I have streamlined my operation because I do not really have that much space for starts. I also do not have a greenhouse. Not a very large one, at least, and what space it offers is taken up by my tomatoes. Actually, it is a rare tribute to prudence on my part, because I am still amazed by how much work just those tomatoes require. I know I will increase my efforts over time, but for now those babies keep me busy.

When starting tomato seeds indoors, it is a good idea to use tweezers to place the seeds where they need to be in a starter tray filled with moist planting medium (a mix a bit lighter than soil). I plant them about a quarter-inch deep, covering them with a little extra planting medium if need be. I always overdo the amount I sow,

We hopeless gardeners get almost breathless as the planting season approaches, even though we were slaphappy from work just a few short months ago.

STARTING FROM SEEDS

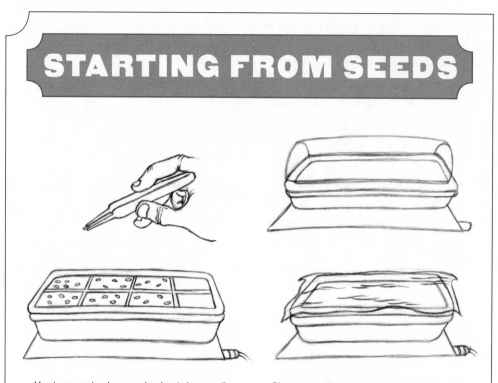

Use tweezers to place seeds, about six per cell, a quarter-inch deep.

Place tray on heating pad set on low. Cover tray with layer of moist paper towel followed by plastic wrap or lid to keep darkness and moisture in.

and invariably every one of those tiny seeds germinates. I tend to plant six or more seeds in each cell of the tray and place the container in a warm spot to allow the seeds to sprout, preferably on a heating pad set on low (there are some made specifically for plant starts). I cover the tray with a little paper towel to keep them wet and in the dark, and I place the accompanying lid or some plastic wrap over it all to keep in the moisture. Generally, it will take no more than a week for them to sprout, but be patient. The main thing to worry about is that they don't dry out, but neither should they be too wet. Setting the tray (or you can use small individual pots if you like) in a shallow pan that has water in it will allow the plants to drink up water as they need it. But leave them in the pan for only a day; that should suffice.

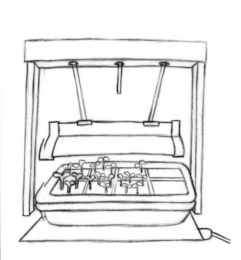

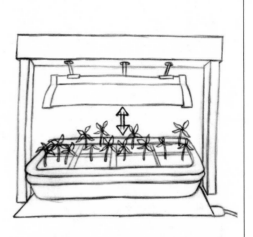

Once sprouts appear, place tray under grow light.

Set grow light about an inch above the plants to prevent the seedlings from reaching too high for light and getting too leggy.

Once plants have at least two sets of leaves and are about two to three inches tall, they are ready to begin transplanting.

Transplant the strongest ones into individual pots and let them take root. Keep the grow light only an inch above the plants as they grow. Once the plants are about twelve inches tall and are bushy, with thick stems, you can move them into a greenhouse during the day to get them used to outdoor light and temperatures.

TOMATO TALK

Along with breeding for traits that are beneficial, like disease resistance, commercial food producers focus on traits that are generally more important for growing large scale, harvesting at one time, and transporting long distances to processing plants and distribution houses, such as skin thickness, consistent maturity, delayed ripening, etc. Taste and nutritional value are secondary.

SOURCE: MIKE DUNTON. WWW.VICTORYSEEDS.COM

More than that, and the soil can get waterlogged and vulnerable to mold and fungus gnats. I give the tray a feel every other day to make sure the planting medium is moist; if it's not, I simply sprinkle on a little water as it drops off my fingertips or from the spray of a water bottle. You can generally tell by the water vapor that collects on the inside of the lid or plastic wrap whether the soil is moist or not. If, as has happened to me, you notice a little white bloom (mold) forming on the planting medium, remove the plastic wrap so it can dry out a bit. This sounds far more complicated than it is. Sprouting seeds is actually quite easy.

Once the sprouts are up, I put the starter tray beneath a grow light set about an inch above them, so the seedlings do not need to reach too high for the light. Otherwise, they will become leggy and have very thin stems. This often happens to plants set on a window ledge—the leaves search for the sun and stretch to find as much light as possible. That is not what you want for your starts. You want them to develop a good, sturdy root structure and stem, and enjoy nice, gradual growth. Setting the lights no more than an inch or two above the little seedlings will produce that result. Once the plants have at least two sets of leaves (I know you may not understand what that means, but watch them—you will) and are about two to three inches tall, I transplant the strongest ones into individual pots and let them take root and start growing a bit more, raising the grow light to the appropriate height (always an inch or two above the plants). Then I let them grow for another month or so. Now, and only if I feel it is necessary, I will transplant them again (by now it is about April). If I do, once again I will wait until the plants have set good roots. At this point, they have grown to about a foot tall, their stems have thickened nicely, and, if I have set the lights properly, they are bushy. Only then do I start moving them into my greenhouse during the day to get them used to outdoor light and temperatures.

THE GREENHOUSE

During these early days, I shield the starts from the heat of the sun by placing a screen in front of them (daylight is actually a lot more powerful than the grow light). And I bring them back into the house at night, because evening temperatures are still a little cold for them and I doubt they have completely adapted to outdoor conditions. So back and forth they go, like little chicks protected from the weather. Soon I let them hang out in the greenhouse without the screens, but I keep a watchful eye on them. I do not want their leaves to burn from the sunlight. By early May, I start letting them sit outside on the raised beds they will eventually be transplanted into. At night they go back into the greenhouse. That seems like a lot of work, but actually it requires attention more than it does work. Since this is my only real commitment to starts, I don't mind. Tomatoes are one of the real power players in my garden, so I am happy to offer them my time.

But lest you consider me a sloth in the starts department, let me explain that I am not a single-variety tomato gal. I like a couple of different varieties, so I order or buy the seeds I am looking for and feel confident (and sometimes a tad smug) that I have the particular variety I am after. And on the subject of garden smugness, maybe it is just me, but we gardeners do seem to make everything into a competition. The more we do this, the prouder we seem to get with our cleverness and the more we like to tell others things like, "Oh, I got my starts in weeeeeeks ago," or some such silliness. I think we can't help ourselves. Folks like to brag when in reality they're almost as clueless as you. And I am still clueless. Well, maybe not entirely, but a great gardener I am not. I am certainly a committed and willing-to-learn householder, but nothing more. So keep that in mind. Do only what makes sense for you. For me, that means nothing more than tomatoes. But boy oh boy, do they keep me busy.

A first-time gardener should have some success with a couple of tomato plants (you can buy them already started, but do not—I repeat, do not—buy starts until the end of May or early June, even though those same stores will tempt you beforehand). And I definitely suggest getting a variety that is suited for your area. In the Pacific Northwest that might mean varieties that ripen early, because we don't have a very long growing season, not in comparison to the Southwest, for example. Try growing a cherry tomato plant because they are easy to grow and you will feel proud of yourself. Besides the tomatoes I have started inside, there are plenty of seeds I sow directly into the ground in March. Unlike my heat-loving tomato seeds, they can germinate in the yard.

OTHER SPRING SOWINGS

In March you may try your hand at sowing chard, kale, spinach, lettuce, and radishes from seed, since all of them are suited to the cool temperatures. Don't be enticed by the cool-weather starts you see in the nursery. Though there is nothing really wrong with buying them as starts, all of them do well from seed, so why not save the money?

YOU'VE MADE YOUR BED, NOW PLANT IN IT

There are two types of garden beds you can choose from: raised or mounded. A raised bed is one you build with a frame and fill with soil. A mounded bed is generally free-form and without a frame. Since the soil in a raised bed is elevated a bit off the ground, it is generally warmer and can be planted earlier than a mounded bed. At least, that is the theory. For a new gardener, I think raised beds are easier, or simply a little neater. If you build them in early spring, you can start planting as soon as they are done—or at least when the directions on the back of your seed packets suggest. My own garden has a combination of both raised and mounded beds, and I do tend to plant early in the raised ones.

To build raised beds, make a frame out of nontoxic wood about one foot high and four or eight feet long by four feet wide (you can also decide on alternate sizes) and plop it down on the grass. Then layer the grass within the framed space with about fifteen to twenty sheets of newspaper. Water the newsprint down, put about three to four inches of good store-bought compost inside the frame, and top it with organic garden soil filled with amendments to get the ball rolling. I put my seeds or starts in that and call it good. At least, that is what I did in the beginning. These days, I rarely buy soil anymore, but you will probably need to when you're first starting.

PEAS AND POTATOES

In the early days of March, I am watching to see if the rain has stopped long enough for the soil to dry out a little, particularly if I am starting with established garden beds, raised or mounded. When conditions seem right, I charge outside to plant my potatoes and shelling peas. There is a little guide I follow: pick up a handful of dirt and squeeze it; if it falls apart nicely when you drop it on the ground, it is probably a fine time to plant the first of your pea and potato seeds. If the soil remains a lump of clay shaped like the fist you wrapped around it, it's probably too soon.

Generally, I plant a couple of varieties of potatoes—early-season new potatoes and russets. Russets are a later variety and great for winter storage. New potatoes are smaller and thin-skinned, suited for summer salads. Though potatoes will grow throughout the

Pick up a handful of dirt and squeeze it; if it falls apart nicely when you drop it on the ground, it is probably a fine time to plant the first of your pea and potato seeds.

SPRING TONIC

I would like to take a moment to discuss the wonder of the spring tonic. Generally speaking, self-reliant rural societies ate from their stores during most of the winter. By early spring they had long run out of fresh greens and were gnawing the last of the dry parsnips and jerky. So when the first dandelions, nettles, and plantains appeared, it was chow time. Not only are they fresh greens to eat, they are also rich in nutrients. The plants that come on early offer a rejuvenating tonic following winter's nutritional drought. That logic made most sense when we were really living from our stores, but spring tonic is still a gift of which we should partake. The fact that we can eat whatever we want all year round does not automatically mean we are healthier as a result. All of us can benefit from these spring plants. I collect young dandelion leaves in early spring and eat them in salads or sauté them with garlic and olive oil. I do the same with nettles, although I am careful when picking them (stinging nettles are called that for a reason) and will only eat them cooked. I have a friend who

has a patch and if I catch it in time there are plenty for the picking. But they have a short season. Just be sure that these wild greens are being grown somewhere that is not toxic, since dandelions in particular pull all the crap out of the soil. Eating wild greens from less than pristine environments is not a great idea (no parking strips for me). Thankfully, however, if you are trying your hand at backyard gardening you will have more than enough dandelions on hand—chances are, more than you can eat. Should that be the case, you can dry them for tea and treat yourself to a fine brew in the winter. I dry leaves for winter teas throughout the season.

summer season to be harvested in the fall, peas need to be sown in March so they can produce their fruit before the sun is too hot. In fact, peas will not be happy growing past June, so don't wait till late April or early May to plant them. Get your seeds in the ground as soon as the soil can be worked. And despite what you see in the nurseries, peas do not like to be transplanted; they are one of the crops that want to be started from seed in the ground. I cannot tell you how often I have seen gardening stores selling pea-plant starts as late as early June. Darn if that doesn't make me mad.

REFERENCE MATERIAL

To help you through all of this information, I advise you to get one or two really reliable guides to gardening. I have my favorites, the ones that simply give me instructions to follow related to my particular region. I like Steve Solomon's *Gardening West of the Cascades*, because I live west of the Cascades. Not that his book doesn't have lots of general information for other regions, but I like the added perspective. I also adore *The Maritime Northwest Guide*, produced by Seattle Tilth and available in most bookstores. It is a month-by-month guide to year-round organic gardening, and if you have anything like that in your region (not all Tilth chapters create publications), I would refer to it. Even if you don't, the Maritime guide will be awfully helpful.

Still, I tend to ignore lots of stuff. It's not because it's not helpful, it's just that my brain can process only so much information at one time. Gardening—really good organic gardening—requires a lifetime of trial and effort. It also requires a lifetime of accumulating knowledge that cannot, no way no how, be reduced to a year, or even five years, for a beginner. That is good news, though. It should relieve you from assuming that you should understand everything quickly and easily.

Gardening—really good organic gardening—requires a lifetime of trial and effort. It also requires a lifetime of accumulating knowledge that cannot, no way no how, be reduced to a year, or even five years, for a beginner.

As I mentioned in the chapter on the January garden, it was extremely helpful for me to make a chart and garden map but only because it was a way for me to streamline the information I was reading into a more tangible context. Goodness knows, a person can get cross-eyed with terms and concepts such as nitrogen, phosphorus, and potassium (NPK) requirements for soil and plants; till versus no-till methods; companion planting; beneficial insects and their evil twins, the plant-eaters; raised or mounded beds; germination dates; sowing dates; succession gardening; compost piles (hot or cold?); worm beds; green manure; crop rotation; fall planting; winter gardening; row covers; and more. Honestly, it's enough to make your head explode. Of course, I think you will love the experience over time, but take it slow, read up a bit, draw a little map, and match your vision to your skills.

MARCH

The Kitchen

The Preserving Game Plan • County Extension •
The Gleaner's Ethic

With the garden still muddy for the most part, March is the time to think about your Preserving Game Plan. It took me three years before I developed any reliable sense of the harvest seasons. Having been born and raised in the Bronx, what did I know about peach season or berry season? Returning to a true understanding of your local harvest takes time and some scheduling.

I used to plan vacations around the same time tomatoes were ripening. Silly me, putting all that effort into growing tomatoes and then being gone when they became ripe. I had to beg my kids to pick them, and I can tell you the results were not the best. These days, I do not plan vacations during the harvest season, because there is no way to predict when it will start or how long it will last. There will be no penciling in the harvest. You might be able to estimate a two-week window of possible ripeness, but that's it.

Making a game plan allows you to think more deeply about what you want to do with the harvest. Not just theoretically—"I think I want to make jam"—but specifically—"I want to make strawberry jam with Hood strawberries and they will ripen anywhere from early to late June." If you are new to the particulars of the harvest, I strongly suggest you make a plan. I have supplied a few charts to support you in that effort. The Preserving Game Plan will assist you in considering the variety of produce you are after (if you are that specific at this stage), as well as providing a system for calculating the amount you should put up to see you through the year. The Canning Yields will help you decide how much produce you will need either to buy or grow in order to fill your pantries (heads up: the amount will astound you). Much of the information contained in these charts came from the county extension office closest to my home. My, if I don't love those folks.

HISTORY OF EXTENSION

The Morrill Act of 1862 established land-grant universities to educate citizens in agriculture, home economics, mechanical arts, and other practical professions. Extension programs were formalized in 1914 with the Smith-Lever Act.

SOURCE: THE NATIONAL INSTITUTE OF FOOD AND AGRICULTURE

LOCAL SERVICES

Look to your local county extension agency for tons of information about varieties, locations, and dates of maturation for anything related to farm produce. I am lucky enough to live in a state that has quite a few active offices, if not one immediately in my own county. In the early days of extension, participation in classes and services required residency in the county, but that is no longer the case. Today, they welcome participation from all over the state, but you might have to travel a bit. The diminishing number of extension offices is a result of funding problems, and because they stopped filling a need. Once city life and its modern shopping systems took hold, few people were interested in the kinds of skills that extension provides. But that is changing. When my county extension office stopped offering food-preservation programs, my friend Marge Braker and I started teaching those skills, because interest was mounting and there was nowhere to go to learn these methods. That was back in 2002, before renewed interest in food preservation had fully developed. Today there are lots of classes around, but few of them have the same type of funding as the original extension programs, which generally translates into higher fees for students. My hope is that extensions (funded by the county, state, and federal government) will renew their programs because, without a doubt, they are staffed by some of the most dedicated employees and volunteers I have ever met, who collectively hold a body of knowledge that is vital to this householding movement.

THE FOOD-PRESERVATION MANTRA

There is a saying in the food-preservation world: Quality In, Quality Out. In other words, you get what you start with. Most products will not magically taste better once you preserve them. I like to pick the best of the season and put it up rather simply, letting the just-ripe and perfect flavor of the ingredient come through. Over the years I have discovered that other than the fancy jams or condiments I can't help but make, I like single-variety products. I know I like Bluecrop blueberries and Veteran peaches. I like San Marzano tomatoes but I also know they ripen later in the season and the weather in the Pacific Northwest will not always provide enough of the sunny, hot days they need. So variety is important but not crucial to me.

All years will not be the same; in fact, they will rarely be the same. Some years I may simply go crazy for raspberries because the growing conditions are perfect—their flavor is prime and the quantity is great. Such conditions lead to a bumper crop, and when that happens I seize the day. Even though you may prefer strawberries for jam, it may not have been their year.

There is a saying in the food-preservation world: Quality In, Quality Out.

On the other hand, if a farmer to whom you are loyal has a bad season, support him anyway. Take those mottled berries and make the best of them. You will probably get a reasonable price since he, too, knows all years are not the same. So for those vendors and farmers you are building relationships with, stay true to the cycle and the effort. They will appreciate it, and you will feel good about yourself. Add to that point the matter of gleaning the otherwise unappreciated fruit from city fruit trees and bushes, and you get my last bit of bleeding heart advice.

THE GLEANER'S ETHIC

Free is a very good price and not letting food go to waste is vitally important. These days, most cities have organizations that harvest fruit from trees on city property or neglected residential lots. If your city does not offer such a program, you can just check out your neighborhood to see if there are any unattended fruit trees. Those old trees may not always offer the best quality fruit, but they are, nonetheless, producing. If the neighborhood fruit trees appear unattended, check with the property owner to see if he or she minds you gleaning from them. And remember to employ the gleaner's ethic, which means, don't pick the tree bare. Leave some for others.

Here, then, is a quick recap of my preserving game plan:

EARLY SUMMER (June/July)—Make strawberry jam (I make 12 8-oz. jars)

EARLY SUMMER (July)—Pick and freeze blueberries (I pick and freeze at least 20 pounds)

MIDSUMMER (late July/Aug.)—Pick and can peaches (About 12 quarts—36 pounds)

Continued on page 104

Over 11 percent of Oregonians experience food insecurity or fear of hunger each year, and many more cannot afford fresh produce, which is vital to a healthy diet. In 2009, Portland Fruit Tree Project harvested over 14,000 pounds of fruit that would have otherwise gone to waste, putting fresh organic produce on the table for over 1,200 families in need. There are organizations throughout the country similarly serving communities in need.

SOURCE: THE FRUIT TREE PROJECT. WWW.PORTLANDFRUIT.ORG

EVEN A GOOD THING CAN BE BAD

I'm not sure exactly when I entered the nerd-of-the-month club, but when it comes to Veteran peaches, I have good company. You can see us on a foggy summer's morning waiting in line for the orchard gates to open. We are the insiders, the ones who have called religiously for weeks to see when the peaches will be ripe. We are the ones who are on the contact list, who have had the presence of mind to put a reminder on the calendar. It hasn't happened yet, but in a pinch, I bet I could scalp my Veteran peaches to the unfortunate person who missed the season. "Yo, you there, you looking for something? Yeah, that's right, I got what you want." And so the deal will go down on a dusty country road with just a few peach pits left to mark the spot of the transaction.

Veteran peaches are notorious for bruising easily, and they go downhill in a matter of days, which is why the loyal followers show up with all sorts of batting material in which to wrap the precious fruit. But good golly, they are sweet and juicy when you get them at just the right moment and in the right year, and they are a favorite for us food preservers, who like to freeze and can them for eating and baking throughout the year. Missing a Veteran peach season means I will have to wait a whole extra year to recover, and it breaks my heart. But on the flip side, there are those who rush out for something they won't end up using. They might think they want twelve quarts of canned Veteran peaches, but, in reality, their family does not like canned peaches. Believe me, it happens. Putting your limited time into an ill-conceived effort won't make you happy in the end.

PRESERVING

RAW INGREDIENT	GROW, BUY, GLEAN	HOW PRESERVED	VARIETY-IF PARTICULAR	WHEN RIPE	SERVING SIZE	
APPLES/PEARS						
APPLESAUCE						
BERRIES (ALL VARIETIES)						
CHERRIES						
PEACHES						
PLUMS						
TOMATOES						
CORN						
CUCUMBERS (PICKLING)						
GREEN BEANS						
EXAMPLE						
APPLESAUCE	glean	can	N/A	varies	1/2 cup	
PEACHES	buy	can	Veteran	Aug. – Sept.	1/2 cup	
TOMATOES	grow/buy	can-crushed	Roma	Aug. – Sept.	1/2 cup	

[1]Once you decide how many quarts you need, check with the canning yields chart to calculate poundage. You will need the same amount for either canning or freezing.

Note on Drying: You will need approximately 25 pounds of fresh fruit to yield 4–8 pounds dried.

GAME PLAN

NUMBER OF EATERS	AMOUNT	BY X'S SERVED PER WK/ YEAR	TOTAL WEEK/ YEAR	TOTAL CUPS	TOTAL QUARTS	POUNDS' NEEDED (SEE CHART)
4	2 cups	2x	2 cups x 52	104	26	78 lbs.
4	2 cups	1x	1 x 52	52	13	32.5 lbs.
4	2 cups	2x	2 x 52	104	26	71.5 lbs.

MIDSUMMER (July–Sept.) —Freeze green beans

MID- TO LATE SUMMER (Aug.)—Ferment cucumbers for pickles (24 pints)

MID- TO LATE SUMMER (Aug.)—Pick backyard Bartletts (20 pints canned, 20 quarts of sauce)

MID- TO LATE SUMMER (Aug./Sept.)—Pick, shuck, and freeze corn (20 pints)

MID- TO LATE SUMMER (Aug./Sept.)—Pick berries for jam (wild blackberries, 6 8-oz. jars) (loganberries, 12 8-oz. jars)

LATE SUMMER (late Aug./Sept.)—Can tomatoes (about 40 quarts—80–100 pounds)

EARLY AUTUMN (Sept./Oct.)—Make applesauce— (20 quarts). Make dried apples (10 pounds) and pears (10 pounds), and 6 jars fruit butter

AUTUMN (Oct.)—Freeze-dry nuts (50 pounds put up in 2–3 pound packages)

AUTUMN (Oct.)—Make sauerkraut (24 pints)

Oh my gosh, just writing that list makes me dizzy— and there is tons of stuff I'm leaving out. There's the vegetable curing (onions, garlic, and winter squash), the herb pestos I freeze, and the miscellaneous condiments I make. There are the currant and berry syrups (for our own sodas) and the seasoned vinegar I add to my "fancy pantry." I make liqueurs, quince paste, and whatever else comes to mind. This year I'm adding barbecue sauce to the menu—and I already make ketchup. I might even work on creating a more exact recipe for my ketchup; for a long time, just getting stuff in a jar seemed amazing enough. But not everything takes the same amount of time: Some things can happen while you sleep. Drying fruit and herbs can be left mostly unattended. And fermenting cucumbers can sit around for up to six weeks without too much

CANNING YIELDS

PRODUCT	Pounds per Canner, Load of 7 Quarts	Pounds Per Canner, Load of 9 Pints	Unit Weight (lbs.)	Yield Per Unit	Pounds Needed Per Bottle
FRUITS					
APPLES	19	12.25	48	16–19 quarts	2.75 lbs./quart
APPLESAUCE	21	13.5	48	14–19 quarts	3 lbs./quart
APRICOTS	16	10	50	20–25 quarts	2.25 lbs./quart
BERRIES	12	8	36	18–24 quarts	1.75 lbs./quart
CHERRIES	17.5	11	25	8–12 quarts	2.5 lbs./quart
GRAPE JUICE	24.5	16	26	7–9 quarts	3.5 lbs./quart
GRAPES, WHOLE	14	9	26	12–14 quarts	2 lbs./quart
PEACHES & NECTARINES	17.5	11	48	16–24 quarts	2.5 lbs./quart
PEARS	17.5	11	50	16–25 quarts	2.5 lbs./quart
PLUMS	14	9	56	22–36 quarts	2 lbs./quart
TOMATOES					
CRUSHED	22	14	53	17–20 quarts	2.75 lbs./quart
WHOLE OR HALVED	21	13	53	15–21 quarts	3 lbs./quart
JUICE	23	14	53	15–18 quarts	3.25 lbs./quart
SAUCE, THIN	35	21	53	10–12 quarts	5 lbs./quart
SAUCE, THICK	46	28	53	7–9 quarts	6.5 lbs./quart

bother. The same with sauerkraut—no need for fussing there.

I hope I've not scared you away with all this information—it might seem a tad daunting. But as I take a breath, I realize that each one of the tasks I mentioned represents a mere day or two of my time. Added together they may take up no more than a month or so of work time. Of course, if I add in all the time I put into growing and harvesting the backyard garden, I suppose I spend six months on and off filling my pantry. But even that is not bad. Half a year on and half a year off. Ebb and flow, sow and reap. A time for work and a time for rest. But I must not speak of rest right now. It is April, and the earth is moving.

APRIL

APRIL

The Home

Spring Cleaning

I feel obliged to offer some information about caring for the inside of your home, since it is where much of the householding work is done. I would imagine most of you know what you need to do in order to live comfortably. I am not suggesting one value over another, but I like a well-maintained home, personally, in line with the value I place on taking care of my things. If I am willing to bring things into my home, I should be willing to care for them. I appreciate organization; it helps me think. I know there are better things to do than cleaning, but I like a tidy home. I enjoy the calm and order it offers. Like a freshly baked pie, a clean home says things are right with the world—at least relatively so.

Here, then, are some simple tools to help toward this end. I suggest you invest in high-quality ones that will last; cheap tools break quickly. I make a point of going to a local shop that carries well-made equipment made of natural fibers. I do not buy them all at once; I've collected them over time. Here are some of the basics for your cleaning arsenal:

- A good mop (I use both a string mop and a flat cloth pad that attaches to a long wand and can be removed and laundered).
- A natural-bristle scrub brush (sometimes you just have to get on your hands and knees).
- Two natural fiber dusters (one long-handled and one short-handled, depending on the job).
- A good natural-fiber dust mop (with removable, washable cover).
- Two brooms (one for indoors, one for outdoors).
- A dust broom for quick pickups.
- A good dustpan (with a good edge).
- A table whisk broom and pan (I like it to remove crumbs from the table).
- Natural sponges.
- Abrasive scrubbing cloths that can be cut to size (I use those all over the house).
- Steel wool (a few different grades).
- A good natural-bristle toilet brush.
- A carpet sweeper that works on carpets better than a broom but is less noisy than a vacuum.
- A vacuum cleaner with good attachments for curtains and upholstery, and for getting into corners where dust loves to hide.
- A bag of rags (old socks, old T-shirts, torn-up sheets) for polishing furniture; another for washing windows and moldings that collect dust neither duster nor vacuum cleaner can reach.
- A window wiper (like the one you use to clean your car windows) for the shower stall. It removes water from the sides of the stall, which prevents mold buildup and water stains (particularly if you have hard water). My mom taught me that.
- A couple of buckets in which to haul supplies around the house.

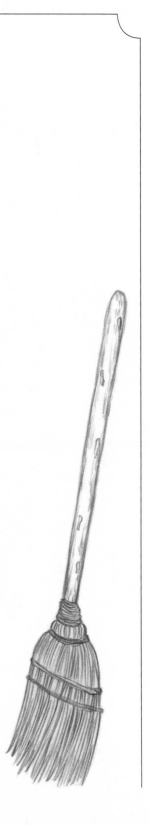

Putting together a bucket of cleaning supplies (two, if you have an upstairs and a downstairs) will make cleaning easier. I put in a spray bottle of my vinegar and water mix, baking soda, my scrubby cloth, a bristle scrubbing brush, and some clean rags. I don't have extras of the bigger items but I do keep a bristled toilet brush and plunger in each bathroom. I don't like to tote those around.

Generally, common household items such as vinegar, lemon juice, baking soda, borax, hydrogen peroxide, and a little liquid soap are fine for cleaning the house. I use them in combination as well as on their own. There are also items I buy in bulk, and specialty items like lemon oil for polishing my wood furniture. I buy my biodegradable liquid laundry detergent in ten-gallon containers and liquid soap by the gallon from a distributor or my local co-op, then refill smaller bottles when I need to. I always dilute these products even when they do not suggest it, because a little really goes a long way. As for hand soap, when I do use soap (I buy it in bulk in a block), I save the little leftover pieces to "melt" in water and use in a pump bottle. Sometimes it gets a little ropy, but it is a good way to use up the little bits. Another great invention is the tightly woven plastic mesh bag that hangs in my shower. You drop the leftover bits of soap into the bag, cinch the bag closed, and use it like a foaming loofah—I really love the thing. I'm sure you could use an old stocking to do that, too, though I haven't tried it. I also have a natural-bristle back brush and loofah in the shower, but that mesh bag is my favorite.

Below is a list of simple cleaning solutions I use. It is by no means an exhaustive list. Many of them I discovered via the Internet. If you have that resource, you will be well-prepared to go about cleaning your home in a healthy and sustainable manner. And since these products come with only the barest processing, they are in line with my values and fit into my world.

One word about vinegar—don't use anything other than distilled white vinegar. I have made the mistake of using apple cider vinegar and ended up with a sticky mess. And depending on what you use it for, I suggest slightly different ratios of water to vinegar. Insufficiently diluted vinegar can erode grout, for example. If you have any doubt, try spraying a little on the surface to see how it reacts. And don't be put off by the smell—it will dissipate. My husband used to claim our living room smelled like salad dressing, but that was right after it had been mopped and because he was being "funny."

FOR THE KITCHEN

Countertops and Appliances

I mix a solution, one part water to one part vinegar, put it in a spray bottle and use it to clean my stove tops, appliances, and countertops. I have old Formica on my counters; vinegar is fine for it, but don't use it on marble countertops—it will corrode marble. If I need a little extra grit I sprinkle on some baking soda (I love to see it fizz). I also use a slightly abrasive cloth that is safe to use on porcelain and Formica counters. You can buy it in large sheets and use it when a little extra elbow grease is in order.

Oven

Moisten oven surfaces with sponge and water. Combine ¾ cup baking soda, ¼ cup salt, and a little water. Make a paste and spread it throughout. Let it sit overnight and then remove with a soft dry cloth or spatula. Rub gently with fine steel wool. Wash down to remove residual cleaning solution. I turn my

> Generally, common household items such as vinegar, lemon juice, baking soda, borax, hydrogen peroxide, and a little liquid soap are fine for cleaning the house.

oven on low after doing this—for maybe a half hour at 250 degrees—before using it again.

Butcher Block

I like to take the heel end of a lemon and rub it firmly on my butcher-block counters. The oil from the rind and the lemon juice work together to clean and oil the counter. I let it sit for at least ten minutes before wiping with a clean, wet cloth followed by a dry one. If I feel the counter needs it, I sprinkle a little baking soda on its surface and rub it in with the lemon heel. After I cut up big pieces of pork for sausages, I spray a very diluted mix of bleach to water (about one teaspoon to one quart) on the counter to make sure it's clean.

Kitchen Floors

Mix ½ cup of vinegar in a gallon of hot water. Sometimes I use just hot water and an old sponge I keep under the sink for spot cleaning. I have Marmoleum in my kitchen, which requires an annual application of Forbo cleaner, a product I get at the environmental building supply shop. I'm not always sure I need it, but I am a good soldier; after spending the money to put down that flooring, it makes sense to follow the instructions for its care.

Bathroom

I use the same vinegar solution to clean the bathtub, toilet, sink, and countertops. Vinegar dissolves soap scum and hard-water stains on your fixtures and tiles. I spray some on and let it sit before cleaning. For extra cleaning muscle, I sometimes make a paste of vinegar and baking soda and let it sit a while on the tub "ring." It's nontoxic, so I don't mind getting it on my hands or putting it down my drain.

Toilet Bowl

You can use pure vinegar in the toilet bowl to get rid of rings. Flush the toilet to allow the water level to go down. Spray the undiluted vinegar around the inside of the rim. Let it sit a while and then scrub the bowl.

Mold

If you do find mold from time to time (particularly around tile grout), get rid of it. Many people are allergic to mold and no one benefits from it. I like to mix one part hydrogen peroxide (3 percent) with two parts water in a spray bottle and spray the solution on areas with mold. Wait at least one hour before rinsing or using the shower. You can also use vinegar or lemon juice at full strength.

Bathroom Floor

You can also use a vinegar/water solution for mopping the bathroom floor. I suggest using ½ cup of vinegar in a gallon of hot water. Sweep the floor first and then mop. If you do it regularly there is no need for rinsing, but when you need a little extra cleaning, add a few drops of liquid soap (I buy it by the gallon from Seventh Generation) for a little more cleaning strength. If you do use liquid soap, rinse the floor with plain water. Sometimes I use an old towel and my foot to sop up the moisture. It works well and speeds up the job.

Laundry Room

You can use vinegar as a natural fabric softener. This can be helpful for people who have sensitive skin. Add ½ cup of vinegar to the rinse cycle (if you use a rinse cycle). I never go this far, but adding a little vinegar to your laundry detergent will also break down any trace elements that you might be sensitive to.

Hardwood Floors

How you clean your floors depends on the finish. If you have had them redone or if they have either a Swedish or urethane covering, then vinegar is not the way to go. You can follow the advice of the person who finished your floors or, if you did it yourself, follow up on care based on the sealant you used. I had my upstairs floors redone with a Swedish finish, so I clean them differently than my downstairs hardwood floors, which have no finish—it has worn off. In either case, one should always sweep, dust, or vacuum floors well before mopping to get rid of excess dirt.

For my floors that have the Swedish finish, I use Bona Kemi, a product sold at the local environmental building supply shop. It both cleans and shines up the floor in a way that is compatible with the finish itself.

For the floors without a finish, I use water and vinegar—about ½ cup of vinegar to a gallon of water. It is best to use a well-wrung mop, because excess water can get between the cracks of the floorboards and cause them to warp. A good squeeze will do the job.

Carpets

For general maintenance, you should use a carpet sweeper (or vacuum) on your carpets to remove dust and general grime. That will improve both the quality of the pile and the overall life and condition of your rugs and carpets. If you have stains to deal with, try mixing equal parts vinegar and water in a spray bottle and spraying the mixture directly on the stain. Let it sit for several minutes and then clean with a brush or sponge using warm, lightly soapy water. You should blot the stain more than rub it. If it is a difficult stain to remove, try mixing ¼ cup of salt (I use kosher salt to provide some grit), ¼ cup of borax, and ¼ cup of vinegar. Gently rub the paste on and leave it to dry for a couple of hours, then vacuum it up.

To deodorize carpets, try baking soda. I sprinkle my

carpets thoroughly with baking soda, let it sit a couple of hours, and then vacuum. Sometimes I mix an essential oil (like eucalyptus or lavender) into the soda before sprinkling it on. This imparts a wonderful scent. Putting a few drops of essential oil or spices in a pot of water and bringing it to a simmer will also give a nice fragrance to your house, at least to the kitchen (if you use oils, don't do this in a pot you use for cooking).

Windows and Mirrors

I use a crumpled newspaper or a cotton cloth and a mixture of 2 teaspoons of vinegar with 1 quart of warm water. Be careful not to use too much vinegar in your solutions, because a strong solution could etch the glass and eventually cloud it. It is best not to clean windows if the sun is on them or if they are warm, as this will cause streaks.

Furniture

As with your floors, how you treat the wood depends on the finish. For varnished wood, add a few drops of lemon oil (you can buy it at a hardware store) to ½ cup of warm water. Mix well and spray onto a soft, slightly damp cloth. Wipe the furniture with the cloth and then wipe down with a dry, soft, cotton cloth.

For unvarnished wood, mix 2 teaspoons each of olive oil and lemon juice and apply a small amount to a soft cotton cloth. Wring the cloth to spread the mixture further into the material and apply to the furniture in wide strokes. This helps distribute the oil evenly.

Water Rings on Wood

Oh, boy, these drive me crazy. They are the result of moisture getting trapped under the topcoat of the finish; they are not on the finish itself. To remedy this I have used the oddest of treatments, with some success. Mix ¼ cup of mayonnaise with 1 tablespoon of baking soda and apply that mixture to the water spots. Use a hair dryer on the spot while you are rubbing in the mixture. As strange as it seems, in a little while the spot will come out. Generally speaking, though, prevention is the best policy. I put a padded table mat under my tablecloth as a precaution and always put out trivets or hot pads when serving dishes whose heat could create a moisture ring. If I decide to dispense with the table-cloth and leave the wood exposed, I put out place mats and give my family the evil eye about where they put their glasses. You might not like to choose the path of intimidation, but it has worked for me.

That's enough about cleaning for now. I don't know about you, but I'm ready for a nap.

APRIL

The Garden

Sowing Carrots • Beets and Greens •
Keeping Out Kitty • Building Raised Beds

La-di-da! It is April, and no one will look askance at me for being out in the garden all day. There are lots of practical things to do. Whatever prudence I needed to exercise in March, I can toss aside in April. My focus is on greens, lots and lots of greens—lettuce (many varieties), chard, spinach, kale, arugula, and cilantro. Though many of them could be planted in March, they are still eminently suited for April. The weather is still cool and that suits these greens fine. In fact, while you might plant lettuce at two-week intervals from now until early June, dark greens like collards and kale are good for one or two plantings in March and early April and then it's best to wait until late summer to sow them again, so that they can grow during the cooling days of early autumn. The logic of the two-cycle growing season will take some getting used to, so don't worry about it now. Just know that April is a fine time to grow greens. Different kinds of greens have different requirements, and you can take your time in winter while browsing the catalogs to learn all the options. Sometimes I am particular and sometimes I am not. For the most part, I still employ the trial and error approach as the easiest way to go.

PRUDENCE, PLEASE

I grow lots of greens because they are what my family eats. They are a solid choice for quick and easy meals, qualities that will probably resonate with many people. A bed dedicated to a mix of salad greens is also a nice way for new gardeners to get started. You can begin with seeds or starts—or plant both, for a long-lasting supply. Succession gardening—following one planting with another—is a brilliant way to extend the growing power of your beds. When planting my garden, I take the notion of using every bit of available space to an extreme. It actually grieves me to see empty dirt, since I know my beds should either have plants, or a cover crop, or compost in them. In fact, I see empty space as a wagging finger, mocking my efforts at maximum production. "If you were good," the finger says, "you could have grown some lettuce or radishes in that space before putting in your tomatoes"; or, "You could have planted your onions or garlic throughout the yard, putting even the smallest of possible spaces to good use." Using my garden space well is a major goal of mine. In the case of your lettuce bed, succession gardening can simply mean putting in one row of starts the first week of April (or thereabouts) and at the same time planting a row of seeds. A week or two later you can do the same thing again—one row of starts and one of seeds. You can do that for up to two months or longer.

A SALAD FOR ONE

I don't wait for a full head of lettuce to develop before I start picking leaves. A leaf or two from each plant will make the smallest salad mix, and since I am home during the day, it seems only fair that I should enjoy it. I could save the greens until they add up and serve them at dinner, or use them just for sandwiches, but I'm not that good. The first of the season's greens end up on my lunch plate, and so they should. The rest of my group will just have to wait, but only another week or so. Once the plants start growing, they will give you what you need for days and nights of salads, which brings me to the topic of too much of a good thing.

I know that when you go to the nursery all those cute starts look harmless, but be assured they will grow, and grow big. If you really like salads, go for it. If you plan to grow other greens, be cautious. If I follow my April planting schedule, by the end of May I can harvest a full load of salad greens, a huge bunch of chard, and a righteous load of broccoli raab all in one day. And how much did I plant? Really not that much. For all my spring greens, I generally plant two beds, each about four feet by six feet, and that serves a family of four nicely for at least two months—certainly until other crops start showing up. Your plants will grow and on certain days you may be overwhelmed, especially if you are not a committed cook. Giving away the excess is a lovely way to go, but if you have limited space try a little prudence, because April is a good time to plant lots of other vegetables, too.

ROOTED DETERMINATION

I take it as a mark of accomplishment to have succeeded in growing carrots. The seeds are very small and require constant watering before they sprout. They also need a

Though recent cooking trends have given them a more exalted place at the table ... beets are a proletarian food.

light soil above and below them so their roots and tender heads may grow. I'm like a mother hen around them. Each day I feel the soil, and if it is a particularly sunny day, I sprinkle them religiously with water, but only until they pop up. Then I am careful not to water too often, lest they perish from "dampening off," meaning the soil got too wet around them. Everything about growing carrots amazes me. How those tiny green hairs grow up to become something as rugged as a carrot is a miracle.

I'm the first to give carrots points for determination, but goodness they are temperamental. After failing for the first couple of years, I was determined to find the path to victory, particularly since my neighbor seemed to do so well with them. Remember that annoying smarminess I referred to earlier? Who knows why something as simple as, "Oh really? I neeeeever have trouble with carrots," fuels the fire of determination. By hook or by crook, I was determined to grow them. Today, I admit to a bit of smugness myself. I have tamed the beast and it is good. I doubt they are sweeter from the toil, but who knows. Life seems to be like that.

Not all things in the vegetable kingdom are so fussy, though. Beets, for example, are an underground glory of hearty nature with the added bonus of edible green tops, as well as sturdy tubers. Though recent cooking trends have given them a more exalted place at the table (roasted and tossed with balsamic vinegar and herbs), beets are a proletarian food. Growing up, I ate them pickled with onions and vinegar, and I still like them that way. I cook the greens with generous quantities of garlic. Oh my goodness, what has not benefited from garlic? I will tell you more about growing garlic in the October garden chapter because that is when you sow it. Garlic stands firm during cold winters and gives you joy come June; I think garlic, along with tomatoes, is my favorite thing to grow. April is still too early, though. That is not its time. But all will be done—despite, I should add, the will of my kitty.

MY DARLING NEMESIS

I love my sweet kitty, Kuddoo, but I hate her instinct to dig in the garden dirt to do what kitties must do. I know I am not alone in my frustration; all my urban gardening friends roll their eyes over this. Between the jays that love to eat my early pea seeds and berries, the slugs that love the tender greens, and the kitties that love a freshly turned bed, I spend at least half my time keeping what's mine, mine. That may not be the most charitable of sentiments—because, after all, I want to be one with the universe—but I dig up enough worms to keep those jays happy, and as for slugs, well, I know a gal who is committed to seeing them as the lowly cousin of the snail and has cooked them on more than one occasion. Not to be cruel, but I always pass over whatever she brings to a potluck—particularly if it looks gray.

But my kitty is another matter. I love her, and I suppose she can't help seeing my nicely turned-over garden beds as a gift to her. She is very spoiled that way. To put an end to her narcissism, I have come up with a number of ingenious designs. I had to, because the solutions I found in gardening stores simply do not work. What work are branches, tiny branches or thin bamboo poles, laid out over your beds (or woven through the spaces

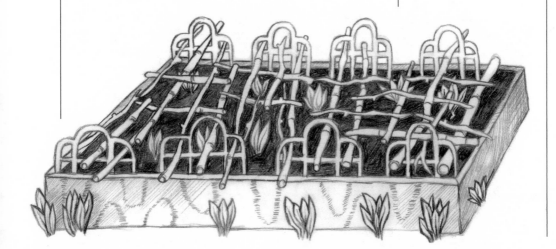

Draw pictures of the birds and slugs and kitties of your world. You will look back at it all with wonder —particularly how you had enough heart to do it all.

of the scalloped garden fences you can buy for cheap) before, during, and after your plants reach their desired height. It is not easy, and the effort will annoy you, because you are constantly having to move the branches or poles around to allow your plants the space to grow; but doing all this is better than finding kitty gifts in your beds. Almost nothing annoys me as much—well, nothing next to the way she can demolish my baby flower starts with the weight of her fat cat ass. Even if her primal urges aren't driving her to excavate my garden, she is an annoying lounger. She can be found late at night in the pea patch or the onion bed, pretty as you please. And why? Because she can. She knows we won't eighty-six her, though sometimes I wonder about it all. Oops, she's looking at me. I didn't mean it, kitty. We would neeeeever get rid of you. Really.

So that is April in my garden. Greens, carrots, beets, and kitty-proof fencing. I could do more. Lots of other vegetables love that climate and a read of your chosen gardening books will tell you what they are. Remember, keep track of what you choose to plant on your gardening map or in your journal. Tell stories about the things you are discovering. Draw pictures of the birds and slugs and kitties of your world. You will look back at it all with wonder—particularly how you had enough heart to do it all. But what am I saying? It is only April—you have miles to go before you sleep.

APRIL

The Kitchen

Building Your Outdoor Kitchen • The Story of Raw Milk •
Making Butter and Buttermilk

Now that you can sense the full growing season that is soon to come, it is a fine time to turn your attention to creating an outdoor kitchen. With the gardens and canning pots still silent, what else do you have to do? Besides, nothing, or almost nothing, will give you as much satisfaction as an outdoor canning kitchen. It will be the thing you are most proud of, and the thing that makes most sense. It will be why, when the weather reaches 100 degrees in summer, you will not mind canning tomatoes. At least it will be better than being inside.

KEEP IT SIMPLE

When I speak about a canning kitchen, I'm not talking deluxe; I'm talking simple, sensible, and way affordable. With no more than a barbecue grill or an outside propane cooking range, plus a little outdoor sink, you can do a lot

An outdoor kitchen has worked wonders for me, if only in the magical way it has resurrected a humble sense of good living.

of damage. My own space was put together beneath an old carport (which has since been stripped of its roof to become the lattice frame for my grapevines). The entire concrete path leading to that carport was hacked up to make room for garden beds and a stone pathway. Today, the path leads to the garden house and, behind it, the backyard canning kitchen. All of it was constructed on the space and framework of that old parking strip. I don't want you to get all dreamy-eyed and impractical. We have a tendency to turn everything into some grand-slam expression when there is no need. Just give yourself a little space to spread out in, to make matters easier. At minimum your outdoor kitchen space should have:

- A burner for your canning pot.
- A counter on which to place your bottles while you're filling them.
- A sink with a bucket underneath to catch draining water.
- A hose from an outdoor faucet that is attached

to your sink (helpful but not necessary).

- And, if you're really going deluxe, another burner on which to cook your jam or sauce, or whatever you need to cook while you are heating up your canning pot.

That is all you need, because the thing you really want is simply to be out of your indoor kitchen when the sun is baking the house. Even if you start canning in your kitchen first thing in the morning, you will bring more heat into your home than is bearable, which is why I would build not only a canning kitchen but also a little attached space for lounging when you want to get out of the heat of the sun. Again, do not get all misty-eyed on me. Though I have refined my outdoor kitchen to suit my classes, it is still a pretty simple structure. Inside, it has a long table on which I can set out fruit (like my peaches) for a final day of ripening, or serve dinner, or sit around with friends while we peel tomatoes. There is a built-in platform for student seating or napping (me, not the students). But you don't have to have a converted carport to do all that. Setting up a table anywhere outdoors will work as long as it is in the shade. Neither your peaches nor your napping will appreciate the heat of the noonday sun.

GOOD LIVING REVISITED

Outdoor canning kitchens used to make sense to us. But like root cellars, pantries, and those little outdoor cubbies for milk delivery, they have been abandoned. Almost no architectural attention is given to the sowing, growing, and stowing of food. With the amount of space allotted to indoor living, what is left for the garden? Are we putting in lawns or vegetable beds, root cellars or basement movie theaters? Are we setting aside space for outdoor canning kitchens or carports? Do we have space in our homes for intergenerational living or are they castles built for two?

Will building an outdoor kitchen defy the logic of industry? Will it free you of the madness? Will it return you to the slow, quiet, circular world of sow, grow, and stow, and thereby to the knowledge that you, like all things, play a part in the pattern language of natural systems? Will it ignite your potato mind and the squirrel in you? Will it explode your senses and bring you to your knees, down to a level at which you may actually see the soil, worry about the soil, care for the soil? Who knows what it will do for you, but an outdoor kitchen has worked wonders for me, if only in the magical way it has resurrected a humble sense of good living.

THE STORY OF RAW MILK (OR FARM SHARES)

Though I drink it throughout the year, spring is an especially nice time to seek out raw milk. With the bursting new green growth providing so much of the cows' diet, raw milk and cream will be richly hued, allowing for the golden butters and cheeses of the season. Due to safety regulations, these raw milk ferments (butter and cheese included) are no longer available in retail shops in the United States but can be reproduced in your home. I understand, however, that raw milk is not without controversy. But so much has been written regarding the pros and cons of raw milk that I will not wade into the subject here, except to say if there is any foodstuff that has been hijacked more than any other by industry, it is milk. Unsanitary conditions in either industrial systems or local farms can leave you in big, sick trouble, but I believe most small-scale dairies offering raw milk are run by responsible individuals with a vested interest in doing things well. If you want raw milk, you should educate yourself on the best practices out there. I offer the following in hopes of buoying the raw milk farm-direct system.

THINK SAFE

When considering becoming part of a farm share for your raw milk, you should first and foremost visit the farm. Farmers should be happy to have you on their farm. Most comply with all state regulations or standards regarding bacterial testing, and so they can track the necessary safety conditions. Ask to see the records if you are interested. Tour the farm—it should be a pleasant place. Many small-scale farmers are very busy but will still be happy and proud to show you around. It is important that you be familiar with the practices of the farm and its farmers.

Raw milk sales are legal in twenty-eight of our fifty states. Groups like the Weston A. Price Foundation are dedicated to making safe raw milk legally available in all states. All that is needed is a sufficient number of inspectors to regularly check farms and logs for safety standards. In the meantime, you, the consumer, must serve as your own inspector.

Unfortunately for raw milk consumers, one bad experience anywhere can create hysteria for everyone. Industry seems to make allowances for E. coli outbreaks in large meat-processing plants without a trace of the witch-hunt tactics that are applied to small dairy farms. I'm not saying regulations are not a good thing, rather that a blind eye is often turned and exceptions are made to every rule when it comes to big agribusiness.

Safety and sanitation are vitally important to me, but so are the systems behind the system. Seasons, forage, weather, and the breed of cow will all make a difference to the quality and flavor of the milk. Issues related to pasture management, calf weaning, and lactation cycles are also important to me, but given that even small local dairies operate for profit, some of my more idealized systems (natural weaning, for one) simply do not pencil out. And while some dairy farmers are honest about those limitations, others are apt to try and convince you of "how it is" vs. "how it is for them." For example, some will admit that they do not follow the exact guidelines for grass-fed animals and will tell you why. Perhaps they do not have enough acreage or time. That is just reality. Others will try to convince you that grass feeding is not healthy for a cow or good for the soil. For good or for bad, many of these farmers are used to justifying their systems to fit them into the model they have chosen. It's better that you understand what is important to you if you are going to spend the money (and it does cost a bit) to support this system. In all likelihood, you will get something close to what you want, but not a perfect situation—that's just where we are right now. The more we support small farm systems, the closer we will come to achieving ideal conditions.

BUTTER AND BUTTERMILK

As you may know, raw cream butter, whether sweet or cultured, is completely unavailable in the United States and very rare even in Europe these days. Once you learn to make it yourself, you will be amazed by its thick, creamy texture and lovely fresh taste. This is butter as it was meant to be. But be advised, it will take a little doing. Butter making is a labor of love. I don't mind, although I don't do it every week—only when I have more cream on hand than I need for everyday cooking.

Making butter from raw milk starts with skimming off the cream. Raw milk benefits from sitting at least twenty-four hours in the fridge to let gravity separate the cream from the milk. The longer it sits, the more it separates, but I would not go beyond two or three days.

In preparation for the skimming, boil a quart jar, a lid, and a small ladle to make sure they are sterile. Use the ladle to skim the cream off two half-gallon bottles of milk. (I receive mine in wide-mouth half-gallon jars, which makes this task very easy. If you get yours in narrow-mouth jars or plastic jugs, pour the milk into a wide-mouth vessel before separating.) Depending on the season, I get anywhere from a pint to a pint and a half of cream from a half gallon of raw milk. Ladle the cream into the boiled jar and add to each pint of cream a tablespoon of store-bought "cultured" buttermilk. Make sure the buttermilk has not reached its sell-by date; you want the culture in it to be very active. Cream that is slightly acidified comes together as butter easier than fresh sweet cream.

You want your cream to be at room temperature for the fermentation process. Old-school butter makers used to just let their cream sit overnight at room temperature to allow it to culture naturally (raw milk will sour or clabber naturally and quickly). When they did that, the cream would not only ferment but also reach room temperature. To be safe, instead of letting the cream sit out all night to warm and ferment, I take the chill off the cream by pouring it directly into the bottle, which is still a little warm from the boiling, and stir in buttermilk for a quicker fermentation time (four to six hours).

To assist in the culturing, I put the cream in an insulated cooler that has enough warm, seventy-five-degree water in it to cover half of the bottle. If it is warm enough in the house, I let the mixture sit out. At this point, the entire process has taken me only five minutes. That's the fast part.

Whether I have placed the mixture in the cooler with warm water or left it out at room temperature, I allow it to sit about four to six hours. If I start culturing the cream in the morning, I will be able to make, or "churn," butter by noon.

After the "culturing" stage, I put the bottle of cream in a bowl with ice water to cool it a bit. Cream should be warm during the culturing process and cool when it is churned. Let it sit until it is cool, which, depending on the starting temperature, could take no more than ten minutes. The cream does not need to be completely chilled, but it should be down to sixty degrees or so to make churning easier. Do not chill it further, as it will negatively affect the churning.

After letting the cream cool to sixty degrees, I shake the bottle (lid attached) up and down to begin the agitation of the fat globules. Shaking the bottle, instead of using an electric beater, incorporates more air and produces greater volume. Using a mixer just gets cream everywhere. It is much better to keep it contained in a bottle.

Churning butter in a bottle will take anywhere from ten to twenty minutes, sometimes less, if all the conditions for proper churning are aligned. Be patient and don't give up. It will happen. Slowly, you will see little butter globules forming. At first they will be loosely suspended in the separated cream (which is now becoming either butter or the surrounding buttermilk), but after another minute or two of shaking (start slowing down the speed of your shaking toward the end), the fat globules will have separated from the buttermilk and cohered completely. When you open the bottle, you will see a separated mass at the top. That is your butter.

Pour the entire contents of the jar through a sieve that has been lined with a boiled and cooled, wet sheet of muslin and set over a bowl. You can use the same muslin over and over, but make sure it is boiled both before and after using it. This muslin (or butter cloth, as it is sometimes called) has a tighter weave than cheesecloth. An old and slightly worn sheet will do the trick if it has been cleaned and boiled, and its color has set. (A friend of mine once had her cheese turn multicolored when she used a piece of cloth with unset dyes.)

After the buttermilk has flowed through the cloth-lined sieve, you will have a soft wad of butter remaining in the cloth. The buttermilk will be left in the bowl beneath. Gather up the corners of the cloth to create a sling for the soft butter, submerge the parcel in an ice-cold water bath, and move it back and forth to remove the milk solids that are still attached to the butter. Removing all these milk solids gives the butter a longer shelf life, because it is these solids that quickly go rancid. Repeat this process a number of times with clean ice water, just dunking and swishing the butter parcel around in the bowl to "wash" and at the same time chill the butter. When the water runs clear (is no longer cloudy with milk solids) and the butter is cool, empty the contents of the parcel into a clean bowl. At this point, you are going to remove whatever remaining liquid (milk and water) is left in the butter.

To do this, take a spatula (also very clean) and start pushing the butter back and forth until you see a puddle forming in the bottom of the bowl. Tilt the bowl to pour off this liquid and start again. Do this four or five times; you can even blot the butter with a paper towel if you see water droplets on it that will not pour off (save that paper towel for greasing a pan or muffin tin, if you like).

The less water the butter contains (and "European-style" butter can have 10 to 20 percent less than many American brands), the flakier pastry made with it will be. Actually, I don't use my homemade butter for baking, for the same reason I don't make hard cheese: I don't have enough cream or milk available to give me the quantities I'd need. I'd rather spread my homemade butter on toast.

After all this work, I generally end up with no more than a half cup of butter. What a lot of work, you are thinking. Yep, I agree. But I also have the buttermilk, which I turn into other things, both for drinking and baking. The buttermilk you buy in the store is really pasteurized skim milk that has had a culture introduced into it. That is why it is thick. Old-fashioned buttermilk is the liquid that is left over after the cream has been turned into butter, and is loose in texture. I am sure I could "culture" my cream with the "old-fashioned" leftover buttermilk (assuming I used it within a week), though I have never done it.

Though it is time-consuming, making butter will return you to the spirit of regional cooking. It is about making good use of what you have on hand, and sometimes embellishing it. When I am feeling really frilly, I press my softened butter into molds meant for candy making and chill them in the freezer (which makes for easier removal). When they come out, they bear the mark of the design and are cute beyond compare. Flavored with something exotic, like truffles or lavender, or something common, like garlic and herbs, these butter parcels become worthy gifts. But be forewarned, serving them alongside dinner rolls will generally elicit something akin to eye-rolling, particularly if your guests are not of the householding universe. Be steady and serve them anyway, because these babies are damn cute.

MAY

The Home

Teach Your Children Well

While many of us boomers must engage in some serious soul-searching before taking on this life, others— such as anyone younger than twenty who is coming of age in this postindustrial, über-technological world— may well be less riddled with indecision. Either they will fall hook, line, and sinker for the promise of the American dream, or they will recognize that there is a hideous narrative facing their generation that must be addressed. Besides the inequity of our education system and out-of-control living expenses, they will inherit grave environmental problems, along with the political strife that is sure to result from them. They will have to watch as the haves go to high ground while the have-nots continue to sink. Sorry, but I do believe this is a likely scenario. So what do we tell them? What do we teach them?

Every so often I read something that opens up a new way of thinking for me. Published in 1908, Sidney Morse's *Household Discoveries—An Encyclopedia of Practical Recipes and Processes* offers a whale of an instructional guide to life and home. I enjoyed reading it, though it is exhausting to consider what a life of householding entailed back then. In the chapter entitled "The Good Old Days," Morse writes:

> It has been pointed out that the American farmer of the past generation carried on in the neighborhood of sixty to seventy different processes on the farm that in modern times have given rise to as many different arts or trades. The pioneer farmer had necessarily to be his own blacksmith, iron worker, carriage ironer, wheelwright, carriage painter, carpenter, cabinet maker, harness maker, boot maker, shoemaker, and so on—just as his wife had to be her own spinner, weaver, dyer, dressmaker, tailor, soap maker and the like. In those days there were no artisans in the vicinity of the pioneer farmhouse. No one could be called in, nor could the work be sent out to be done by others. Hence so many necessary tasks accumulated that the boys and girls of the family were obliged at a very early age to master a large number of domestic arts and processes. The natural desire felt by all children to equal or exceed their models resulted in the acquisition of considerable skill, which was thus transmitted from father to son, and from mother to daughter through generations.

That's a bunch of work. I can't say I'm jealous, and I certainly do not mean to romanticize a life I have never lived (after all, I want to nap after baking bread). Yet I am inclined to idealize that kind of childhood. At the same time, I am equally aware of the well-documented narrative of farm kids waiting breathlessly for the moment they can leave the farm. So where is the balance? Once

again, I am reminded of my friends' kids who participated in 4-H programs during their youth. Though it
will not provide the full measure of self-reliance defined
by Morse, I do believe 4-H is designed to give children a
farm-centered experience and a sense of pride in their
relationship to the natural world. Unfortunately, 4-H is
also a big agri-marketing campaign. The organization's
official Web site gives some history:

> The seed of the 4-H idea of practical and "hands-on"
> learning came from the desire to make public school
> education more connected to country life. Early
> programs tied both public and private resources
> together for the purpose of helping rural youth.
>
> During this time, researchers at experiment
> stations of the land-grant college system and USDA
> saw that adults in the farming community did not
> readily accept new agricultural discoveries. But,
> educators found that youth would "experiment" with
> these new ideas and then share their experiences and
> successes with the adults.
>
> So rural youth programs became a way to
> introduce new agriculture technology to the adults.
> A.B. Graham started one such youth program in
> Ohio in 1902. It is considered the birth of the 4-H
> program in the U.S. When Congress created the
> Cooperative Extension Service at USDA in 1914,
> it included boys' and girls' club work. This soon
> became known as 4-H clubs—Head, Heart, Hands,
> and Health.

I am buoyed by that history if only because it
trumpets the notion that children are the way toward
opening their parents' hearts and minds. Today, in
addition to teaching big agribusiness ideology (corporate agriculture is certainly still at work in 4-H and
land-grant universities alike), some school programs
attempt to teach children the value of growing food pri-
vately and on a smaller scale. That is in part the work

of chef, writer, and small-farm advocate Alice Waters (of Chez Panisse fame), whose movement to create "edible schoolyards" is catching on all over the country. The hope is that, because of their participation in and enjoyment of these schoolyard gardens, children will bring the gospel home. The common denominator between Waters, Morse, and 4-H seems to be children: if you teach them well, they can advance any agenda. But here is where I need to ask the question: how will we keep children interested as the realities of modern life take their toll?

Just as we adults are dealing with the conflicting demands of our busy lives, so are our children. They too are attracted to the ease and excitement of modern living and technology. We teach our children to "respect the earth," and buy chickens for them to raise in the backyard—but we also indulge them with cell phones, iPods, and the latest video games. We want our children to understand the issues of global warming, but we load them down with extracurricular activities that have little to do with the solution. I am not trying to dismiss the value of physical activities such as T-ball, soccer, gymnastics, football, or swimming, nor the importance of more academic pursuits like science and math clubs. I just wonder what we are really telling our kids. When, in their busy lives, would they have time to pick up a hoe? Even more than that, I wonder, will they ever want to?

Perhaps you are one of the lucky ones. Perhaps you have started from scratch with a family that has grown up around the values of home and land stewardship, and there will be no teeth to pull. I was not so lucky. As I mentioned earlier, I inherited a family late in life. I have my own child, a child I have been attempting to pull from the jaws of addiction (for the record, he played T-ball and was a Talented and Gifted student), but I also married a man with a son who has grown into a lovely young man—though one not inclined to

How can
we truly
communicate
the full scope of
this life without
committing to
it ourselves?

love the householding life. It is one thing to romanticize a life of urban/rural familial bliss; it is another thing altogether to live such a life. It is somewhat idealistic to think we can recruit children happily into a householding system, particularly if we have a hard time recruiting ourselves. And that is the point I really want to make. If you, like me, feel the world would be better served if we powered down and returned to a hands-on existence— to skills, trades, and systems of householding—then why should we not teach our children ourselves? More specifically, why not model our behavior so they might consider it reasonable themselves?

The notion that we can teach children the full scope of householding, when we ourselves are busy with careers that do not resemble anything like it, is deeply problematical. To expect schools and extracurricular activities to provide such lessons (worm composting for toddlers?) would be ironic, indeed. How can we truly communicate the full scope of this life without committing to it ourselves? Do we simply expect children to take on the task on their own? Why not set a better example? Why not offer them the opportunity to get out of the rat race of higher education, debt, and an unsustainable cost of living by first getting ourselves out of it? Why not offer them a "farm" that is well cared for and systems that will supply their needs? Why not tell them (after we have told ourselves) that leaving the "family farm" or backyard homestead for a life of independence and adventure is not really, not now, such a responsible plan? Why not shift the conversation about "place" from the academic to the practical? In fact, why not take on the concept of academia in general? The assumption that children need to get a college education (and now a master's degree seems to be the standard) is so entrenched in our cultural psyche that we tend to accept it without thinking too much about it. I understand why we think it is important, but I still challenge its logic. For one thing, who can afford such an education anymore? But as much as I think cost is a big obstacle, I also wonder more generally about education in the first place, particularly as it relates to the world today.

If we, as world citizens, need to power down, what sense does it make to keep talking about the next great industry of the future and expanding the frontiers of market opportunities? Why, in essence, do we keep training kids to take part in an effort that is more about the status quo of a growth economy than anything else? Who are we asking them to work for? It does not take a huge imaginative leap to see colleges as engines for tomorrow's corporate workforce. Industry has always been involved in planning the college curriculum, and I suspect this state of affairs will only worsen the more privatized our educational system becomes. Those who would reject this argument need only look to Washington to witness the hold that corporate culture has over our elected officials (and hence over the citizenry). So why assume it will be better in our universities? Just as the University of Chicago, with its history of free-market ideologues, has sent a million little Greenspans into the world, so Exxon, Chevron, Mobil and Shell, Glaxo, Pfizer, and Monsanto, with their generous donations and support, work to seed the world with their own disciples. Frankly, the world they are seeding is a frightening one.

I am not completely contrary; I do understand the concept of job creation and the self-perpetuating way the producer/consumer/distributor model works. I understand that we, as a national economy, are attempting to move away from the hard manufacturing jobs of yesteryear (most of which are now overseas, anyway) toward the soft technology and green industries of tomorrow. I understand how the service industry serves, how the support industry supports, and how research is supposed to move the world forward toward equitable global living standards. But let's be honest here. First,

"Powering down" was coined by Richard Heinberg in his book *Powerdown: Options and Actions for a Post-Carbon World* (New Society Publishers, 2004). Powering down is a strategy to reduce per-capita resource usage in wealthy countries, develop alternative energy sources, distribute resources more equitably, and slowly reduce the human population.

It is all well and good to become environmental scientists and researchers and to throw ourselves into tomorrow's burgeoning "sustainability" industry, but how about becoming a farmer?

I do not believe the equity they (the corporations who really run our economy) promote will ever really happen. Vested interests and market-based solutions are way too committed to keeping wealth where it has always been, so I need to distinguish between theory and reality. But secondly, if the world is in meltdown, how much knowledge, or rather what kind of knowledge, will we need to repair the planet? It is all well and good to become environmental scientists and researchers and to throw ourselves into tomorrow's burgeoning "sustainability" industry, but how about becoming a farmer? How about growing food and tending animals and home and hearth and community? Who will be doing that as we all go off to save the world? Who will be the neighbors and citizens in the community, understanding and upholding the needs of any given place, if everyone is moving from this place to that place?

To go from home to college to one job or another, from one city or country to another over the course of your career means, frankly, you're going to be on the road a lot. So I always wonder what all this fancy talk about "place" is really about. You know that conversation. The one that says we cannot fix the soil or know our environment unless we stay in place. It is perhaps an inconvenient truth to suggest that "place," as we like to talk about it, means staying put. It means staying put to do the task of caring for the place you have been given, the place that needs tending, the family, community, garden, soil, and habitat you call home. It also means inviting children along on the journey. Not outside our homes but in them. So why not move back in and invite them along with you? Why not teach children and, in the process, learn right alongside them?

MAY

The Garden

Rain • Meals at the Table • Onions • Beans •
Eating Dirt • The Love of Herbs

It is not that the rains have stopped, or that the soil has dried out enough. Really, whoever coined that old saying about April showers bringing May flowers simply did not live in the Pacific Northwest, at least not in Portland, Oregon. In the Pacific Northwest, it is the March, April, May, and June showers that are responsible for the lush greens of summer. But, oh, how lush they are when the rain does stop. Still, come May, I start getting mad at the weather, though I know I should be more charitable. I mean, with the world facing a water crisis, I should be overjoyed by the rain. I hate to think of those folks living in, say, Arizona or Southern California, where so much of the "blue gold" goes toward establishing housing communities. Really, talk about poor design and a bad use of natural resources. So I do not really mean to complain. I just want some sun. Which is not to say it never shines.

May normally offers misty weather and sixty-degree highs, but one year we got blazing-hot, ninety-degree weather, with cloudless skies of blue, for three straight weeks. Three weeks? In May? That was unheard of. I was sure the signs of global warming were upon us. I protected my tiny carrot starts like a frantic jay protecting her nest.

Rain or shine, blazing heat or cool, cloudy days, May is the month my year in the garden really starts. If you put your garden beds in during the fall and planted a cover crop (more on that later), they will have a better tilth (soil quality) and will dry out a little faster than garden beds that you start in spring. Those of you first starting out in spring should probably build raised beds and buy decent soil (from the nursery or a wholesaler).

GROWING SOIL

I have heard many great gardeners say they don't grow vegetables, rather they grow soil. After these few years of my own efforts, nothing makes more sense to me. Good soil, soil that is healthy, light, well-composted, rich in nutrients, and teeming with a healthy and active microbiology is like manna from heaven to plants. You can get the best of the best bagged soils, but in a way it will be a dead product. You will also, when getting soil from outside sources, be bringing in the good and the bad from those outdoor sources. But don't let me scare you. I just want you to understand that as you continue on this path, you will begin to understand by touch, feel, and intuition just how important healthy soil is, and you will begin to know it by sight and smell. In fact, I often wonder if the day will come when I will be able to do something that is currently only a rural legend to me—namely, taste the soil and know what it

> **Many great gardeners say they don't grow vegetables, rather they grow soil.**

JAYS AND NUTS

Darn if I don't know what a jay on patrol sounds like. Get anywhere close to their nests and they screech your ears off. I try and tell them they should go easy on me, because I've saved more than one of their fallen chicks from my fat-ass cat (as if she doesn't get enough food!). I can always tell when Kuddoo is stalking something; she gets all low to the ground and stealthy. I know she can't help herself, but since I'm out in the garden more than she is, she has a hard time getting away with being her bad kitty self. And that's what I tell the squawkers, though they do not show the least respect for the way I take their side in the dance of primal instincts. They should surely feel some gratitude, given all those fat worms I turn over for them, or the nuts and seeds I supply in an attempt to win their favor. In fact, I have put out whole bowls of hazelnuts in the shell and watched as the brazen birds flew right up next to me for their treats. Occasionally, when I am eating what could only be considered my fair share, they give me a dirty look and do this head-tilt thing as if to say, "Girl, I don't know who you think you are, but you're eating our nuts . . ." Luckily for them, I have better things to do in May when the sun is blasting my carrot starts, or the argument would be on.

needs. Now that would be something. I'm far from having that sort of knowledge and I suspect none of you has it, either. But who knows? Eventually we might all put a new spin on the term "eating dirt."

PLANTING A PRESERVING GARDEN

As I mentioned before, I grow a side-dish or preserving garden. I grow things I know I will preserve in one form or another for eating throughout the year. As a result, much of what I already have growing by May are things I planted the previous fall, things that need the winter months to get settled—garlic and shallots. In May, I add another member of that family to my brood, the wonderful yellow-skinned Copra onion—if properly cured and stored at summer's end, these onions will last me throughout the year.

I have yet to grow enough Copra onions to last the year. I say "Copra" because that is the variety of storage onion I like. There are others; just be sure when you buy the young starts that the sticker reads "storage onion," or else read up on the different varieties. I have tried many times to start Copra onions in my home from seed, but have had little success. They are always too weak to be successfully transplanted outdoors. I'm sure I will get better at it, but for now I accept that I have to buy them as starts. They look like tiny scallions when you buy them that way, just long green stems coming out of their soil beds. The ones I buy have been grown from seeds by someone else, and they are different from what folks refer to as onion "sets." Onion sets look like little onions, and you plant them in the ground in May. They are said to be the easiest to grow, but I have never done so. I guess it's a toss-up, because some say the best way to get large onions (the ones they depict in the catalog) is to go with transplants, as I do. I can't say either way; I've always gone with transplants, and they work great for me.

Planting onion starts

I have always planted storage onions in one bed, but they can be planted throughout the yard. There are no rules to keeping onions by themselves. In fact, when you read about companion plantings, you will discover how well-suited onions are to most other plants. They act as an insect repellent, keeping away many unwelcome garden critters. So put them wherever you can, as long as where you plant them is not next to something that will need a lot of watering come late July and August. Once the stems and bulbs of your onions have grown large and begun to dry, they are telling you they want to begin "curing" in the ground. That is when you should stop watering them so much. The same is true of potatoes. Some tubers and bulbs need to dry up before you harvest them. That is especially true of storage varieties. But aside from this one concern, go forth and plant where the space is available. A perfect spot might be around the base of an established fruit tree, which already has long roots and will not mind being ignored in the heat of the summer.

To plant onion transplants, dig a trench about two inches deep and lay the individual onion starts (carefully separating them from one another) into the trench about four inches apart. Water them well and then fill in the trench with the dirt that was removed. This gives the starts a nice anchor in the soil and enough room between them to grow nice and fat. You can start them as early as April, weather permitting, but very early May should be fine. With a little tending, your babies will fatten up nicely by the first of June. It is hard to believe that those puny wisps could grow up to be big, fat onions, but it will happen. My first effort reaped great results and I have been hooked ever since.

BEAN COUNTER

By mid-May the weather and soil in most regions will have warmed up enough to plant your beans. Unlike my early sweet shelling peas (which by this time are at least a foot or two tall), beans like heat. But what peas and beans have in common is that they like to be planted directly in the ground. Don't be fooled into thinking you need to go with starts. Just pop those beans about one inch underground (read the directions on your seed packet), water them well, and then wait. Keep in mind there is a difference between pole beans and bush beans. Know which one you are choosing. As the name suggests, one likes to grow tall and twine around a pole while the other grows as a bush. The bush variety is a fairly new invention. Much in the modern world of fruit and vegetable horticulture has more to do with industry than with the backyard. In the case of the bush bean, it was about eliminating the cost of trellises and enhancing ease of harvesting—the lower to the ground the plant is, the more easily it can be harvested by machines (at least in Oregon's Willamette Valley, commercial bush beans are virtually always harvested by machines). But you and I don't have that problem, and I think folks who love beans love the taste of pole beans more. I like pole beans for other reasons, too: they grow up and out of the way and tend to be more productive.

Over the years I have been growing beans, I have settled on Romano green beans. They are green and meaty and meant to be eaten fresh. They freeze well, too. Since I don't have the space to raise a great dried-bean crop, Romanos work the best for me. Some years ago my friend's father built me a round metal trellis about three feet wide and eight feet high; it is made out of fencing material that gives the vines plenty to grab on to as they grow. I can grow twelve to twenty seeds on each trellis (I have two), which gives me a substantial harvest. Like a lot of things, my Romanos have been selected for their preserving quality. What I don't eat fresh will be frozen. Their texture holds up better in freezing than most green beans, which makes me happy. Those I do not pick in time or freeze I let dry on the vine, and I save the seeds from the dried pods for next year. What a simple miracle it is! I just hull the dry, yellowed pods to remove the hardened seeds and save them in a jar to plant the following year. It has been

Some 80 countries, constituting 40 percent of the world's population, were suffering from serious water shortages by the mid-1990s. Increasing water demand has been caused by population growth, industrial development, and the expansion of irrigated agriculture.

SOURCE: *SYNTHESIS GEO-3.* A REPORT PUBLISHED BY THE UNITED NATIONS ENVIRONMENTAL PROGRAMME, 2002.

years since I have had to buy seeds, and each year the ones I've saved from the previous year yield a boatload of beans. In fact, I get cross-eyed looking at all those beans when they are coming on. Day in and day out, it is beans for dinner. Only when we can't imagine eating any more fresh do we freeze them. What a welcome sight they are in winter, when I sauté them with garlic and dried oregano from the garden. Which reminds me—I haven't spoken about herbs yet.

TEA FOR THE TILLERWOMAN

Drying leaves is really rather simple. Put a wicker basket on the top of your cabinets or refrigerator. As you collect various herbs, lay them in the basket. If you have a big haul, lay the herbs flat so they can dry easily. I do that with dandelion, mint, nettles, raspberry leaves, and lemon verbena if I have it. I leave them to dry, and once they have, I strip the leaves from the stems and put them in a bottle. I mix them to make a female toner tea to enjoy all through the winter. And do I like not having to buy boxes of those silly little individually wrapped and double-wrapped tea bags? You bet.

SPRING HERBS

Spring herbs, particularly perennial herbs, are a lovely thing. They burst forth with great vigor just when you need them. Everything from chives to early oregano, sage, tarragon, marjoram, thyme, and parsley (actually a biennial) will give you inspiration during the early days of spring. The way to grow parsley is to plant it in spring for summer harvesting; if you don't harvest it too aggressively, the remainder will make it through the winter and give you a nice new bounty in early spring, after which it will bolt (create seed heads). That overwintered parsley will give up the ghost around May, so don't expect it to get you through the summer. Parsley flowers, however, are great for attracting beneficial insects, so don't be in a hurry to remove them. You can save the seeds, too. Just plant more with the rest of your annual herbs come early June. If you time it properly, you can have fresh parsley throughout much of the year.

Whether they're perennial or annual, herbs are a must for any serious food gardener, if only because they offer so much for so little investment of time. Established perennial herb gardens are the workhorses of the kitchen. Once planted, such a garden will provide a source of inspiration throughout the year, since most will stand up to all but the frostiest of winters. A word to the wise, though—some herbs will grow quite large, and unless you want a rosemary tree in your backyard, be careful about where and how much you plant. Give them time to grow and in a few short years you will find plenty to harvest. In fact, you can probably find more than you need of many herbs just from the overgrown plants around your neighborhood. Folks overplant them or grow them as hedges for precisely the reason I mentioned—they are low maintenance. But they do grow, and they'll take over if you do not harvest and prune them regularly.

> Everything from chives to early oregano, sage, tarragon, marjoram, thyme, and parsley … will give you inspiration during the early days of spring.

Given all the summer squashes, tomatoes, beans, cucumbers, carrots, and God knows what else that are overflowing by late July and August, having winter squash cured and stored to eat later seems sensible beyond compare. I am so glad nature thought of them.

WINTER SQUASH

Another favorite of mine to plant in May is winter squash—butternuts and delicatas. I generally hold off planting them till the middle of May, but I stake out quite a bit of space for them, because these guys like to run. Delicatas are amenable to staking up, butternuts less so. I'm not sure if butternuts are really suited for a backyard space, but I can't help myself. I love them, and they make for really great eating and storage—much better than delicatas, which wither come February. I usually plant enough seeds for five or six healthy plants—generally two to a hill. Winter squash likes to be planted on a raised hill or mound. The hills can be up to a foot high and two feet wide, but smaller is fine. Just set the hills about four or five feet apart. The notion is not unlike vertical gardening, in that it provides extra space for the vines to grow. If weather and growing conditions work in my favor, I get four or five squashes per plant, which means upward of twenty butternuts for the root cellar. That's without counting the delicatas.

Given all the summer squashes, tomatoes, beans, cucumbers, carrots, and God knows what else that are overflowing by late July and August, having winter squash cured and stored to eat later seems sensible beyond compare. I am so glad nature thought of them.

By the end of May, I have planted my potatoes, peas, lettuce, chard, spinach, arugula, kale, broccoli raab, carrots, and beets. I have planted pole beans, winter squash, and onions. My garlic and shallots are looking promising, and my perennial herbs are full of verve and vigor. Some of my vegetables, like carrots and beets, I repeat plant throughout the season (every two weeks until July or August), whereas I plant cool-weather crops once in early spring, then wait till mid-June to plant again for a fall harvest. If I want an overwintering crop, I plant certain varieties again in August. A lot has been written about winter gardening, and I encourage you to read about it. But just by drawing your map and noting the growing conditions—upright or sprawling; the length of time for maturation; whether, and if, you can follow that earliest planting with something else— you will slowly learn the cycles of the garden. I also suggest keeping track of how much of what you hoped for actually came through, because hoping and wishing won't make things come true.

THE LAW OF DISTRIBUTION

Let's call the distance between what you hope for and what you get the Great Law of Distribution. Some of the stuff you're gonna get, and some of it the hungry backyard critters (or the weather, or the gardening learning curve) are gonna get. I would say that if you set your mind to accepting at least a 25 percent crop failure, you will not be disappointed. Who knows, it might be less than that, but you definitely could lose more. The natural world will show you who is boss. Some years, for example, the weather doesn't let bees make it to that sweet, blossoming apple tree. Sometimes, the slugs will come in greater numbers than can be imagined and they will eat more than their fair share of your tender starts (they can eat stuff right down to the nub). Some years, despite all your coddling, certain seeds will not germinate, or when they do they will perish due to what I have already described as dampening off. Actually, when you think about it, it is a miracle that anything grows at all. The truth is, modern agriculture (modern in the sense of the last couple of centuries) is a human invention. The minute we discovered that we could plant seeds ourselves, the genie was out of the bottle. Folks could now put down roots and build communities and whole civilizations. Taking things to their most odious extreme, industrial agriculture has now turned

> If you set your mind to accepting at least a 25 percent crop failure, you will not be disappointed.

Truth be told, living this householding life is about as radical an act as I can think of, especially if you do it well.

the genius of self-reliance into a diabolical plot to own seeds through patents, which is about the nastiest thing I can think of. Who the dickens do they think they are? I don't want to get started again, but if there is one thing that makes householding so delicious, it is the way I can, in a couple of years, sidestep most of the industry's madness—as long as they haven't patented all the seeds by then. By hook or by crook, I will learn how to save my own seeds, or at least make sure I buy or exchange my seeds with those I believe are on the same path as I am. Even if it is frustrating, even if I lose a big portion of my crop every year to the fickle hand of nature, it is still worth it. Growing your own food and restoring the tilth of the soil, fighting the prevailing paradigm and industrial systems make it worth it. Truth be told, living this householding life is about as radical an act as I can think of, especially if you do it well.

The Kitchen

The Story of Meat,
from Pasture to Table

Because the issues involved in eating and raising animals are loaded with both environmental and moral concerns, I did not make the decision to include meat in my family's diet lightly, and I have made it a priority to buy my meat from a sustainable farmer and to understand all the issues involved in responsible farm-share purchasing. When it is eaten in moderation, meat can play a vital role in meal planning for the year, I believe—which is why a friend and I visited a number of farms, talked to a bunch of farmers, and read a whole slew of information regarding the opportunities and limitations involved. What follows is an account of some of the issues you will face along the way. Hopefully, as you consider them, you will be able to make decisions in keeping with your own personal needs and preferences.

One of the ways farmers are able to sell to you outside of the standard USDA-certified system of meat production, processing, and distribution is for you to become an "owner" of the animal before it is slaughtered. The rules for processing animals for owners or shareholders are different than those that apply to the retail market. To become an owner yourself, you pay for the animal before it is brought to slaughter. Farmers are willing to enter into this agreement with you because it cuts out a million middlemen and allows them to raise animals according to a different system. Do not think of this as just a sneaky way to get around a system, however. For you to support the conditions you are after and to ensure a great product, there are things you have to do and things you should know. Here are a few of them.

FARM SIZE

Though I would like to assume small farming is always the best, it is not always the case when it comes to sustainable cattle farming. If a farmer is selling only a few animals on the side, he is likely not a farmer in the traditional sense (one who farms for a living), but rather a hobby farmer—someone for whom farming is merely a sideline. Though this is not always the case, most small or hobby farmers will not take on the immense amount of time required to focus on raising an animal in the way I want to support. Small farms raising only a few animals may not have enough ground to rotate pastures or engage in the type of management practices that are critical to raising cattle with a low footprint (high-density stocking, frequent moves, etc.). Livestock producers who are doing it full-time are dedicated to raising high-quality, sustainable livestock, and they have devoted their lives to it. These farmers will have good relationships with processors and will be very selective about the animals they choose for their shareholders. Of course, some small-scale farmers will be just as selective. You should talk to your farmer and decide if he operates in a way you are interested in supporting. Large or small, intention is key.

GRASS-FED: FACT OR FICTION?

Be clear about the distinction between grass-fed cattle, on the one hand, and cattle that are grass-fed by rotational grazing on pasture grasses, on the other. The former suggests a diet, the latter an approach to sustainable farming. Grass-fed cows (as properly defined) don't simply need pasture; they need a fair amount of it. They also need different grasses at different times of the year. This management of pasture grasses and rotational grazing takes a particular skill set that many farmers of "grass-fed" cattle do not have the space, time, or ability to embrace. If a farmer says his animals are grass-fed, but he has fifteen cows on five acres, you can begin to wonder. Depending on the grasses and regional terrain, a good rule of thumb is at least an acre of true pasture (not just landmass) per cow. You can research the rules at www.americangrassfed.org or through the Food Alliance at www.foodalliance.org.

> Depending on the grasses and regional terrain, a good rule of thumb is at least an acre of true pasture (not just landmass) per cow.

FARMER OR BROKER?

The next question to ask when buying your meat from a farmer (as an owner) is whether to work directly with the farmer or with his representative, the broker.

Farmer

Personally, I prefer working directly with the farmer who raises the animals. He should be able to clearly explain the history of breeds; why he chooses one over another; how pasture conditions, irrigation systems, terrain, the weather of the region, herd size, age of cattle, weight gain (when and how), and overall animal health are vital to an animal. And he will know about the processing—who does it and why.

Broker

Brokers are a little more removed from the process. Often, they represent farmers who are uncomfortable working directly with shareholders (not every farmer likes city kids coming to his farm). Brokers contract with farmers (they may work with more than one farmer) and interact with the customers to help figure out their needs (cuts, delivery dates, etc.). Brokers cannot legally arrange for the animal's processing, but they can help you decide what you are after. Understand, however, that brokers must get paid somehow, either by the farmer or by you. The price will be added to the per-pound price for the animal, since brokers cannot legally tag on an additional fee, because the shareholder system is meant to be a direct farmer-to-owner relationship. Even so, brokers can be perfect when you want a small order of beef or are new to the system. Just be careful; as with farmers, there are honest brokers and less honest ones.

THE PROCESSORS (THE SLAUGHTER, THE BUTCHER, THE HANGING, AND THE CURE)

All the players between the farmer and your neat little bundles of meat packets are called the "processors." They are, more specifically, those folks that either slaughter, butcher (cut up), or cure your meat. Each state has slightly different rules, but broadly speaking, some facilities may perform all of those services and others only one. Some are USDA-certified; others, as in Oregon, are "custom-exempt," meaning they do not

> The shareholder system is meant to be a direct farmer-to-owner relationship. Even so, brokers can be perfect when you want a small order of beef or are new to the system.

need USDA certification but they may not sell retail—they are the processors of meat provided by hunters and farmers for family use or for you, the owner. Even though most "owners" don't understand, or want to understand, the choices, I think you should.

WHERE TO SLAUGHTER?

The choice of slaughter site affects who, in the end, can do the butchering. The animal will either be slaughtered by a small mobile unit that comes to the farm or it will be taken to a slaughterhouse. Sorry to be so grim, but this piece matters. Where and how the animal is processed is becoming an increasingly challenging part of the sustainable meat industry.

On the Farm

A farmer who chooses to have his animal slaughtered on the farm will use a mobile slaughtering unit. These units are equipped to kill, clean, and hang the animals in a refrigerated locker in the back of a large trailer, then transport the carcasses to a facility for further processing. Farmers like these units because they create less stress for the animal. Stress can release enzymes into the animal's muscle mass, which negatively affects the quality of the meat; more importantly, though, on-farm slaughtering is considered a much more humane process than trucking your animal to be slaughtered off-site. There are, however, some consequences to on-farm slaughtering. A farmer who uses the mobile slaughter unit cannot sell his meat for retail because, although these units are often state-inspected, they are usually not USDA-inspected. This is not much of a concern for shareholders (farmers are selling directly to us, not through retail), but it is important to understand that "custom-exempt" status means that these mobile units are visited only once or twice a year (if that) by the state sanitarian. That doesn't mean that they are less sanitary; it just means they are not as heavily regulated. The fact is, whether USDA- or state-inspected, good mobile slaughter units can be hard to come by and are often booked early. That seems like a market opportunity for new mobile units, but licensing, regulations, and costs for establishing them are often prohibitive.

At a Slaughterhouse

A farmer who wants/needs to drive a *live* animal to a USDA slaughterhouse (the USDA facility will not take an animal any other way) does so for one of two reasons. He might want to use a mobile slaughtering unit but cannot find one available when he needs it, or one that meets his standards. Or he may also want to sell retail, in which case he must use a USDA facility. Unfortunately, there are not many facilities for farmers to choose from, and they are often an unreasonable distance from the farm. This situation has only gotten worse in the past few years.

As it stands today, most of the meat production in America is run by four large conglomerates. Much of what we dislike about the meat industry comes from their operating systems, which is why I suggest this piece is important. Supporting the types of facilities (either USDA or custom houses) that cater to the ethics of the sustainable meat industry, and understanding the issues that challenge them, is vital. It will also translate to having great food for your family, because even an animal raised perfectly, and on perfectly stewarded land, will be less than perfect if processed incorrectly.

The farmer's choice of slaughtering process will be personal, but you should ask him to explain it. Often the decision is based on trust—does the farmer respect the processor behind the counter, so to speak. Often he will choose based on what is available to him, and each region is different.

AGING BEEF

Before your meat is butchered, you have a chance to have it aged. Each butcher has an opinion about this. Some processors will age the animal ten days, fourteen days, or up to twenty-one days or more. Others will not hang the meat at all. For a comprehensive description of the issues regarding the aging of meat, I suggest *The River Cottage Meat Book* by Hugh Fearnley-Whittingstall.

BUTCHER VS. CUTTER

It is important to know that there are few real butchers out there. Most folks who "butcher" your meat are really called "cutters." It takes years and years of apprenticeship to become a competent butcher, whereas it takes a week to train as a cutter. With so much risk related to inappropriate butchering, most facilities have given up the service and gone with a process that requires little finesse. When doing custom butchering (and I'm not talking about the custom cutting most facilities suggest they do, but real, old-world butchering), a single misplaced cut can render an entire animal useless or greatly compromised (those who understand dressmaking can appreciate the similarities—making a single mistake either laying out or cutting a pattern on expensive fabric can be costly). Though most facilities have a butcher on site, the cutting is done by "cutters" who follow a simplified formula with very little room for deviation. A traditional butcher can theoretically make all the fancy cuts you might want (though they rarely want to spend the time), but a cutter can't. Knowing who will be butchering your meat may or may not be important to you, but knowing the process of butchering is important, because butchers, too, have had their industry turned upside down by

> It takes years and years of apprenticeship to become a competent butcher, whereas it takes a week to train as a cutter.

corporate competition and an uninformed consumer culture. Before you start to think about the cuts of meat you want and how to ask for them, you have a choice to make in butchering facilities—a choice that has in large part been made for you by where and how the animal was slaughtered.

WHERE WILL YOUR MEAT BE BUTCHERED?

Custom Cutting House

According to the USDA, the number of USDA slaughterhouses fell from 1,211 to just 809 nationwide between 1992 and 2008, while the number of small farms has grown by more than 100,000 in the past five years.

If you, the farmer, or the broker have chosen a mobile slaughtering unit, then the choice for butchering will generally be a custom cutting house (a USDA butcher cannot take meat that was slaughtered anywhere but in a USDA slaughterhouse). Like a mobile slaughtering unit, these houses will be "custom exempt." They may be USDA-certified (if they do both custom and retail business), but they don't have to be. The butchers (or rather cutters) in a custom cutting house will work with you, the owner, to decide cuts, but these cuts will be very standardized. You might want something special, but it will be difficult for them to oblige you, given the cost of personalized butchering.

USDA Butcher

If your farmer or broker took your animal *live* to a USDA slaughterhouse, the meat can be butchered at a USDA facility. Having your animal butchered at a USDA facility does not mean your meat will be cut to your specific instructions. These facilities are largely staffed by cutters as well, and they follow strict cutting systems that vary little. Whether you get specialized cuts has more to do with the particular butcher with whom you are working. For the farmer, however, the decision to use a USDA butcher means the meat can legally be sold to retail markets, if he is interested.

Do-It-Yourself Butchers

Some facilities are popping up to teach "owners" how to do their own butchering. Theoretically, you can ask for your meat not to be butchered after the slaughter and do it in your own home or in someone's certified kitchen (this is true no matter where the animal is slaughtered). It is your animal, after all. I haven't tried this, but it does interest me with regard to a pig. It's a whole different ball game with half a cow. A half a cow has an immense weight. Rocky Balboa did not look all buff for nothing. There is no way I could handle that body mass. Besides, do not mistake these hip new butcher boys who are popping up to teach these skills for seasoned old-world artisan butchers. They may be cute, but when push comes to shove, they are still novices. That means they, too, can make wrong cuts.

THE CUTS

Though you would like to imagine a great selection of cuts when you buy a whole or half share of an animal, you may be disappointed. According to Chris Roehm, of Square Peg Farms in Forest Grove, Oregon:

> The primary problem with the butchering business is the same as with the rest of the food world—it has become industrialized and consumers expect to pay factory prices. After a few decades of this approach, all of the craftspeople have been driven from business or for cost reasons cannot provide the great service they are capable of and still compete with larger chains—groovy or otherwise. (Whatever people say, for 99 percent of them, the price at the supermarket is the baseline they use to evaluate all other food.) There are a few customers who would pay twice the price to get a real custom cut/wrap job, but most people just want cheap meat, and

when you buy conventional pigs, the butchering can be 40 or 50 percent of the cost. I think the demand for really good butchering has finally grown to the point where someone can make a real business doing it—taking the time to do it correctly and increasing per-unit prices to make up for the decreased throughput that high quality requires. This leads us to the secondary problem facing the butchering business.

The federal regulations facing someone who wants to start a meat-processing business are daunting. Another qualification—I am not a ranting anti-government, anti-regulation lunatic. However, U.S. food-safety regulations are very clumsy, usually fail to address root causes, and generally serve as a barrier to entry to small would-be operators. Giant companies bitch about regulation, but they know it keeps small guys from taking their markets.

If industry has taken control of the system of cuts, we the consumers have allowed it. Frankly, we don't know the difference between great butchering and simple cutting. We don't even know what cuts are available on an animal. I once overheard a woman who was so confused by the prospect of ordering her cuts that she asked for the whole cow to be processed into ground beef. And I know that even many of you reading this will not get how completely crazy that is. Most people are more than happy to follow the processor's lead just because they don't know any better. Before we can support and encourage a return to old-world, artisan processors, we must know what we are supporting—and not just in concept. Before we can get the variety and sorts of cuts available just a few decades ago, we must know what they are. That will take a lot of rethinking and relearning from us and a certain degree of cooperation from the processors, who are already strained. If we want their participation, we

> *"The federal regulations facing someone who wants to start a meat-processing business are daunting... Giant companies bitch about regulations, but they know it keeps small guys from taking their markets."*
>
> —CHRIS ROEHM
> Square Peg Farms

must shoulder the cost of changing the system together. On our part, it will require a willingness to pay more for what we get and an increased understanding of the cuts—all the cuts, not just the fancy ones. How to utilize your animal from snout to tail is, after all, what grandma and grandpa used to know.

WHAT GRANDMA AND GRANDPA KNEW

A knowledge of bone and muscles, along with the skills related to in-home butchery, was something almost all of our grandparents had. In fact, during the Depression, the ability to utilize every cut of meat on an animal as well as possible was vitally important. Today, this ethic should still appeal to us, albeit for different reasons. Which is why I make such a big fuss about it. Unfortunately, until we start learning about—and asking for—the right cuts, we will remain captive to the old processing systems. It is those old systems that allow for the grinding of everything into hamburger (lots of miscellaneous fat gets hidden in it), the boning-out of roasts that would be better if the bone were left in, and for the theft of certain cuts by processors if only because most people don't know enough to recognize it (this happens more often than I care to mention). It is that old system (theirs and our own) that allows the shanks best suited for osso bucco, the oxtails that are excellent for stews and soups, and the disrespected tongue and liver to be tossed into the waste bin. We householders should be utilizing every cut of meat on our animal—not only for frugality's sake, but as a mark of respect for the effort and resources that have gone into raising an animal well. If there are objections to the morality and carbon footprint of raising animals for our consumption (and I know there are), our ability to put everything (and I mean everything) from the animal to good use will go a long way toward mitigating some of the complaints. At least it will suggest that we take those concerns seriously—or that I do, at least.

THE BASICS OF BEEF CUTS

After a beef carcass has been eviscerated, the carcass is generally cut down the middle so that there are two "sides" of beef. Each side of beef is then separated into a forequarter and a hindquarter.

Then each quarter is separated ("broken" is the word used in the industry) into the nine primal cuts. These primal parts are the wholesale cuts that are customarily distributed to retailers.

The first five primal cuts are from the forequarter:

> Beef Rib, Primal
> Beef Chuck, Square Cut
> Beef Foreshank
> Beef Brisket
> Beef Plate, Short Plate

The next four primal cuts are from the hindquarter:

> Beef Round, Primal
> Beef Loin, Short Loin
> Beef Loin, Sirloin
> Beef Flank, Flank Steak

These are the names for the primal cuts as they appear on standard beef charts today. Within each of those primal cuts, there is a group of secondary cuts called the sub-primals. Unfortunately the names of these sub-primal cuts not only vary from region to region (the history of butchery charts is fascinating), but also, taken as a whole, they constitute not so much a list of *all* the cuts available in a single primal section but rather *some* of what is available. Ordering one particular cut will often cancel out another. That was one of the most confusing things for me to understand and why I went on such a long journey to demystify the ordering process. I felt endlessly baffled when ordering my cuts or simply buying my meat at the grocery store. I know I'm not alone in this; it's why most of us go for sausages—what's to know? The reason we are so confused is twofold: first, the markets do not carry certain cuts anymore; and second, we no longer understand the skeletal and muscular structure of an animal.

I know this may seem like a ridiculous (and somewhat morbid) requirement, but I cannot emphasize too strongly how important it is to understand both the skeletal and the muscular structure of your animal. Though it will be difficult to comprehend at first, gaining a deeper understanding of your animal's structure will not only change the variety and quality of cuts you have for your householding kitchen, but ultimately will help change a processing system that has been defined by industry's bottom line and not by the talents of sustainable farmers and artisan processors.

THEM BONES (AND MUSCLES)

Understanding the bones and muscles of an animal will revive the availability of the sort of cuts that used to be in the butcher shop or meat case. Understanding bones will help you locate where, exactly, the cuts come from on the animal. Do not imagine that those bone-in cuts have been eliminated from the market for your convenience. Removing bones from the primal and sub-primal cuts at the processing plant resulted in lighter, cheaper, more compact packages to ship to retailers. Removing bones allowed for less skilled cutters on the assembly line (they use high-powered water spray guns to free the muscle groups from the bones). Removing bones allowed mistakes to be hidden from

Gaining a deeper understanding of your animal's structure will not only change the variety and quality of cuts you have for your householding kitchen, but ultimately will help change a processing system that has been defined by industry's bottom line.

view (you can tie up almost any piece of meat to make it look pretty), and over time created a consumer culture that imagined every chuck roast, sirloin steak, or package of stew meat to be the same as any other. Outside of the traditional rib primal, what the cutters behind your meat case usually receive from their wholesalers today are big bags of beef that, while designated as coming from a particular primal section on the cow, don't have a single bone in them—which is odd, since almost every primal section (save the flank) has bones. And what they do with those boneless bags of beef is cut them up into the array of other boneless cuts—the roasts, stew meat, stir-fry, sausage, ground beef, and kebabs that you see in the case. Convenience for you? Not really. And while understanding bone and muscle structures is important for the retail shopper, it is absolutely vital for those buying an animal through farmer share, particularly if you are splitting the animal in small shares.

THE SPLIT

Not everyone is inclined to order half a side of beef; many prefer to go with an eighth or quarter share (be advised, some farmers and processors will not work with such small orders). If you do want to split your animal into smaller shares, it is important to understand that certain cuts may be lost unless you give very specific cutting instructions. This again may take some rethinking. Many choice cuts (the brisket, the flank steaks, tenderloin, and standing rib roast, to name a few) come one or two to a customer. Should you have your heart set on a few brisket roasts, you should know there is only one large brisket to a side of beef (which is typically cut in half); this means you can't really split it four or eight ways with your friends unless you want really tiny roasts. You should understand that you cannot have both porterhouse steaks *and* the tenderloin roast from the sirloin primal. You can have one or the other. Do you want a standing rib roast for the holidays? Well, you can't have individual rib steaks and standing rib roasts; they simply cancel each other out. Few folks understand that when you split an animal into even or similar packages, lots of the choice cuts will get lost. It would be better to sit down together and decide who gets what—if, that is, you can figure it out. I suggest you try.

RESOURCES

One of my favorite books is *Cutting Up in the Kitchen* by Merle Ellis. Written in the 1970s and designed to encourage cooks to make the most use of inexpensive cuts, it offers a great visual guide for sorting things out and supports the very thing I have been saying: understanding, and recognizing, bone and muscle structure is key to being a savvy consumer—whether through farm shares or at the market. I also like *Beef and Veal* (in the Time-Life series); it has great illustrations and information. Remember, most of what you find that was written before 1980 will refer to things that are hard to find in markets today. In fact, the further back you go in time the more thorough the butchering and cooking charts will be because, as I've said, true butchering is a lost art.

MY FIRST YEAR'S EXPERIENCE

Frankly, it took me a long time to figure all this out. It entailed not only poring over charts and books, but also finding a butcher who would review my order to see if it made sense, or if I had missed something despite all my efforts. Unfortunately, I never got a chance to do that in my first year of ordering farm-share beef, because I worked with a broker. I never got to visit the farm, see my animal, or meet the farmer who raised it (my broker said farmers don't like "Birkenstock types" on their land, which is funky but true). I simply trusted my broker, which, in retrospect, was not the best approach. My animal was not raised and fed, hung and aged, or even cut as my broker promised. I do not blame the farmer or the processors. They would have told me themselves that none of what I was promised was possible. Which is why I suggest you speak with your processors directly (in fact, as a farm-share owner, legally you should) and get involved with all aspects of the system. Being aware of the issues that challenge them (knowing about existing and upcoming USDA regulations, for instance) can change farmers' and processors' perception of you from a pain in the ass (sorry, guys) to an advocate for change and truly sustainable systems. As the "greenwashers" take hold of the marketplace, small-scale farmers and processors will need your help.

One other point I need to make (because if it can happen to me, it can happen to anyone). When I noticed I had not received any of the bones that were boned out, I asked my broker about it. About a week later they were delivered to my house (was I supposed to think my animal's bones had been sitting around in a refrigerator bin somewhere for a week?)—and, to make matters worse, the broker charged me extra for them. Which is the point I absolutely have to make. When buying a farm share of an animal, you pay for everything ahead of time and there should not be any add-ons for the animal itself. But like I said, brokers and farmers can be on a learning curve themselves—or, more simply, they can be dishonest. It can happen. Knowledge will be your best defense.

THIS YEAR

Luckily, after that experience, I bought a farm share with Carman Ranch (a fourth-generation farmstead run by the fabulous Carman family). Cory Carman then introduced me to Kevin Silverira, her butcher and the owner of Valley Meat Service in Wallowa, Oregon. I traveled to Wallowa and met with Kevin, who sat with me and looked at my list and indulged my questions. He even let me in the cutting room while he butchered the animals. I've been invited to watch my own animal be processed, and I will do it. I will go to the Carman Ranch to see my steer, note his body structure, weight, and age, and then follow the system through its process. Cory has already taken me on a tour of her land, explained what is meant by rotational grazing, and shown me how she is returning the pastures to their native grasses and restoring the surrounding wetlands. Today, I feel I have a small clue as to what is involved, but only that. It will take years for me to truly understand it all, but between Cory at the Carman Ranch, Kevin at Valley Meats, and Chris and Amy at Square Peg Farms, I think I have relationships that will last me well into the future. I am so grateful to have found them, and I pray they will not go away as the costs of keeping up their small, sustainable systems rise.

THE CURE

After the cuts comes the cure. I have not had good experience with traditional cures at smokehouses. The meat is oversalted, injected with nitrates, and quickly smoked. Finding a good cure house is very difficult, which is why more folks are doing it themselves. As part of a rural lifestyle, curing is a food preservation tool that has existed for centuries and was another vital part of creating stores for the year. Here is the perspective of Chris, my pig farmer:

> In my opinion, in the current environment, the best
> way to manage curing meat from a custom hog is to
> do it yourself. Especially with a food-buying group

Continued on page 174

MORE MEAT STUFF

LIVE WEIGHT

Calculated on the hoof. Most farmers can give you the approximate weight.

HANGING WEIGHT

With head, hide, and hoofs removed and eviscerated (organs removed). This is the weight that farm-share owners should be charged by.

AGING WEIGHT

Though technically not a figure most processors keep track of, you should know that aging subtracts anywhere from 2 to 15 percent from the hanging weight, depending on how long the meat is aged (2–6 weeks or longer). This loss of weight translates to less meat to sell, which is often why butchers don't like aging meat. They also don't have the room to allow the carcass to hang around that long. If you do have a butcher who's willing to age your carcass (not all carcasses are suitable for long aging), be prepared to pay more and/or get less meat.

PROCESSED (FINISHED) WEIGHT

This is the weight of the finished product after it has been cut and wrapped for the customer. Many processors have standard cutting forms that work within the system they have developed. Though this works well for those who do not understand (or do not want to understand) the full range of cutting options (as I mentioned, it can be challenging to do so), I do suggest you try to figure them out yourself.

The formula below shows the approximate loss of weight between live weight to hanging weight and between hanging weight and finished weight. Knowing all three weights, and following the formula, will help you track the changes. And while some brokers or farmers like to both arrange for and charge by the "finished" weight (as well as occasionally adding their fee for negotiating your deal), it is neither technically legal nor advised. You, not the farmer or broker, should be working with the processors, since you, not the farmer, broker, or processor, should know what you want.

CALCULATIONS BETWEEN LIVE, HANGING, AND PROCESSED WEIGHTS

Live weight x 0.60 = hanging weight

Hanging weight x 0.60 or 0.80 = finished weight (use higher number if bones, organ meat, shanks, tails, etc., are included in your order)

For example, a 1,000-pound live-weight steer will yield about a 600-pound hanging carcass, and about 360 to 480 pounds of finished, wrapped meat.

A half hanging weight is 260 to 350 pounds, which will give you about 160 to 220 pounds of meat for the freezer. I have heard of some customers wanting

every single scrap of meat, bone, and fat from the animal, and some processors will oblige them. If that is the case for you, you will receive the entire hanging weight, or close to it, but you will have a lot of bits and pieces packed up in a number of boxes to sort through. All of it can go to making soup stock, but it can be a bit of a headache if your freezer space, time, and skill are limited.

PRICE

Hanging-weight price varies from farm to farm, but typically runs from $2.50 to $4.00 per pound. My own cattle farmer charges closer to the high end, but he deserves it.

Finishing fees (cut and wrap) run an additional $0.50 to $0.85 per pound on the hanging weight and should be charged separately.

Kill fees (charged by the slaughterhouse or mobile unit) usually run from $50 to $60.

Curing fees vary greatly. Check with your curing house. These fees will apply only to the meat you have cured.

Note: Some processors do it all— slaughter, cut, wrap, and even cure—and they will list the fee for each of these services separately, or they should.

LABELING

Just as it will take extra effort to make special cuts, you will have to convince your processor to label your cuts appropriately or, absent that, be willing to make sense of them when you open up your packages.

STORAGE

For every 50 pounds of meat you receive, you will need 2.25 cu. ft. of freezer space, which is the size of the freezer compartment on most average fridges when empty. I suggest purchasing a chest freezer.

QUANTITY

The number of packages you receive will vary greatly depending on the weight of the carcass, its breed, and your finishing order (cut and wrap). The following list was based on my cutting instructions for half of a 600-pound hanging carcass. My cutting instructions were very specific, and it took a special processor to oblige me. Even if you don't find a processor who's equally adaptable, the standard processing forms will not be bad—they just won't be as good as it gets.

CUTS

I've listed these by each primal section and by standard and not-so-standard sub-primal cut names. I've also listed the cutting instructions and/or weight, the number of cuts I want in each package, and the number of packages I expect to receive (in parentheses). The exact amount I receive can vary based on the particulars of the animal (muscle and bone structure). My advice is to meet your processor in person and then trust him to do the very best for you. Word of mouth is often the best way to find a great processor. Cherish yours when you do.

FROM CHUCK

Short ribs - Three to a pack (2)
Arm roast - Ground. 1-pound packages (6–8)
Cross-cut chuck - Blade, center, and 7-bone. 3–5 pounds each (5)
Neck - Cut for stew meat. 1-pound packages (6–8)

FROM RIBS

Roast - Ribs 9, 10, 11, 12 (1)
Steaks - Ribs 6, 7, 8 - Cut for 1-inch steaks. Caps left on. One to a pack (3)
Short rib ends - Four to a pack (1)

FROM PLATE

Cross-cut short ribs. Cut 1½-inch thick. Four to a pack (3)

FROM FORESHANK

Shanks - Cut in 1½-inch cross-sections. Three to a pack (2)

BRISKET

Roasts - Point-cut and flat-cut roasts. 2 pounds each (2)

FROM ROUND

Heel of round - Ground for hamburger. 1-pound packages (2)

Top round steaks - Cut ¾-inch thick. One to package (8–10)

Bottom round roasts - 3–4 pounds per package (2)

Eye of round roast - 2–3 pounds per package (1)

Boned sirloin tip roast - 3–4 pounds per package (2)

FROM SHORT LOIN

All cut for 1-inch-thick steaks with tails left on

Porterhouse - One to a package (3)

T-bone steaks - One to a package (10–12)

FROM SIRLOIN

All bone-in, cross-cut, and cut 1½-inch thick

Pin bone - One to a package (2)

Flat bone - One to a package (2)

Round bone - One to a package (1)

Wedge bone - One to a package (1)

FROM FLANK

Cut ¾-inch thick

Whole trimmed flank steak - One to a package (1)

ADDITIONAL CUTS

Skirt steak - 1 pound per package (1)

Hanging tender - 1 pound per package (1)

Tongue (1)

Liver - 1 pound per pack (8)

Heart - Split (2)

Oxtail - 1-inch cut. Four to a pack (1)

Soup bones (6-8)

Miscellaneous cuts ground for burger - 1-pound packages (10 or more)

like the one you are involved in, the few items you
need can be purchased cooperatively and any heavy
lifting can be shared. To be clear, I am not suggesting
you slaughter an animal. Get it killed and even
cut into pieces. Let someone else cut and wrap the
fresh meat, if you like. But get the shoulders, bellies,
and legs fresh and cure them yourself. Buy some
industrial pork at industrial prices to practice. If you
screw up one of those bellies, who cares? Twenty or
thirty bucks and a few hours time is a cheap way to
learn. Chances are you won't screw it up, however,
and you'll have some really tasty fat to chew.

I agree. I'm working through it with more or less success.

HOW IT WORKS IN THE HOUSEHOLDING KITCHEN

Today I know I can take one large bone-in chuck roast
out of the freezer at the beginning of the week and cut
it up into four or five meals—some for stew, some for
steaks (in the case of the blade roast), some for smaller
roasts, soups, and stir-fry, or ground up for burgers.
Cutting up a large section of meat into smaller pieces
and using them over a week or two is just fine, since I
know my meat is very fresh. I am beginning to understand what each muscle group is best suited for, and
cutting it up myself will allow for a variety of uses.
Finally, though we may have no hope of getting some
of these old-school cuts at the retail market, we may
when we order them at the farmers market or from a
small processor who understands what this movement
is really about.

JUNE

JUNE

The Home

The Happy World of the Generalist

I am always amazed, and a little awestruck, when I meet folks who knew early on what they wanted to be when they "grew up." You hear these stories told like near-apocalyptic visions, and maybe it is just like that. Perhaps you can know by the age of five, ten, fifteen, or even twenty that you want to be a doctor and then follow a straight path to get there. I suppose that is why we are asked so early and so often what we want to be when we grow up. Someone must assume we should know. Personally, I never understood that question; in fact, I still don't. I think most folks are like me, searching for a fit. At least, that was how it used to feel. Then, late in life, I discovered the happy world of the generalist.

I think they used to call us jacks-of-all-trades, implying a failure to master anything in particular. Considering my history, that assumption is fair. While I have dabbled in everything from perfume making to fabric design, from fashion, sales, office work of every stripe, event planning, catering, and restaurant work to writing, I never had a total aha moment until recently. More common to my work history was a fleeting commitment, particularly when it came to the routine most jobs require. Not that I am afraid of hard work or the requirement of detail; in fact, I love an orderly system. I just needed some tacit faith in the overriding purpose of it all, because, in the end, who can love selling widgets? Who can do the same thing, day in and day out, and not get bored? Which is not to say it has all bored me; it has not. I have worked for many wonderful people and opened a number of restaurants that carried the mark of my own creativity and expression. Yet bracketing those efforts was a life without context, a life of business that would always, somehow, bore me. Today I understand that I was not so much bored as fragmented. That my experience of work as separate from the everyday tasks of everyday life was a relatively recent phenomenon. That what I took as the norm was more accurately the reversal of a long-standing narrative of work as something one *does*, not something one goes to.

PURPOSE MATTERS

Somewhere between the insufferable toil and degradation of forced labor and the misty-eyed accounts of country comforts lie the stories of lives marked by the joy of self-sufficiency, the stories of work before industry, wages, and "labor-saving" devices took over. They are the stories of people buoyed by the pride of doing what was needed on the land and having the skills and trades required for it. It is hard to know whether all this work gave folks a sense of value and purpose, or whether it was nothing more than utility born of necessity. What I do know is that purpose matters. That is the sentiment I read in accounts of the past—that once those things produced by and attached to a unique combination of

> My experience of work as separate from the everyday tasks of everyday life was a relatively recent phenomenon.

skills among people, communities, and the land were transformed by industry into easily replicated widgets, something was lost to human experience, something akin to pride, purpose, and a sense of place. During the industrial revolution and beyond, a modern "scientific" ethic emerged to support the sweeping displacement of place by the mass-produced products of no-place. What was offered as justification for this deliberate disconnect from the cycles of the natural world was the freedom from hard work. Has this proved to be the panacea that our forefathers imagined?

In that same book of essays by Wendell Berry I mentioned in the introduction, he asks: "We are being saved from work, then, for what? The answer can only be that we are being saved from work that is meaningful and ennobling and comely in order to be put to work that is unmeaning and degrading and ugly."

Of course, this is Wendell's charm. He lures us with the nostalgia of honest work, hard work, work done on and for the land. Clearly he knows what he is talking about, while my nostalgia is entirely more obtuse. Really, I am a city girl. A born-and-bred Bronx girl. I have never lived on the land. Other than my summer pilgrimages to Vermont to play farmer, and an attempt to hack up a city golf course to grow food (yep, that was me, coppers), I am not from a rural culture. I am every bit the child of immigrant parents who came to this country and to the city for the chance at something better, and in a certain light I have to say they accomplished just that. Were it not for my parents' hard work (my father was a tailor, and my mother, after raising us kids, worked for Ma Bell), I would not have had the life I've had. In retrospect, I understand their middle-class success as a moment in time when government policies, incentives, and unions encouraged the distribution of wealth between industry and its workers. Though some may have understood how unique a time it was, I did not. I did not understand that the comforts of my home, my

> "We are being saved from work, then, for what? The answer can only be that we are being saved from work that is meaningful and ennobling and comely in order to be put to work that is unmeaning and degrading and ugly."
>
> —WENDELL BERRY

parents' jobs, and the access to education I enjoyed were an atypical episode in the history of human progress.

THE PEARLY GATES

Would I have run through the gates of middle-class opportunity had I better comprehended that story? I'm not sure. What I do know is that at the time I did not feel the allure of that safety my parents wanted for me: a home in the suburbs, a job with benefits, marriage, children, and a two-car garage. Certainly that is how the second-generation middle-class story presented itself, at least in part. Who knows why we refuse what our parents feel is best for us? All I can say is that my sensors were aligned to another story. Growing up in the Bronx one could not avoid that other story. Because right alongside the tales of success and opportunity within our middle-class culture were the narratives we don't want to acknowledge—stories of urban racism and isolation, of poverty and despair. More than the middle-class security I was promised, it was the sadness I wondered about during my long, silent subway rides to college through the dark, dingy neighborhoods on the other side of the American dream.

WINNERS AND LOSERS

I never understood who was running the show, why some folks were winners and some were losers. I never understood why some of my peers could run unfazed into the great big world of opportunity while I could not. Was it a refusal of my parents' vision, or a vision of another kind? Or was it the lack of any vision at all? That, I suspect, is more the truth of it, since what supplied the wind beneath my wings was something less inflating than hope. Without knowing why, the darkness of the human experience appeared entirely more honest to me than the jingles of middle-class lifestyles. I do not credit this sensitivity to a particular social consciousness alone, but to a personality that leans toward the melancholy.

DARK IS AS DARK DOES

Though it never happened, I have a funny image of myself at a pool party, dressed in black and nervously smoking a cigarette, railing, "What about the Holocaust?" It's a metaphor for my temperament because—well, I can get a little heavy (no duh). Which reminds me, what's up with cheerleaders? God forgive me, but I can never figure out what the hell they are so happy about. Where do they get such commitment? Such unbridled enthusiasm? What the hell is with those pom-poms? Even more puzzling to someone with my temperament are those beer hats and furry mascots. Not that I want to dis sports fans, but the spectacle of so much enthusiasm frightens me a bit. Perhaps that's not such a surprise. Except for a few second-generation anomalies, we New York Chekhov types will wet our panties during an Ingmar Bergman festival but flatline during the Super Bowl. Cheetos? Really? Oh, the horror. Can somebody find me some pickled herring?

Sorry, I digress. I just wanted to own a bit of my melodrama. Still, the point was, and is, that I did not understand the life being promised to me. Which does not mean I ran to the world of reasoned protest and civil disobedience, or that I marched in the streets defending the right to rights. Certainly, that would have been a logical expression of my discomfort, but I was born in 1953 and was a little too young during the early '60s, when the pot was being stirred. I experienced little of the counterculture or social unrest while I was sowing my wild oats in the Bronx. More common to the backdrop of my

What all this unraveling has offered me—at this late date—is a life comforted by the clear message of everyday acts.

stomping grounds were the dregs of the cotton (I will leave that reference for those who get it) and the lingering sentiment of the Beat generation who, by all accounts, were a less than cheery lot. *Howwwwwwlllllllll.*

EVERYDAY ACTS

As I sought to make sense of life amid urban ruin, its effects on me were toxic and disillusioning. It has taken me four decades to sort through the mixed messages of history, society, and my own folly. It has taken time and brutal self-reflection to find explanations for the disparities I witnessed during those train rides. What all this unraveling has offered me—at this late date—is a life comforted by the clear message of everyday acts. Messages like Wendell's, which encourage a simple life without the rose-tinted vision of upward mobility. Messages like the Zen proverb, "Before enlightenment, chop wood and carry water; after enlightenment, chop wood and carry water," which suggests a life that honors hard work, simple work—before, after, always. These messages carry the powerful notion that no great horizons are to be found in the right job, house, neighborhood, marriage, or income bracket. Rather, those horizons are in the silent workings of self-reliance, in quiet reverence for "the least of these"—that idea not frozen in a biblical context, but applied to all things, be they in the soil or on the land, your neighbors or someone somewhere who has less to eat than they deserve. Behind my life as a generalist is the world I think Wendell and many others before him allude to. It is that world of purpose, place, and pride, before they were transformed by industry into the same large, uppercase notion of success that my parents promised me. If today I live as a generalist, it is not from lack of heart but more *because* of it. If today I practice the trades of running a household and hanging on to a notion of place and purpose,

Between 2002 and 2006, the average inflation-adjusted income of the top 1 percent of earners increased by 42 percent, whereas the bottom 90 percent only saw an increase of 4.7 percent.

SOURCE: *THE MIDDLE CLASS SQUEEZE*, A REPORT PREPARED BY THE UNITED STATES HOUSE OF REPRESENTATIVES COMMITTEE ON GOVERNMENT REFORM – MINORITY STAFF SPECIAL INVESTIGATIONS DIVISION, SEPTEMBER 2006, FOR DEMOCRATIC LEADER NANCY PELOSI AND REP. HENRY A. WAXMAN.

it is not because of the fable of American promise but *in spite* of it. If I am saying no, it is because I can see no good coming from saying yes. If today I have become a generalist, it is not purely a result of my *Sturm und Drang* nature but of something resembling hope and, I must say, happiness.

THE NEW POM-POM

As it turns out, I love my life as a generalist. I love trying on one skill set after another. I love flitting about from plant to tree, from garden to home, from soil to kitchen, and from ceaseless activity to the long winter days of rest and projects that can only be imagined when the harvest is underfoot. I love discovering the fundamentals of really good cooking, of discovering my ingredients as they go from seed to salad. I love the conversations with my children and the guidance I can offer them against the madness of this world. I love the meals at our table, the decorating of our rooms, the cheer of the holidays and the traditions they bring. I love looking out my window in every season to see how the world changes and yet stays the same. I love walking out, in every season, in the cool morning while the world still sleeps and surveying all that is around me. Oh, how lovely it looks in the cool breeze of a new day.

I can live this way because of my parents' position at that unique moment in human progress, but I am not without respect for the sacrifices that were made. I am privileged, but it is not without knowing what is owed to the world. I am a householder in an effort to imagine a way out of a formula of diminishing returns, because if ever the middle-class experiment has been abandoned, it is now. This is not a lament for that life but an invitation to understand both what it meant and what we have allowed it to become. Somehow, in the mad dash to capture a life in the suburbs (or even one

Somewhere in the natural and rightful world of progress we came to believe our destinies meant something bigger than the small things that we do every day.

of urban sophistication), we abandoned the principles of hard work, equality, and stewardship that stood as the bedrock of those middle-class values or, more certainly, of our rural roots. Somewhere in the natural and rightful world of progress we came to believe that our destinies meant something bigger than the small things that we do every day. I do not agree. I think a correction must be made—and if not by us and for ourselves, then where and when? Though householding will not be the answer for everyone, in spirit it suggests that the work "in here" is as valuable as the work (and careers) "out there." Today I do not go to work, but rather work as I go. Here and there, in a rhythm entirely more suited to my nature, I do what must be done. Today, because I am so inclined, I take on the hard work of endless tasks and, in so doing, become a jack-of-all-trades and a master of none. Perhaps this will encourage you to try this out, and perhaps it will suit you as well. And now I realize I am my own kind of cheerleader, only without the pom-poms.

JUNE

The Garden

The Guilt of the Gardener • Transplanting Tomato Starts •
The Wild Kingdom • Slugs Be Damned

I must be honest. I always feel a little guilty buying plant starts. I feel guilty when I don't buy heirloom seeds or plants. I feel guilty that I don't save all my seeds. But though I would like to do more, I can do only what I have the time to do. The matter of time is no joke, since once planting season begins I am kick-ass busy with all my chores. Remember, this householding life is that of a generalist—a little here, a little there. If all I were doing was growing food, it might be different, but not only am I the farmer, I am also the farmer's wife. I am the one meeting me at the door as both the bearer and receiver of the harvest. Such is the way of our oddly fragmented family systems. Chores that can be effectively managed with two or three sets of hands can be overwhelming for just one set—mine. Which is not to suggest I can jump ship. No, no. In June I am just getting started.

Late May or early June is when I focus on the heat-loving vegetables of summer—peppers, eggplants, cucumbers, beans, and summer squash. That list is not comprehensive nor is it a list of what I always grow. I keep it simple. Growing what you love is all the more important in a small backyard garden—which seems obvious, but I can't tell you how much food goes to waste simply because a preference was not taken to heart. Melons and corn, which I do love, never show up in my garden, because neither takes kindly to transplanting and direct seeding is a game of chance given the sunny-day shortage in Oregon. They will grow, but not always to the point of great fruiting. Still, folks around here can't seem to resist trying their hand at growing corn or melons in their backyard. I love the idea, just not the logic—too much space with a questionable return.

Cucumbers are one of those summer vegetables I do plant in fair quantity, since I pickle quarts and quarts of them once they are fully fermented (as opposed to quick pickled). Like many other vegetables and fruit, they should be direct seeded, since they don't prosper when transplanted. And while I go heavy on the cucumbers, I go light on the summer squash. What summer squash I do plant is mostly pattypan squash. Rather than bearing its fruit on runners, like the prolific zucchini, pattypan squash is a compact bush. Could there be a single gardener alive who has not heard the cautionary tales about zucchini? Simply put, unless you want to eat lots of the things, a single plant will do. One morning you will have a properly sized squash waiting for you; the next day, if you failed to pick it, it'll be a monster. That is the way it is with lots of produce. Growing your food is not like going grocery shopping; it will be the harvest, not your palate, that dictates what's for dinner. There is likely no better example of the shift required in householding than this: it is the harvest, not your mood, that calls the shots. Even I, despite all this talk,

> Growing your food is not like going grocery shopping; it will be the harvest, not your palate, that dictates what's for dinner.

have salad greens withering in the fridge because I haven't used them. That's also why I like to focus on a preserving garden, since what I do not cure and store in my "root cellar," I can preserve for future use in the freezer, on drying racks, or in cans.

SOMETIMES A GREAT NOTION

No matter how great your intentions, there is still only so much fresh produce a person can eat during the summer, and sadly I have heard many urban farmers admit that they are too tired to cook or eat what they grow. How many people growing backyard gardens still rely on beer, pizza, and burritos as their main food sources? Lots, I'm sure. The sheer volume of our harvest, or the fatigue that results from raising our food (particularly if we are balancing the effort with other full-time obligations), or the mixed metaphors of our life (we are both stewards of the earth and creatures of the night), mean that we often do not find the time to use what we grow. To be sure, there are food banks and neighbors to take the surplus produce off your hands, but unfortunately I start looking for someone to whom I can give my produce only after I have accepted that I can neither eat nor process it in time. By then, it is a little long in the tooth and not worthy of being a gift. One feels a little sheepish passing off lettuce that is a tad bitter or zucchini (to get back to them) that are too large and seedy for most palates. At the other end of the spectrum, there are those who grow an extra row of crops for just that purpose. Supplying others with produce when they would otherwise not have access to it is a valuable endeavor, so I will not discourage it. For my part, however, having excess is a sign that I need to rethink my sowing and harvesting schedule. Poor planning is a luxury that limited space cannot support, which is another reason I don't plant unruly zucchini. My pattypans, on the other hand, are compact, more reasoned producers. At their peak, they give off two new orbs every day or two, something I can manage. This is another reason I plant a preserving garden—it fits my temperament and lifestyle. It allows for my squirrel consciousness—the tempered rhythm of putting up stores in summer and fall to enjoy in the winter. If we were to follow that code instead of practicing 24/7 shopping, we might more successfully embrace the goal of stewardship, but that is another story. Right now I am thinking about my tomatoes.

THE TOMATO STRETCH

In late May or early June, I finally plant my tomatoes. Still safe and warm in their pots, they are now ready to stretch out their roots. Though I love my slicing tomatoes, I devote my greatest attention to plum tomatoes destined for canning. I often say that if you are going to preserve only one thing a year, it should be tomatoes, since they are so versatile in the kitchen. After selecting a nice spot that gets at least six hours of sunlight, I transplant them. This involves digging a hole in your bed, adding a generous heaping of compost, watering the hole thoroughly, and then carefully setting the beauties into their new home. Once they are settled, I water them again, let the water soak in, and cover them with soil to tamp down gently around the roots so they are steady. If you notice the ground is very hard when you're digging the hole, loosen it up and add compost to the entire area around the tomato start. Remember, plants like to have room to grow, particularly their roots. If your soil is very hard, the roots will not be able to spread through the soil very well. Some plants will thrive in very dense soil, but not many vegetables will. If you don't yet have the best soil (and your efforts and amendments will improve it over the years, if you have a mind to do so), I suggest planting in raised beds.

I allow at least two feet between starts, which looks spare and stark in the beginning, but, believe me, those tomato plants will fill out. Many a mold and disease problem has been precipitated by overcrowding, so give them room to grow. I stake them when I first transplant them, since doing so will prevent possible root damage later, once the roots have taken hold. I place a six-foot bamboo stake (one foot goes in the ground) right by the central stem of the tomato plant. I will attach the main stem of the tomato to that stake as it grows. I put a tomato cage around the rest of the plant to provide some structure and keep the plant from flopping over. Some folks I know allow the plants to flop over, or put branches around the base of the plant so that it will have some support when it gets heavy with fruit. I prefer tomato cages. I like my plants to grow upward as much as they can.

Tomato growers refer to their varieties as being either "determinate" or "indeterminate." I have been able to remember what that means by thinking: determinate varieties are determined to be exactly what they want. Other than being staked and having their bottom leaves trimmed (so they don't touch the wet ground and become more susceptible to disease), they want to be left alone. Their growth and fruiting pattern are determined, and pruning them will interrupt that coding. Indeterminate varieties are more indecisive, so to speak, and allow for more fussing and pruning. If you can keep that in mind, you should be okay. If you choose to fuss over an indeterminate variety (remember, it will allow it), a good way of thinking about it is to consider how much energy the plant has. How many stalks and flowers and fruits can it support? Left to its own devices, a tomato plant is greedy and will put on as much fruit as it can. This is true for lots of other plants, particularly fruit trees; it's why agriculturists thin some of the fruit from the tree, allowing it to put all its vitality into the remaining fruits so they can grow big and ripen without too much competition. The same logic applies to pruning an indeterminate tomato plant. You're giving it a trim so it can put its energy into a smaller quantity of larger tomatoes, along with less leaf production.

Pruning also gives the plant room for good air circulation and allows for easier staking—which reminds me to give a shout-out to the person who invented green Velcro plant ties. Now, there's a product that was worth putting on the market. They come in various widths and I use the stuff like crack—constantly, and without any shame about what the neighbors might think. Okay, bad comparison, but I do go through that stuff. If I am really obsessive, I can reuse it from one year to the next because it holds its Velcro-osity. New or recycled, it holds the stems to my stakes very nicely. It is easy to apply and never digs into the tender stems as a string might do. I use it for my other vines, raspberry canes, and just about anything else that needs to be reined in at my house (note to self: try on teenage son).

TOO LITTLE, TOO LATE

Once the tomato plants are in place, I stand back and watch them do their thing. I have been lucky over the years to have had few viral, insect, or bacterial invasions, but I have suffered from growing the wrong, late-ripening varieties. It may not seem like much at the beginning of the growing season, but fifteen days is a big difference when you are trying to outrun the frost. Pay attention to the maturation date listed on the package of seeds you buy. Varieties will be designated as early-, mid-, or late-ripening. Sadly, some of my favorites are late-ripening varieties, which in the past I have ignored. One only has to go through one season of waiting for the lovely green orbs to turn red and ripe before an early frost turns them flaccid and inedible to know what a shame it is when you lose the battle to nature. That's when you know what a difference a

How odd it is to see folks running or jogging miles in specially designed sports gear when they could be working up a sweat growing food.

day makes. Even if you do beat the clock on the first winter frost, you may not have enough lusciously hot summer days for your tomatoes to truly ripen.

As with berries, hot, sunny weather brings out the best (i.e., sugar) in tomatoes. Even one extra sunny day can turn a merely good tomato into a sublime one. Nature has its demands, which is why I pay attention to genetic coding. Sometime I beat the clock and sometimes I don't. Growing food can be such a crapshoot that you understand how blessed you are when the seasons and weather align themselves with your gardening agenda. That is another way that life will straighten you out. You will stop seeing the weather as a backdrop for your weekend activities. Not that anyone wants a rained-out picnic, but, on certain occasions, rain will be such a welcome guest in the garden that you will almost delight at the way it overturns your vacation plans. Actually, I think about that a lot. Not so much maliciously, but when I think about a world pegged to recreation and leisure. How odd it is to see folks running or jogging miles in specially designed sports gear when they could be working up a sweat growing food. I understand that not everyone wants to grow food, but it is curious how thoroughly convinced we are of the logic of jobbing out food production to industry. Sure, it has allowed us time for sports, but given what poor condition the food supply is in, I think it may be time to trade in those running shoes for a shovel.

These days the only time I do feel a little bad about a rained-out affair is when I think of some bride and groom having their special day ruined. But even weddings have turned into oddly disconnected photo ops with all manner of country-comfort aesthetics thrown in for effect. How many weddings are held "down on the farm" for folks who wouldn't know the front end from the back end of a cow? Well, I guess they'd know that, but you get what I mean—nature is merely a backdrop. Might there not be a better way to keep nature a

real enemy to keep their numbers in check. Under the circumstances, I am only doing my part to keep the garden world balanced. That's my theory, anyway.

By late June I have planted my potatoes and peas, my lettuce, chard, spinach, arugula, kale, broccoli raab, carrots, and beets. I have planted pole beans, winter squash, and onions. My tomatoes, summer squash, and annual herbs are all in place. A large share of my early spring vegetables—my sweet shelling peas and earliest lettuce—has been eaten. Now, and for some time to come, I will turn my attention to serious harvesting. I can feel the heat approaching.

Whatever it takes— scissors, slug bait, copper tape, salt, beer, or nighttime raids—slugs will not roam unchallenged in my backyard.

JUNE

The Kitchen

Berries • Patience • Genetic Modification • Wild Things •
The Alchemy of Jam-Making

Perhaps it is the magical sweetness of strawberries after a winter of turnips and stew; perhaps it is their illustrious color, the way they pop like jewels from the sea of green that surrounds them; perhaps it is that they represent all that is to come as summer begins. Whatever the reason, nothing gets everyone quite so excited as the first display of berries in our garden or the markets. It can send us racing to the jamming pots, even though prudence suggests we wait.

Over the years, I have witnessed the proud and determined stride of early-season jam-makers as they negotiate flats of strawberries through the throng of market shoppers. You can almost see a glint of craziness in their eyes as they take their babies home. Understandably, it has been a long and lonely winter and somehow, they imagine, the waft of sweet stuff cooking will set the world back on its sunny axis. It is quite true that jam-making smells sweet after the last of our morning toast has grown tired of being neglected (if your basement stores of jam have run out), but that is still not a good reason to rush to the craft. With every aspect of food preservation, the quality and the specifics of the ingredient, rather than breathless, reckless enthusiasm, should guide us. It is hard, but trust me, variety matters. I have learned that the hard way.

BERRIES FOR THE BABE

Several years ago, I planted three impressive beds of strawberries just to endear myself to my youngest son. His favorite fruit was the strawberry, and I thought it would make him happy. As luck would have it, just as the beds grew wild and prolific, he grew indifferent. In fact, I think the two were intimately connected. I suppose he didn't like the crushing responsibility of liking what I did, or the weight of admitting it (and eating them would have been a tacit admission). Not that I objected. I knew stepchildren only slowly become close to their stepparents, but hell if I didn't have a lot of berries.

Here is the thing, though: no one with limited gardening space needs three beds of strawberries, even if those strawberries are Shucksons, Bentons, and an ever-bearing variety called Tri-Star. I picked those varieties from a sea of options without ever tasting them. The mark of a novice. Besides their intruding abundance, I never loved those varieties of strawberries enough to dedicate so much garden space to them. I have since turned their three beds into one and lost any sense of how much of each variety is there. Soon I will forgo them altogether in favor of other, more productive things and return to picking berries at the berry farm. That's the sort of thing I suggest you consider before laying out your garden. Consider not only your space but also your palate, and not only your palate but also what you will do with what you grow. Knowing what role these foods will play throughout the year is an important consideration for

Consider not only your space but also your palate, and not only your palate but also what you will do with what you grow.

the householder. Growing strawberries to eat fresh and for making jam was a lovely notion but, given their space requirements, they could not match my onions, garlic, winter squash, or beans. Though I still make strawberry jam for the kids, I long for the variety best eaten quickly (while fresh) in June.

THAT FRESH MOMENT

There is a moment in early summer when the strawberries I've been longing for arrive. They are sugary sweet and offer a fleeting presence in the garden and the market. They do not transport worth a spit. They are bright red through and through and, when sliced and sprinkled with sugar, make lovely sauce. At their supreme sunny best, Hood strawberries require no embellishments. How wonderful to know that it is in June—and only in June—that you can eat them fresh. Unlike the ever-bearing varieties, Hoods will not stay on the scene. Some folks freeze them (as they do many berries), but so sweet and fragile a creature should be consumed as it rises off the bloom, which is why I suggest eating them with abandon in everything from strawberry short-cakes to yogurt, in crème fraîche with brown sugar or bathed in sweet chilled cream. Really, what could replace any of that? California strawberries with Cool Whip? You see what they have done to our palates?

I do not want to sound fussy here, but something is lost in the quality of your seasonal world when you imagine all things are like one another. Even here, in Oregon, where we have so many choices, I see folks reach for the first local strawberries they see in the market, or worse, California strawberries, all puffed and pretty without a whiff of flavor or substance. And why? Because they do not stop to consider it. They have not been taught. And what do they lose? Mostly texture and sweetness, because it is the sweetness and dewy-fresh tenderness of Hoods that makes them impossible to ship. I am sure each region has such a fruit, something fleeting that is unsuited for anything other than the moment. We must all take the time to seek these fruits out, lest they fade from the field altogether—which, sad to say, is exactly what's happening throughout the world.

EVERYWHERE IS NOWHERE

Those in the business of reviving old heirloom and traditional varieties of produce do so, in part, in reaction to the onslaught of industrial agribusiness that has defined "good" as that which withstands disease, and has higher yields and longer storage and shelf-life. None of those traits is corrupt in and of itself, but these goals come at the expense of breeds and varieties (produce and livestock) that could not make the grade. The more farming became a business, the more farm products became commodities. That is simply the logical outcome of that system. I do not want to suggest I know what faces those involved in commercial agriculture, nor would I dismiss out of hand all the changes that were made over time. Being able to grow an apple that is less prone to disease is a nice thing. Hybridization and selection for healthy and productive traits are good things. In fact, most backyard gardeners, when saving seeds of a particularly healthy or vigorous plant, are doing the same; they are self-selecting for certain conditions. A variety of tomato that is normally late-ripening in my garden but happens to put out early fruit is a tomato I want to save for its seeds. Something in its genetic coding supported my personal agenda—an early fruit that will ripen before the Oregon chill comes on. So who am I to disregard the logic? I think it is more that I object to those who have hijacked it.

Continued on page 200

A variety of tomato that is normally late-ripening in my garden but happens to put out early fruit is a tomato I want to save for its seeds.

CRÈME FRAÎCHE

If you are buying raw milk, a happy thing to do with all your cream is to turn it into crème fraîche. Besides giving the cream a little longer shelf life (in some cases up to thirty days) due to the fermentation, it is lovely to have on hand. As opposed to sour cream, which is 20 percent butterfat, crème fraîche is 30 percent butterfat, which means it will not curdle when heated or combined with acids. Not surprisingly, it is made much the same way butter is, at least in its early stages. The fact that the two are so connected makes me somewhat giddy. Playing with milk has offered me a number of lovely surprises, not the least of which is that with very little time and the best ingredients you can achieve the quality of product that food lovers dream about.

Perhaps I am being dramatic. Perhaps it is because I am making crème fraîche with the cream of a Jersey cow, a breed whose milk has a high butterfat content. But having delicious crème fraîche to cook with is like having a new toy in the kitchen. It leads you to prepare things that you would not normally cook or eat, or treats you had only dreamed of. It could be why, in years to come, my kids will want to know how I made those hot caramelized pears in lavender syrup to serve with cool crème fraîche. Get the point?

Even though I make dairy fermentations with raw milk, you do not have to. You can keep it simple by buying a pint of heavy cream, adding two tablespoons of buttermilk, and letting it sit at room temperature anywhere from twelve to twenty-four hours to thicken. Since I start with raw milk, I need to take a few more steps. Either way works. Just go with your comfort level.

To make crème fraîche, you follow the entire process as if you were making butter, except that instead of putting one tablespoon of buttermilk in a pint of cream, you put in two. After that, you follow exactly the same steps, but at the early culturing stage, you let the cream sit for eight hours, rather than four. If you are starting out with pasteurized cream, you can set it out on a counter at room temperature, in which case it can take up to twenty-four hours to set up. Since I use raw milk, which is full of live cultures, the culturing process is quicker. I can have a nicely thickened pint in as little as twelve hours. If I want the process to go even faster, I put the mixture in a warm water bath inside my cooler, where it takes no more than four to six hours to congeal. But be patient—every batch will be different.

Once it is thick and congealed, I put the crème fraîche in the fridge to chill, generally for four to six hours. What emerges is a fully thickened, mildly tart cream that is so close to butter in texture (at least at the top), that I can't help but spread it on my morning crackers or toast, topped with a little finishing salt—oh, my. Other times, I dollop it on fruit, blintzes, soup, stews, or whatever my fancy dictates. It is easy to make and worth adding to your cooking repertoire. And given the price of crème fraîche in the grocery store, it is a great way to add value to your raw milk purchase.

Throughout its history, the Extension Service, as the field extension of the land-grant universities, has worked to select breeds for greater yield, flavor, and resistance to disease—which, as I said, is in no way a crime. If there's been a crime, or at least a wrong path taken, it is in the way extension's efforts became merged into the agenda of an industry that has made small-scale family farming obsolete. More and more, the focus and activities of extension agents and research facilities are directed and funded by industry. For a while, that was considered a good thing. We were on the move toward a green revolution, with all the benefits it promised.

Unfortunately, it backfired. Varieties that had always grown very nicely in garden patches and on small farms across the United States and beyond were displaced by the ever-expanding agenda of big agribusiness. Up against the industrial logic of economies of scale, government subsidies, and global competition, small-scale farmers simply couldn't survive. And as much as anything, it was the single-track agenda of agricultural monopolies that destroyed their livelihoods.

TALK ABOUT THE GREED GENE

I want to make a distinction here between traditional cultivar development and genetic modification. As I mentioned, the self-selecting effort of cultivar development can happen in our backyards or in a research lab. The process involves the cross-breeding of varieties within a similar genus. A trait from a European red raspberry crossed with an American blackberry will yield my much beloved loganberry. Sometimes cross- or open-pollination occurs naturally (plants exchange their "juju" in the air or on the wings of bees, birds, and humans), other times with the aid of tweezers in a lab. What results from this natural crossing is a hybrid. Hybrid plants are different than heirloom varieties—or,

Tuesday, May 24, 2010—*The Wall Street Journal* reports that ConAgra is working with Louisiana State University to turn the unruly, knobby yam into "something that looks like a brick" so that it will fit into french-fry machines. ConAgra is spending $155 million to build a sweet-potato processing plant with the help of a federal income tax credit and 30 million dollars from the state of Louisiana. Jan de Weerd, a potato expert and VP of Global Agriculture Strategy Services at ConAgra, humbly describes this as "a revolution in the making."

rather, they are distinguished by the length of time a particular hybrid has been around. This is not always the case—and it depends a bit on whom you ask—but usually a hybrid or cultivar that is over a hundred years old is considered an heirloom. Others believe that to be considered an heirloom, a seed or plant must be of single origin, while still others suggest it is a plant or seed that has been handed down from one generation of farmer to the next. Regardless of the definitions, both naturally crossed cultivars and heirlooms are born and created the old-fashioned way—they swap spit in the wild or with a little help from a friend.

Genetic modification, on the other hand, is a form of plant and seed development done in a laboratory. It is a process of hybridization that crosses qualities not only from plants of a similar genus but also qualities from a totally foreign genus. Such crosses cannot happen naturally. Genetic modification involves attempts to cross genes from different species: an animal with a plant, for example; it is hybridization gone the way of science fiction. The main concerns about genetically modified seeds and plants are that they have been removed from the natural system and that there is insufficient research regarding their impact on the biodiversity of the natural world. These plants have been released into our fields and our markets and our stomachs. Many of us are eating genetically modified foods without knowing it (currently, no labeling is required by the FDA). I find that creepy. But what makes it even worse, from the perspective of traditional farming practices, is the way these genetically modified plants can then cross with traditional hybrids or heirloom seeds and turn them into things they never wanted to be.

Some genetically modified seeds are sterile. They simply will not reproduce in the field and must always be "made," as it were, in the lab. They will never spread their juju in the wind, which, from the perspective of corporate seed developers, is a good thing. They don't

> Many of us are eating genetically modified foods without knowing it.

GREEN REVOLUTION

The green revolution refers to a mid-twentieth-century movement toward increased production of food grains (especially wheat and rice), driven in large part by the introduction into developing countries of new, high-yielding varieties. Early dramatic successes were obtained in Mexico and the Indian subcontinent. But the new varieties required large amounts of chemical fertilizers and pesticides to produce their high yields, which raised concerns about not only cost, but also potentially harmful effects on the environment. Poor farmers, unable to afford the fertilizers and pesticides, have often reaped even lower yields with these grains than with the older strains, which were better adapted to local conditions and had some resistance to pests and diseases.

SOURCE: ENCYCLOPEDIA BRITANNICA

want farmers to be able to save seeds for future sowing, as has been the practice since the earliest days of agriculture. By developing a seed that cannot reproduce naturally, they hope to entice farmers to buy their seeds directly from the lab each year. Why would a farmer want to do that? Why would farmers knowledgeable about seed saving buy seeds each year? Well, because the lab (or corporation) producing genetically modified seed makes it attractive to them in the beginning. I won't go into the politics or economics of it, since I want to make another distinction first.

THE REAL FOOD FIGHT

While some genetically modified seeds or plants can never reproduce naturally, others do. And that is where the real fight comes in. When, for example, a farmer takes the bait and grows genetically modified seeds, he is unwittingly participating in a sad chain of events. By planting those seeds, he is introducing some of the traits of those seeds into the wild. The pollen from genetically modified seeds can, unfortunately, cross with a native variety and infect it. Its pollen can fly over to the plants of a neighboring farmer (one who may have been raising a particular heirloom variety for generations) and alter the plants' gene pool. That, for a traditional farmer, is a tragedy. But worse than the destruction of an established hybrid or heirloom seed stock is the ensuing legal nightmare. It is a nightmare from which we can only wake up once generations of good farming practices and lifestyle have been destroyed.

Strange as it may seem, if the errant pollen of the genetically modified seed makes its way to the farm next door, the traditional farmer must pay. Once his seeds or his plants carry a single trait of the genetically modified seed (whether he wanted them to or not), he must pay royalties to the manufacturers of

the GM seeds. Unlike those who use the natural process of selection (hybridization, or cross-pollination in
the wild), those who genetically modify seeds do so for
profit—big, big, monopolized profit. The companies
that modify seeds genetically (or the corporations that
support their research) patent the seeds they develop.
They sell them to farmers (or even supply them free,
at first) by suggesting the seeds will produce disease-
resistant crops and an increased yield. They convince
farmers that the return will be great. Sometimes, over
the first year or two, it is true. These plants yield big,
disease-resistant crops.

But over time the return is not as great as the farmers have been led to assume it will be. When there is
a bumper crop, the commodity price (what big companies pay for crops) may go down. Big yields lead to
surpluses and poor returns. At that point, not only
must the farmer keep paying for the next crop of patented seed (now at a higher cost), but he also begins
to question this logic. He begins to wonder, from both
an economic and an environmental perspective, what
he has signed up for. It is not true that all large-scale
farmers do not care. They have been seduced by a system that has captured us all. Many large-scale farmers
understand that they are caught and do not like it. In
the game of big agribusiness, only a few farmers will
make it to the top. This game, as they will discover, is
a brutal game. Unfortunately, in the case of genetically
modified crops, when farmers sign up, they are stuck.
Once the pollen has made its way into the air, there is
no going back—for the farmers or their unsuspecting
neighbors. Patented-seed distributors are watching to
see if their plants are crossing with older seed stocks in
the neighborhood, and then they move in for the kill.

I doubt there is anyone (at least, anyone who has
picked up this book) who has not heard about the fight
of seed activists trying to hold on to their right to use
their indigenous foods, seeds, and plants. Who has not

heard of the small farmers in India who committed suicide when the promise of greater crop yield landed them in debt? Who has not read of the small farmers who, in a brutal showdown with corporations, have lost their ancient traditions of farming, seed saving, and harvesting to the invading ideology of private owner-ship? It is not at all dramatic to suggest that the roots of civilization are being privatized. In the world of agri-business and resource commodification, controlling all the water (a whole other story) and the seeds is nothing short of brilliant. It may take a fiendish mind to design such a system, but if profits are what you're after, what greater assurance could you have than by controlling seeds and water? This is why my stomach turns every time I think about where this is all going. What child has not played Monopoly? When folks are hungry and thirsty, what will they not pay? What is the outcome of high demand and limited access? Who cannot see what will come of this?

We do not think about all of this for a reason. Some-times it's because we don't want to, but more often it's because they (whoever "they" are) are adept at convinc-ing the public that all is well. They will tell you they are only working to feed the poor, and that the movement toward genetic modification and seed privatization is one of stewardship. They will say it is for the good of mankind, that the growing food scarcity and threat of world hunger demands it, that they will distribute these limited and precious resources equitably and with care.

But is that how you think profit-driven enterprises are run? Think it through. This system does not bode well for the masses, which is why I think seed activ-ists are some of the most brilliant and radical folks out there. It is also why I think that learning how to sow, grow, and stow your food and seeds is essentially a political act. But so is knowing what you are buy-ing in the marketplace. It is important to figure out what is what, and why it is grown, but this can be a

---

Almost 96 percent of the commercial vegetable varieties available in 1903 are now extinct.

SOURCE: "AGROBIODIVERSITY LOSS: CONFLICTS AND EFFECTS," A PUBLICATION FOR THE WORLD RESOURCE INSTITUTE.

slippery slope—which is the point I was trying to make about strawberries or any plant that is grown mostly for the way it holds its value in the marketplace—be it the grocery store, the fields, or the farmers market. For example, when I start seeing oceans of organic Seascape strawberries in the marketplace, but nary a Hood, Shuckson, or Benton (let alone the more elusive Marshall), I begin to wonder what is going on, why a new mono crop is making the scene. I wonder how different it is from any other industrial practice. If the Hood, for example, is being discarded for other, more durable varieties of strawberry, where will it all lead? I should emphasize again that I am not a small farmer trying to make a living. I don't have to go to my berry fields and see my tender strawberries decimated by heavy rains. If I did, and if I'd lost a big part of my income as a result, then I too would most likely shift my crop to an ever-bearing variety that better withstands the conditions of the region. But when organic and local farmers start shifting toward the practices of agribusiness (selecting varieties of produce that offer higher yields rather than the best flavor), they are aligning themselves more with industry than with the fleeting brilliance of the moment. Can I blame them? No. Do I see a common thread here? Yes, I do.

> It is not at all dramatic to suggest that the roots of civilization are being privatized.

THE SLIPPERY SLOPE OF MARKETS

Over and over, I am reminded of all the concessions, large and small, that we make whenever we take nature into the marketplace. Though there is not a straight line between the varieties of produce hybridized in your backyard or by your local Extension and those genetically engineered in a lab, there is a faint connection, if only in terms of the agenda. Each, in its own way, is working to control the market. In my idealized world of small-scale subsistence farming, I imagine a more holistic system.

Our appreciation for these products amounts to buying in, not living in. And that is a shame, since commodification will always offer only a shadow of the things we are really after.

It is a system outside the market. It is about varieties grown by generation after generation on the family farm, by and for the people who live on the land. In that world, there is no marketplace or, if there is, it is one of back-road farm stands and bartering between neighbors. What idealism. What hopeful posturing. But those are the lives and systems I believe we are most enraptured by. Those are the experiences and traditions that give us the transitory seasonal fruits and perennials of the region, as they appear not in our markets but in our homes or on our land (one and the same if we are lucky). These are the truths behind the "artisan" foods we adore—prosciutto, cheese, grappa, balsamic vinegar, good wines and oils, or *les confitures* (French for "jams"). That is the mystique that intrigues us. Is it just the flavor of these foods? I think not. I believe it is the humble birthright of these ingredients that gives them their appeal. It is their honest place and function within an agricultural society that seduces us. More than the products themselves, it is their attachment to traditions that sets us on fire. And we glorify them even though we will never do the work ourselves. Our appreciation for these products amounts to buying in, not living in. And that is a shame, since commodification will always offer only a shadow of the things we are really after.

It is important to remember that all these things, these valued artisanal products, have their origins in the world of self-reliance. These were the stuffs of old-world stores, resulting from people's need to live off the land. We have turned them into designer foods only because we have forgotten what they were. We have forgotten that we, and not industry and markets, are responsible for keeping them alive, first with our own labor, and then (if we cannot pick up a shovel) by knowing where and why they exist. I am always cautious of shopping my way toward sustainability. I am not sure the beast can be contained that way, which brings me back to berries and jam.

These days, when I make jam for myself, it is from wild blackberries. I have grown to love wild blackberries for a number of reasons. First, there is the smell. When you're making wild blackberry jam you're enveloped in an intoxicating fragrance of berry and roses, because they share a common genus. I had forgotten that connection, but was reminded of it as the jam cooked. Standing over that bubbling brew, I took in the scent and wondered if previous generations were aware that no amount of hybridization could match it. Yes, there are varieties that have fewer seeds and some that are fatter. There are varieties of blackberries that are thornless, and those "easier" varieties stand up better to the demands of the marketplace. Not one of them is as singularly rugged and fragrant as the wild variety, however. I know they are considered invasive, but had they remained our only blackberry, would we have watched over them better? Have they grown fierce in our neglect? Did we forsake them for tamer creatures? Can we blame them for taking root in abandoned fields and along back roads and refusing to become extinct? They are not the newcomer. They deserve to be where they are. This gets me thinking about the lives we lead. Will we endure? Will we stay free and wild, fragrant and feral? Will we, like the wild blackberry, be sweeter for our thorns? Will we stand up to the beast of industry? Will we claim the right to *be*? Will we remember our heritage, our traditions, our natural and rightful place in that plan? Or will we only be the cultured and civilized version of the real thing? Who knows. But when I make jam for my morning toast it is with the wild blackberry.

> Will we, like the wild blackberry, be sweeter for our thorns? Will we stand up to the beast of industry? Will we claim the right to *be*?

THE ALCHEMY OF JAM-MAKING

In teaching the art and science of food preservation, I have found almost no endeavor to be so fully mystified as jam-making. I blame this, at least in part, on the box—boxed pectin, that is. I think the box has done more to confuse jam-making than anything else. Did they not make jam before there was boxed pectin? Sure they did. They just knew that when extra pectin was called for (which is not always the case), you could find it naturally in fruit.

Anyone can make jam. But to become a really good jam-maker you must learn not only what pectin is and isn't, but also what role all the other ingredients in the recipe play. Here is the information I give my students. It is a list of subjects as they relate to the category more inclusively described as "sweet spreads."

To begin with, sweet spreads refer to many things, including the following:

JELLY: Crystal clear, juice only

JAM: Crushed or chopped fruit

CONSERVE: Mixture of fruit and nuts or raisins

PRESERVES: Large or whole pieces of fruit

MARMALADE: Citrus suspended in syrup

BUTTERS: Smooth spreads, with or without sugar

The distinctions between these spreads have to do with how the mixture is prepared or combined. For ease of instruction, I'll describe the process as it relates to jam-making, since that is the type of spread most folks are after. You can, however, follow these same steps in making conserves, preserves, and marmalades—the variation lies in the ingredients used in those particular products. Butters and jellies are different enough to require a separate set of instructions but, generally speaking, involve many of the considerations I offer in what I call the "Formula of Jam-Making." Here is the formula:

Fruit(s) + Sweetener + Pectin + Acid + Cooking Time/Equipment = Jam

Let's address each part of this equation separately.

Continued on page 211

WILD BLACKBERRY JAM

The thing about wild blackberries is the seeds—there are lots and lots of them. Which is why folks like cultivated varieties. But since my last intoxicating and perfumed experience with wild blackberries, I can't resist them when making jam. My solution is to remove the seeds from half of the berries I will be using, although you could certainly remove them all.

To remove seeds, put the desired amount of fruit (½ of the whole weight) in a pot with enough water (about ¼ inch) to steam the berries. Reserve the remaining berries in another bowl. Cover the pot, bring it to a quick boil, turn off the heat, and steam for a minute or two. Pour the steamed berries and steaming liquid into a sieve placed over a bowl. Using a spatula, push the fruit pulp through the sieve into the bowl.

Scrape the bottom of the sieve every so often to remove the pulp. In about five minutes you will have a bowl of smooth pulp, with most of the seeds left behind in the sieve. If you touch that mess of seeds, you will notice it is slightly tacky. That results from the residue of the pectin that is found on the seeds. I like to capture that pectin when making my jam, though you may not want to.

To capture the pectin, put the seeds back into the pot with enough water to "wash" them. Depending on how much you are starting with, add ¼ to 1 cup of water and swirl the mixture around a bit. Bring the "washed" seeds (water, too) back to the boil and let it simmer a minute or two. Then put the mixture through the sieve again to capture the liquid and remaining pulp. You

WILD BLACKBERRY JAM

4 cups wild blackberries (partly or completely seeded)
2 cups sugar
Add lemon and additional pectin as needed and before cooking
   (most likely no more than 1 tablespoon of each)

Marinate fruit and sugar as described below. Cook as described on
pages 222–23 and can in a boiling-water canner.

will feel that the remaining seeds are less tacky. Even though what you've captured in your bowl may not seem like much, it is full of pectin. You can test it to see, if you like. I was happily impressed. But again, you can skip that whole step, if you prefer—it is not entirely necessary. Just remember, if you are seeding the entire amount of berries for your jam, you are removing all or most of the pectin found in the seeds. My process seems to offer a happy compromise—few of the seeds but most of their pectin in the jam.

I combine the sieved mixture with whatever quantity of whole berries I have reserved and measure it. I add half as much sugar as the combined amount of fruit. If, for example, I have four cups of fruit (seeded and unseeded along with pectin "wash"), I add two cups of sugar. I allow the sugar-and-berry mixture to marinate at room temperature for four to six hours, or refrigerate it overnight.

Wild blackberries will be tart enough that you won't need to add lemon juice, though adding some won't hurt. Taste the mixture. If you want more punch, add the lemon juice. If you use some cultivated blackberries (which can have a very mellow taste) along with the wild blackberries, add a tablespoon or so of lemon juice.

You can do all of this prep the day before, if you want. You can adjust the quantities as you wish, as long as they don't exceed the capacity of your pan. You can use more sugar, though I have never found the need. One additional note: once a jar of this jam has been opened, I suggest you store it in the fridge, since low-sugar jams are more likely to grow mold if left out in the cupboard.

Fruit

Even within a single variety, every fruit is different. Some will be sweeter or tarter than others. Some will be denser and some will contain more liquid. Some will have a large number of seeds (like wild blackberries), while others are bred to have few. The things that affect those individual qualities are not just genetics but also the particulars of the season. Berries within a particular variety that are picked at the end of their season will generally be smaller and have a denser texture then those picked early on. They also tend to be a bit sweeter. These are the ones I pick for making preserves, since I prefer their smaller size.

Weather plays a big role in the quality of your fruit. Some years, you will have the perfect amount of rainfall and a great many sunny days to enable the fruit sugars to develop. Other years, rainy, overcast skies will soak the berries and allow none, or little, of the sun—and sugars—to come through. Besides the variables of the season, there are also those of the day. I tell my students to pick their berries after a few days of sunshine, for maximum sweetness, and in the cool of the morning, while the fruit is firm. You want your fruit to be fully ripe, but not so soft that it can easily be crushed by the pressure of your fingers. If you wait until the afternoon to pick them, the heat of the day can oversoften them. You also want to get them quickly to the canning pot or fridge, because they will only deteriorate from the time you pick them until they become jam. Don't store them in a hot car or you'll be sorry. Buying them from the farmers market eliminates some of these considerations, but before you take them home, keep in mind what conditions the berries (or any fruit) were grown or picked in, and for how long they have been stored.

You can start with sliced or mashed berries (or whole ones, for preserves). You can combine some of each; there is no rule. Mashed fruit jams set well due to the dispersed fruit fiber in the mixture (jelly is at

Along with the loss of diversity has come a loss of quality. The nutritional content of many of our grains and vegetables has dropped between 5 and 40 percent, which means we have to eat more calories to get the same nutrition.

SOURCE: "WHO WILL FEED US—QUESTIONS FOR THE FOOD AND CLIMATE CRISES," A REPORT FROM THE ETC GROUP, NOVEMBER 2009. WWW.ETCGROUP.ORG the opposite end of the spectrum; it uses no fruit pulp and must therefore rely on additional sugar and pectin for setting). No matter which method I use for jam-making, I always marinate my fruit with sugar for at least four hours, or overnight in the refrigerator. Marinating the fruit does two things: it enables the sugar to penetrate the fruit's fibers and preserve its shape (most important with whole-fruit preserves), and it pulls out the liquid from the fruit to form the syrup that surrounds them after they've been marinated.

Sugar

The role of sugar in jam-making is threefold. It sweetens; it assists in the gelling process; and it preserves the color, texture, and shelf life of the fruit. But do not be fooled into thinking you need as much as the box or most recipes suggest. Over the years, I've reduced the amount of sugar I use to half the volume of the fruit, with good results. You can choose other sweeteners besides sugar. Honey can be substituted, but use half a cup of honey for each cup of sugar in your recipe, and use a very light honey unless you want the flavor to overwhelm the fruit. Given its texture, honey will also add a little more liquid to the mixture, which could result in a longer cooking time. Either way, once I measure my berries and add my sweetener, I let the mixture marinate. Be warned, however, that leaving berries and sugar out all night on a summer evening will invite fermentation. Do refrigerate them.

Sugar's role as a preservative is to discourage mold growth. As you may recall from your childhood, the strawberry jam bought at the supermarket was damn near indestructible—you could keep it in the cupboard for years without it getting moldy. Much of that had to do with commercial jam's extremely high sugar content and very long cooking time. My process involves neither of these things, so the jam is more susceptible to mold growth; that's why I like to seal the jars in a water bath and then, after opening, store them in the fridge.

When making high-sugar jams (where sugar constitutes 60 to 70 percent of the total mixture), I just invert my hot jam jar to seal it. That is what our grandmothers (or great-grandmothers) did, and it is a perfectly acceptable process for high-sugar jams. With these jams, I am less worried about a little air getting in, because the sugar content is so high, and it is therefore not a happy place for mold spores. But I recommend that you seal low-sugar jams in a water bath (read your book) and store them in the refrigerator after opening. Remember, mold spores and bacteria are everywhere— and praise the Lord for that, because we would be dead if we brought about a world without those happy dwellers. But you don't want them setting up house on your food source (not just jam, but many foods), even though they will not kill you if they do.

Some people are allergic to mold spores, but most people are fine even if they ingest a bit. I was taught that mold on the outside of a very dense substance (such as a hard brick of cheese) can be safely removed by cutting away a good quarter inch of cheese all around the mold. Jam and other foods (applesauce, for one) are less dense, which means the spore tails can wiggle down into the mixture (normally, you see only the bloom of the mold growth). According to my teachers, you shouldn't just scoop off the bloom and call it good, though I know that can be tempting. If I cannot bear to toss out an otherwise full jar of jam, I remove the bloom from the top and then put the jam into a pan, bring it to a boil, and cook it down a little to kill off the spores. But that's just me. You have to do what makes you comfortable. I am not all that frightened by a little mold, particularly after I have removed it and cooked down the remaining jam again. But to avoid the need to do this, I recommend you do the right things—use a water bath to seal your product and then store it in the fridge after opening.

For added safety, I suggest you keep dirty spoons and knives (like the one you cleaned off with your tongue) out of the jar. No need to tempt fate. But lest I scare you off, you should know that jam—in fact all fruit preservation—offers a high-acid environment. You might have to watch for mold growth (and you will see it), but you don't have to worry about the scary things most folks worry about with food preservation. Those scary things require a low-acid environment, which fruit does not have. So relax.

I like making low-sugar jams for the obvious reason that I don't want too much sugar in my food if I can avoid it. But as a result of lowering the amount of sugar I use, I must often increase the pectin. There are some boxed pectins that are designed for making low-sugar jams, or jams without any sugar at all, but I don't like them very much. To me, they give the final mix an odd taste and texture. I would rather make my own.

Pectin

Pectin, like sugar, exists naturally in all fruit. It is found in the seeds, pulp, and skins of fruit and shows up in greater or lesser amounts depending on the fruit. In the pages that follow, I've supplied you with a reference guide, as well as instructions for making your own pectin. Knowing how much pectin your fruit contains will help you decide how much more you should add. Wild blackberries, for example, are packed with pectin while domesticated seedless varieties have less of it. Some people pick unripe fruit along with their ripe fruit, because underripe fruit has more pectin. I don't like to do that because I'm after the flavor of fully ripe fruit. Some folks will just combine their fruits, since tart early-drop apples or crab apples (as opposed to fully ripened green apples like Granny Smiths), fresh currants, and gooseberries are all great sources of pectin. Think about the way your cranberry sauce sets up so nicely—pectin. You will see many old-school recipes that call for adding crab apples to berries in jam-making. I am an advocate for single-variety jams (though currants and strawberries are a favorite combo of mine). What I do instead is to follow another old-time system and make my own liquid apple pectin. Apple pectin has a very mild flavor that will not overwhelm my fruit. I offer a guide for making it, but few people are as committed to it as I am. I think that's foolish, because I can often cook up enough liquid pectin in one year to last me for several years. Once canned, it keeps.

Using your own liquid pectin will give you the flexibility your fruit requires. The chart on page 217 explains which fruits need a little pectin boost and which do not. Boxed pectin is less adaptable. It does not allow you to follow the lead of the fruit. It does not allow for the alchemy that jam-making is all about. I love that alchemy. I love knowing that I can, if I so choose, throw a couple of tablespoons of currants or gooseberries into my low-pectin strawberries or peaches to give them what they need. I like seeing how the subtle pink hue of my crab-apple liquid pectin tints the nectarines I have combined it with. I love the experimentation. I love using what grows locally. I love the symmetry of it. I like following my nose and not a recipe.

Acid

The fourth element in the formula is the acid found in fruit. As you can see on the Pectin & Acid Level Chart, the amount of acid varies from fruit to fruit. If you are starting with a fruit that is low in acid, you can add some lemon juice. Taste the fruit. If it is not very tart, it is probably low in acid. Generally speaking, the same fruit that needs a little extra pectin will need some extra acid. And as with pectin, you can combine fruits to add what doesn't exist already in the fruit you start out with. If you examine some of my recipes, you will be able to follow that logic.

Equipment

Knowing what equipment to use in jam-making is very important. Using a wide, shallow-sided pan with a larger surface area will greatly reduce your cooking time. Conversely, a tall-sided pot will slow things down. Since I like to cook my jam as quickly as possible, I use the widest, shallowest pan I can that will hold my mixture and still provide the additional space required when it boils. Your pan, along with the heat of your stove top, will affect the time it takes for your jam to set.

Cooking Time and Technique

When cooking jam, you will notice two stages of evaporation. The first stage involves the evaporation of the liquid in the fruit. During this stage, I do not stir my mixture. I let it come to a boil (a mashed fruit mixture will bubble less), and then I cook it without stirring for at least the first five minutes. Every time you stir down the boil, you are adding extra time to the cooking process, so let the mixture boil without stirring for the first five to eight minutes. During this stage, you will see large watery bubbles; that's because the water in the fruit is boiling off.

The second stage of evaporation allows the sugar syrup around your fruit (remember, I like to marinate the fruit in the sugar overnight) to cook down and combine with the fruit fiber, pectin, and acid, so that the mixture congeals. It is during this second stage of evaporation (beginning anywhere from five to eight minutes after the fruit mixture first comes to the boil) that I begin to stir the mixture. At first, I do so infrequently, probably no more than once a minute, just enough to make sure it is not sticking to the pan. As the fruit-and-syrup mixture continues to reduce in volume, I start stirring more frequently. Toward the end of this process, I stir constantly to prevent sticking.

I have become familiar with the way the mixture will feel as I move my spoon through it. I look for something

Continued on page 220

PECTIN & ACID LEVELS

FRUIT	HIGH PECTIN	MED. PECTIN	LOW PECTIN	HIGH ACID	MED. ACID	LOW ACID
APPLES: SWEET	X					X
APPLES: TART	X			X		
APRICOTS			X	X		
BLACKBERRIES: CULTIVATED		X		X		
BLACKBERRIES: WILD	X			X		
BLUEBERRIES		X		X		
CHERRIES: SOUR		X			X	
CHERRIES: SWEET		X				X
CITRUS FRUITS	X			X		
CRANBERRIES	X			X		
CURRANTS	X			X		
ELDERBERRIES		X			X	
FIGS			X			X
GOOSEBERRIES	X			X		
GRAPES		X			X	
LOGANBERRIES	X			X		
MELONS		X				X
NECTARINES			X			X
PEACHES			X			X
PEARS			X			X
PLUMS: SOUR	X			X		
PLUMS: SWEET	X				X	
QUINCES	X			X		
RASPBERRIES		X		X		
RHUBARB			X	X		
STRAWBERRIES			X		X	

HOMEMADE PECTIN

Making Homemade Pectin Stock

1. Slice about 4 pounds of washed green apples (not Granny Smiths, but tart under-ripe apples, found in early summer). Place apples in a nonreactive saucepan. Add enough water to barely cover and bring to a boil. Lower heat immediately and simmer until soft, approximately 20–30 minutes.

2. Pour your apples and liquid through a fine sieve into another pot. Without stirring, let this liquid drain overnight.

3. Bring liquid to a boil in the pot and cook till it has reduced to half its original volume.

4. Allow liquid to cool, then test pectin content (instructions below). Continue to cook if necessary.

5. Once liquid pectin has reached the desired strength you can store it in your fridge, or for longer shelf life, process the hot pectin in sterile pint jars for 5 minutes in a boiling water canner. (Oh, don't worry. You'll understand in time.) You can also freeze your liquid pectin.

Testing the Pectin Level

I admit to loving this part. I suppose it comes as close to chemistry as I get these days (what with Mr. Leary long departed). To determine the amount

BASIC LOW-PECTIN BERRY JAM

4 cups mashed or sliced berries (or combination of fruit)
2 cups sugar (half as much as the quantity of fruit)
4 tablespoons lemon juice
2/3 cup strong homemade apple pectin

Follow cooking instructions on pages 222–23.

OLD-FASHIONED
STRAWBERRY PRESERVES

(This technique uses whole berries. Try to use small, bite-size berries that will hold their shape when cooked.)

6 cups sliced or whole strawberries

3 cups sugar

6 tablespoons lemon juice

²/₃ cup liquid homemade pectin

Follow cooking instructions on pages 222–23.

of pectin in your liquid, put 1 teaspoon of the cool liquid on a plate and add 2 tablespoons of rubbing alcohol to the mix. Swirl the mixture around until clots start to form. It will amaze you, but it will happen, and you will know the strength of the pectin by the size of the clots. Basically, the formation of a fairly large, viscous clot will indicate strong pectin. Weak pectin count will show up as several small, scattered clumps. If that is the case, just bring the liquid back to a boil and reduce further. And please toss out the test batch. You don't want to return that to the pot. Once it reaches the desired strength you can refrigerate, freeze, or "can it" until you make jam. I would not keep it in the fridge for more than a week, however.

Using Homemade Pectin

As a general guide ²/₃ cups of liquid pectin will be enough to set 4 cups of low-pectin prepared fruit or juice. So here again you have room for whimsy. If you are using strawberries (low pectin) alone, I would use the full amount. If I wanted to throw in a few currants (high pectin) with the strawberries, I might use less. And if I were using half currants, half strawberries, maybe none at all. And you can use less if you start with less fruit. For example, 2 cups of low-pectin fruit will need ¹/₃ cup of liquid pectin. This seems obvious, but is news to all of us. In the end, it will be trial and error—and the willingness to love whatever the outcome is—that will win the day.

STRAWBERRY JAM

2 pounds strawberries (a low-pectin fruit), mashed or sliced
1 pound sugar (about 3 cups, but I have used only 2)
3–6 tablespoons lemon juice
$^2/_3$ cup strong apple pectin

Marinate berries and sugar overnight in refrigerator.
You will have about 6 cups of berry/sugar mixture, sometimes more, depending on variety of strawberries. Make sure sugar is dissolved.

Mix all ingredients in a large, wide pan; bring to a boil and cook for 15–20 minutes as instructed on pages 222–23.

in my pan that I call "parting the waters." That's the moment when, as I move my spoon through the mixture, the bottom of the pan is revealed for a moment or two before the liquid flows back over it. You will know what I mean when you do it. You will also note that the color of your fruit is changing, growing deeper in shade. You will smell the sugar caramelizing. In fact, you will smell wonderful aromas the whole way through the process. I love standing over my jam pan, inhaling the deep, seductive fragrance of cooked fruit. I make much of my jam outside in the summer and wonder if the neighbors are lucky enough to smell it.

It is during these last few minutes of the process that folks go through all sorts of gyrations to figure out if the jam has set. There is the drip-off-the-spoon method, where you take a little of the jam in a spoon, raise it high over the pan, and let it fall from the spoon in droplets. The idea is to allow the sugar syrup to emulate the consistency of a cooled-down syrup, since cool syrup gels differently than hot syrup. So keep in mind, if you cook your hot jam to the consistency of cool jam it will be much too stiff to spread nicely on your toast when it has cooled.

Another technique is the cold-plate method. You put a plate in the freezer before you start making the jam. Toward the end of the process, you remove the plate and place a droplet of jam on it. You do that for the same reason as the spoon drop; you want it to cool to the consistency of cooled jam. If, after letting it sit for five seconds or so, it does not drip quickly when you tip the plate a bit, your jam is ready. If not, cook it another thirty seconds to a minute.

This last minute of jam cooking can be a little maddening, I admit. You will ask yourself in a tizzy, Is it ready? Do I have to cook it longer? Really, do not sweat it. I have done this long enough that I just go by the look of the jam. I don't use the spoon or plate method anymore; I look at my jam and smell it and say it's ready when I see fit. If, in the end, it has not set after cooling for a full day (natural pectin continues to set over time), I do one of two things. Either I call it good and enjoy it as syrup or loose jam on my scones, or I cook it down again for another few minutes. You can do that with jam that has been thickened with natural pectin. Boxed pectin is way more fussy. When making jam with natural pectin (or when you need none), you can always just go back and cook it down a little longer. That will work. To be honest, though, I would rather just let it be. I can think of nothing wrong with allowing my luscious nectarine-and-crab-apple jam to slither across a hot biscuit. Oh goodness. I just might have to pop it in my mouth a little faster. What a shame. And if I have cooked my jam too long, it will be perfect for making jelly cookies or diluting with a little juice or vinegar in a pan to use as a glaze in the bottom of a tart shell or on top of pork roast. Truly, you will find a use for all of it.

So there it is. Work through the formula. Get to know each step. And remember, when processing your low-sugar jam, I recommend the traditional boiling-water canning method. Though it is not strictly necessary, I would hate for your hard work to go moldy.

THE TV DINNER
During World War II, women entered the workforce in large numbers for the first time. After the war, many women kept their jobs, creating a need for quick, easy meals for two-worker families at the end of the day. Clark and Gilbert Swanson of Omaha, Nebraska, responded to the need and in 1951 began selling frozen pot pies on a national scale. A lawyer, Cecil Johnson, had earlier trademarked the name "TV Dinner." The Swansons acquired Johnson's trademark and began preparing complete dinners in sectional aluminum trays in 1953.

SOURCE: "WOMEN'S ROLES IN THE 1950S." AMERICAN DECADES. 2001. ENCYCLOPEDIA.COM

HOT TIPS FOR MAKING JAM

Wash fruit right before making jam out of it.

If using strawberries, rinse, drain, and lay them out to dry on a cloth. Blot dry, or air dry for an hour. Remove caps.

With cane berries or blueberries, rinse and drain. Dry. Some cane berries are fragile when wet. If they are organic, I often do not wash them at all, or if I do, I just let them drain in the sieve instead of turning them onto a cloth.

With peaches or other stone fruit, blanch, peel, and slice if you want the skin off or just slice with skins on. Leave skins on apricots. Using blanched fruit will actually cut down a bit on the cooking time. Fresh fruit has more liquid in it.

Check the chart for pectin and acid count.

Making jam with strawberries requires more acid and pectin than jam-making with wild blackberries, for example. Adjust the amount of pectin and lemon juice for the type of fruit you are using. I generally use no pectin with high-pectin fruit and a varying amount when I am mixing fruit.

With regard to sugar, I follow the half-as-much rule whether I am using weight measures or liquid measures. You will notice that the first recipe calls for cup measures while the second one calls for weights. It works either way, though I prefer to use weight measures, since I buy my berries by weight at the farm or market. Your pan should be at least twice as high as the layer of marinated fruit in it. And it should not be too tall, or it will hold in the steam.

Directions for cooking all jams

In a large, wide, heavy-bottomed pan, bring the fruit mixture slowly to a boil, stirring very gently to avoid breaking up the fruit. Add your homemade pectin and acid as needed. During the first half of cooking, stir only occasionally. Each time you stir you are slowing down this stage of the evaporation process.

If you like, you can remove the foam that forms on the surface of the jam. I remove it by "slicing" it off with a spoon. Not all fruits make as much foam; strawberries make more than most. The only issue with not removing the foam is that you can end up with a cloudy layer of foam when you ladle the jam into jars. It's just a matter of appearance.

The entire process, from the beginning of the first boil until the end, should take about 18–20 minutes (8–12 minutes if you're making a small batch), but you will develop a sense of how much time is appropriate. Depending on quantity, it could take a couple of minutes more.

Remove from heat and test for gel. If you like, return to heat for another minute. Remember, jam will "set up" when cool, so do not judge merely by eye, since the consistency will be very different when it cools.

Once the mixture reaches the desired consistency, remove from heat. Pour into jars that have been washed in hot, soapy water and air-dried. If you are not going to set them in a boiling water canner, I would boil the jars first (remember the discussion on low-sugar jams). Use a jar funnel when ladling in the jam and fill to ¼ inch from the top of the jar. Make sure the jar lid is clean and free of any jam drips before putting on the lid and ring. Either invert the jars or put them in a boiling water canner for 10 minutes, as instructed in your preserving book (I like the *Ball Blue Book* as a basic guide to food preservation). If

inverting, turn right side up after 10 minutes and leave to seal.

Set aside for 24 hours to cool and fully seal. Do not test seals early. Let them seal on their own. In other words, resist the temptation to touch them with your finger until they have rested overnight. This is particularly true for inverted jars. After 24 hours, test the seal by running your finger over the top of the lid. If the lid is flat and does not give under gentle pressure with your finger, it is sealed. If it does not, and you can hear and feel a buckling sound, it is not sealed. You will easily sense the difference. If a jar did not seal, either store it in the refrigerator or start over. Just empty the jam into a pan to reheat, refill your jar, and reseal in the water bath. This will require using a clean jar and a new lid (the rings can be reused). Once you are sure it has sealed, store the jam out of the light in your cupboard or pantry.

Note: Jam can easily boil over, so don't turn your back on it. If it begins to act up, stir it down quickly. If it is really close to overflowing, take the whole pan off the stove and stir quickly (make sure your pan handle is insulated). As you make jam more often, you will learn to adjust the temperature on your range to the right setting.

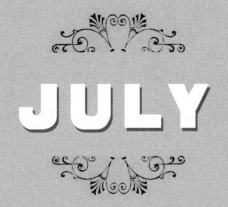

JULY

The Home

A Home of Mom's Making

My mother, Sonja Fasenfest, is a "balaboosta," which means, in Yiddish, "great householder." Its superlative, "richtecker balaboosta," or badass homemaker, suggests supreme competence in the home. In the 1950s, many of the older women I know (most of them born in Europe) stayed home to raise a family. In the homes of my friends whose parents were not foreign-born, it was a little different. Many of their mothers seemed a bit more modern. They worked part-time and served TV dinners. They were the ones inching toward new horizons. Not that Sonja was old-fashioned; she was just inclined to a different life. I could chalk it up to tradition, but I know it was something else.

I remember Mom telling a story about a neighbor who wondered why Mom sang as she worked. "Why should I hate taking care of my own home?" my mother asked the woman. My mother told me that story after the neighbor committed suicide. It was the first time I'd encountered suicide, and when we speculated about the cause, we imagined our neighbor had felt trapped, though we never really knew by what. What gives one person's life hope and meaning, when another's life has none? What allows you to carry on? My mother seemed to think that life and home are valued to the degree they are denied. She thought it took a constancy of will to move between the cracks of a broken life. But Sonja was a hardheaded pragmatist. Those who share a similar family history will understand the tenacity of spirit that reigns within the homes of survivors. Once you've been dispossessed and left for dead, you do not take things lightly.

My parents come from opposing sides of a certain history, though somehow their stories are the same. They are stories of tragedy and redemption. My mother came of age in Nazi Germany, while my father was a Polish Jew attempting to survive in the camps. They met after the war in Frankfurt and decided to build a life together. My brother was born in Germany; I was born some years later in the States. I offer that simply as context for the indomitable spirit that existed in my home and for my mother's "don't cry for me" attitude. Both determined and grateful, my mother took to making a home with a vengeance. If a job needed to be done, she would do it. Repairs, great and small, were her domain. She would take on small construction jobs, house painting, plumbing, and electrical work, if they were called for. She had been a draftswoman during the war and felt that no job was beyond her intellectual and technical capacity. Besides those maintenance jobs, Mom could stretch the budget, knit our sweaters, paste-polish floors, hang out of four-story windows to wash them, sew clothes, and, together with my father, who was a tailor, make curtains and bedspreads for the home. It would only be honest to admit that the entire endeavor was conducted with a fastidiousness

Continued on page 229

> What gives one person's life hope and meaning, when another's life has none?

SHOPPING UNDER THE L TRAIN

Jerome Avenue was a great old shopping district under the L, the Lexington subway line that runs from the most northern sections of the Bronx all the way to Coney Island. We often walked from our apartment on Sedgwick Avenue along the Moshulu Parkway until we reached our destination.

The walk took no more than a half hour and we took turns pulling the tall, wire-framed shopping wagon behind us. Once on the avenue, we walked beneath the speckled shadows of the overhead subway track into a sea of merchants holding court on either side of the crowded street. In and out of shops we went, buying our weekly supplies amid the occasional roar of a passing train. It was Sonja who showed me how to shop the markets, who introduced me to the fish guy and the cheese man, told me to watch that the butcher didn't have his hand on the scale when he weighed the meat. These were the old merchants, whom you needed to watch. I never knew if she was serious, because she would tell him to his face in a Yiddish-infused cadence, "Be so kind as to keep your finger off the scale." Awkward, but funny, to be sure.

In a world still spared big-box stores or fancy shopping, Jerome Avenue had all the right stuff. And what made it right was its size and environment and the everyday expression of trade done by vendors and shoppers who knew their stuff. Hell if I don't remember Sheff's bakery—the sights, the staff, and the not-too-patient shoppers all crowded together to get a slice of the sheer goodness of the place. And the smell? Kids today cannot really imagine it. Sure, we have bakeries today, but back then the smell of butter, yeast, sugar, and eggs could knock you over. It was the smell of a bakery that had been in business for fifty years. It was the smell of a bakery whose recipes and creations had fused with the walls and ambiance of the place to create an aura of danish-ness. Here in the doughy center of Yiddom, there was a luscious and inviting rightness to the world, not just in the combination of butter, flour, and sugar, but in the particular expression of cultural pride and values that encouraged me, as a child of that tribe, to eat and be happy, to enjoy what comes when suffering finally ends, to celebrate what the tenacity of spirit and memory and a handful of old-world traditions and recipes can offer.

And that is the reason we Jews love to eat so much—at least, that's why I think we do—and why serving meals at the table for our families is so important, or used to be. After all that has happened and all that has been endured, a mother feeding her child is a victory beyond belief. Our love of food is legendary—not simply because we are orally fixated (oops, that's personal), but because it all used to be so damn delicious. It was not like we were being fed "dreck," as the ladies shopping on Jerome Avenue would refer to anything substandard. No way. Just try and pass off an inferior piece of meat or fish or anything that good money had paid for, and you would be marked for life. But that was back then. Standards slowly changed and the world seemed to forget. There came a time when the old merchants started leaving (or dying), and their kids, now "professionals," didn't want to continue the trade. There came a time when few people knew the difference between a good cheese danish and dreck. In time, an entire culture succumbed to the double whammy of modernity and new management. But for a fleeting moment, the moment of my childhood, I experienced what a cheese or poppy-seed danish should taste like, and I am a better woman for it.

bordering on obsessiveness, but what I inherited from them is the joy and pride of making a home, along with understanding that in doing so, you create a safe place for your children to return to at the end of the day.

I remember coming home from school for lunch (we still did that in my day) or coming to dinner knowing that something good to eat would have been prepared. In fact, I played a game related to it. Starting on the ground floor I would ascend the stew-scented stairway, trying to guess what she had made for dinner, thinking of the groceries she and I had shopped for that week on the avenue.

There was a comfort in knowing that the smells related to our meal, on our table, for our family. This was not a piggish sentiment, but rather one of safety. The feeling was tangible and, in the mind and taste buds of a child, I can assure you it was no small thing. We should not fool ourselves into thinking the family meal has no value. I have few memories as significant as waiting for my father to come home so we could sit down to dinner. The value of those meals, the effort and the unity they embodied, has stayed with me through the years. It is why I call my own family to dinner most nights of the week. Whether they come when I call is another story, but I do call them. Sometimes I turn the entire business of cooking dinner over to someone else in the family—I'm just too tired or unwilling. I would hate for you to imagine that I'm completely a woman of convention. I am like everyone else in feeling it can be a burden at times, which is why I get so annoyed every time my mother, during her long stays in summer, asks me, "What are we making for dinner tonight?"

However fitfully, I have come to love my mom's summer visits. They begin in July and generally end right after my birthday in September. Though neither of us will admit it, we are desperately holding on until then, trying to behave in a way we can both be proud of. Even in the best of situations it can be hard, though

> The feeling was tangible and, in the mind and taste buds of a child, I can assure you it was no small thing. We should not fool ourselves into thinking the family meal has no value.

I am one of the lucky ones who's grown closer to her mother over the years, not further apart. That is a miracle, because we are two equally hardheaded women trying to determine who is boss—which is also why I hate it when she asks me what's for dinner. I hate her assumption that there will be a dinner. I want to exercise dominion over my home. Yet I know she is right. I know Sonja knows what I would rather forget at times, which is that there is a solidity to the dinner ritual that cannot be replaced. At the table, we talk about our worlds, tell our stories, enjoy our blessings, or, sometimes, simply feed our faces. The tradition, and our determination to create it and hold on to it, gives us the strength to continue. That is what my parents knew. When my family sits down together, I think what an odd little patchwork quilt we are. Survivor with survivor, this family and another, this son and that one, and the occasional friend, neighbor, and stranger that we invite into the mix. Together, we create the stories we will pass on to the next generation and we rebuild, in whatever ways we can, the hope that war, cruelty, and displacement sought to take away but could not. Today, I take on the mantle of the balaboosta as an exercise of constancy and willpower in the face of our broken lives.

JULY

The Garden

The Truth behind Gardening Guides •
The Importance of Mulch • Thinking Like a Plant

A t this point in my householding life, I have learned it is almost impossible to plan your garden by the planting guides. You can approximate, but when it gets down to it, the weather makes the rules. Planting carrots and beets in July for your fall garden will work only if the sun is not blazing. You need to keep an eye on the weather and do your gardening when it permits—which can be challenging when most folks have a busy work schedule. During the times best suited for planting or harvesting, or for watering seedlings both early and late in the day and shielding them with screens, many of us are in offices behind closed doors. Being away from home at those times can certainly hurt your chance of success, particularly if you are a novice.

Planting your garden according to the weather around you, rather than the static advice in guides, will require you to use your eyes. Those who do not will continue to depend on the easy advice of others, which can often be misleading. I walk through the neighborhood and see hopeful tomato starts that were planted too early or too late in the season and as a result now stand stunted or withering under the cruel rays of the summer sun. I see front-lawn gardens that were started in soil that is hard and unyielding to sensitive root systems. I see plants for sale in nurseries at the wrong time because, as the sales staff tell me, people want them and they do not want to discourage them from trying. I'm not sure that is exactly their motivation. But I wonder how many of those people will succeed, how many will take failure with a grain of salt, and how many will try again, year after year, to repeat the miracle and effort of tending soil and growing food.

ONCE, TWICE, ONE HUNDRED TIMES A GARDEN

As I write this entry, it is blazing hot. The forecast predicts temperatures of over 100 degrees for the next week. The heat reminds me that if I want to buy loganberries, I'd better do it today and not wait until next week, when I would have more time. Another week of blazing sun will burn and dry up the last berries of the season, so I must take action immediately if I'm to make the jam my husband likes. Because of the heat, I must put off sowing seeds until I am sure the soil has cooled a bit. I must water and shield the lettuce starts, which, despite the shade of the tree they sit under, will need my attention to survive. The subtle and constant requirements of my garden remind me of something a friend once said. He found it funny that folks would say, "I've got my garden planted for the year," as if it were a one-time affair and you could simply put in the starts and seeds all at once, sit back, and watch it flourish. If you were focusing on just one or two varieties, that might work, but even then attention is required. If you are thinking about a serious alternative to grocery shopping, then you'd better be prepared. Staying on top of things is a serious commitment.

A SUDDEN BLAZE

Some might think I'm being a tad fussy here, but really I'm being honest. With its odd combination of chill and blaze, July can be confounding. This year's sudden heat has pushed the pickling cucumbers to maturity, sent the summer squash and green beans into overdrive, and laid the ground bare in the now-harvested shallot and garlic beds for too long (the planting or transplanting of new seeds must wait for cooler days). The early-variety slicing tomatoes, those two tiny transplants put out in late May, have started to fruit in earnest, and I know the plum tomatoes for canning will not be far behind. I wonder how my turnips will taste, given that I planted them in early July and now, still small, they are taking this heat on the chin. What makes them bitter or sweet, I wonder. I try to note on seed packages which varieties are more tolerant of the hot weather. How shall I remember all of this? My basil plants, put in as transplants in early June, are coming on strong and tall and remind me that I'd better start thinking about the pesto I will make and freeze. Can the basil wait until the walnuts I want to buy are ready in October? That would be the best scenario, but perhaps I have misjudged the timing. I'd like to put in my spinach and chard seeds soon, but they will have to wait a while. Many things must wait until cooler temperatures return.

MULCHING AND MAKING SHADE

When the world turns torrid, there are a few things one should do. Mostly, they have to do with keeping your beds cool and mulched to hold enough moisture. Actually, you should mulch throughout the season, but especially during full-on summer weather. Putting on too much mulch early in spring can keep the soil from warming up; now you must think in the opposite direction and keep the soil cool. Over the years, I have come to use all manner of things as mulch, everything from compost to straw, grass clippings to pulled pea vines, bolting lettuce, and chard. If I clip long-departed rose blooms, I cast them on the ground beneath this plant or another. The tops of garlic and shallots, dry and brittle after curing the bulbs, make a fine cover for my seedlings as they attempt to sprout in the heat. Actually, I have devised a number of techniques for shielding my starts; I am very proud of some of them. For example, just by placing screening material over the entire kitty-defense structure, I'm able to create a lean-to of sorts. If the sun is particularly hot, I cover the screens with whatever additional mulch I have on hand (dry straw works nicely, since it is light) and keep the ground moist both morning and night with a shower from the garden hose. If I time it properly (and the universe cooperates), I can sow a different row of seeds every two weeks under that tent and have a nice crop of vegetables to enjoy throughout the fall and winter growing seasons. This technique works particularly well with root vegetables, carrots in particular, since they are sensitive to the slightest loss of moisture in the soil. I must also watch that their roots are covered once they emerge, because the seeds have not all been planted at the same depth. A carrot that is emerging and whose roots are edging out of the ground gets a mounding of soil placed around its tender top for protection. These techniques seem to work, but they require attention. It also requires you to think like a plant.

PRACTICE PLANT MIND

I remember being in my friend's garden when he pointed out how big the leaves of his rhubarb plant were. He imagined it had to do, in part, with catching water. Their big leaves were like hungry hands cupped to catch the rain. He took his lead from their natural design and gave them what they wanted—enough moisture to be vigorous. His plants were enormous and healthy. My own rhubarb was thin and frail with brown specks on the stalks, and withered at the base. The previous year, I had been able to harvest rhubarb throughout the spring, summer, and into fall, but this year offered only meager pickings. I didn't understand what was different until I realized that moisture was being taken from the plant's roots by the currant bushes and apple trees I had planted near it. Did the growing trees cast too great a shadow on plants that had once had no competition for either sun or moisture? Until my friend showed me the leaves of his rhubarb and told me what he had discovered, I hadn't thought about it. But once I gave a greater ladling of moisture to my plants, they seemed to rebound. Not as vigorously as his, but they were better than they had been.

One should not get discouraged by the unpredictability of the weather or ups and downs in plant health. What grew very healthily one year may limp a bit in another. It is only our plants telling us something we have yet to understand. Taking the time to walk around daily, to look at each leaf and branch, to notice the buds and sprouts, to feel the soil and keep a keen eye on the weather is what turns a decent gardener into a great one. But even the great ones will have their failures. Great gardeners are not magicians with special powers. Rather, they are in love with the little bit of land they have been given. They are astute servants of the soil and stewards of the harvest. They have empathy and respect for the seeds, the starts, and the fruits of their labor.

THINK LIKE A PLANT

Plants are capable of detailed sensory perception, information-processing and integration, decision making and control of behavior, learning, memory, choice, self-recognition, foresight by predictive modeling, and computation to efficiently sequester resources.

SOURCE: TREWAVAS A. "ASPECTS OF PLANT INTELLIGENCE." *OXFORD JOURNALS ANNALS OF BOTANY,* 2003.

Beautiful and bountiful gardens come with a price. They require commitment—not "I put in my garden for the year," but "I put in the garden day in and day out," until it has given you your leave.

They have come to think like a plant.

Remember this when you see the gardens that inspire you to grow food. Beautiful and bountiful gardens come with a price. They require commitment—not "I put in my garden for the year," but "I put in my garden day in and day out," until it has given you your leave, which, in July, is nowhere close to happening. Nope, July is full-time duty and a sentry's constant watch. You need to stand up to the challenge if you want to turn goodness into greatness, and understand that, as with all things, what stands between here and there is simply will and commitment.

JULY

The Kitchen

A Quick Cup of Coffee • Mama Darden •
Blueberries • Napping

It is late July, and I have finally sat down after a six-hour work stint. Once the harvest starts rolling in, I sprint from the garden to the canning kitchen to the house and back in a mad multitasking orchestration of chores. Being an early riser, I am able to do quite a bit before the heat sets in (and this week it is blazing), but I always underestimate how much there is to do in a day. I start, as always, with my morning coffee, but without fail it starts to cool before I can finish it. I imagine I can do just one little thing before sitting down with the paper. This morning, I tell myself, I will sit down and read the paper with my coffee before checking my list for the day. But first, I will just take the loganberries out of the fridge and weigh them and put half of them in a sieve to seed them and mash the other half with sugar to let them macerate until

I'm ready to make jam. Of course, that little task takes about an hour, between the extra steps I take to get the pectin out of the berry seeds and washing all the pots and utensils and then the kitchen, before my husband and Mom come down to make their breakfast and my second cup of coffee, a latte my darling husband makes each morning. That second cup goes down in a few good swigs while I whirl around the kitchen in a burst of caffeine-infused, focused energy.

The refrigerator must be cleaned out quickly (I think) to make room for the fruits, vegetables, and daily foodstuffs it will need to accommodate. It amazes me how things accumulate, and how all those tiny bottles of jam or chutney I acquire from the classes I teach pile up. There is a half-full half-pint jar of last year's quince chutney; some curried green-tomato pickles; apple butter; plum butter; strawberry, raspberry, and peach jam (at least one or two of each, thank you); dill pickles; yogurt; feta (floating in a large bottle of brine); roasted pork loin; a pot of stewed tomatoes waiting to be tended to; vodka-infused cherries; currant syrup for sodas; portions of this and that leftover side dish; and, now, two full produce bins of summer fruit and vegetables. And that is just what I have grown, picked, or made. There are also the store-bought condiments I am trying to get rid of and all the new stuff that Mom likes having on hand during her long summer stay (slowly, she is giving them up). There are the four half gallons of raw milk, as well as whatever cream I have separated off the top to use fresh or ferment. There are eggs (I keep them in the fridge, although I have been told I do not have to keep them cold), and a brimming cheese drawer with bits and pieces waiting to be used in some mac and cheese. And so what I'd hoped would be a quick once-over of the fridge ends up taking another forty-five minutes of my day.

It is now pushing 8:00 a.m. and I think I should quickly mix some of the blueberry compote left over from my fruit-canning class the other day with some fresh blackberries to make a cobbler. I got the idea from a recipe in a book called *Spoonbread and Strawberry Wine*, which I picked up at a community book sale. The book, a compilation of family recipes, was written by two sisters, Nora Jean and Carole Darden, in 1976. Given the life I am promoting, I was struck by the section entitled "Mama Darden's Canning and Preserving," which begins with a note about Mama:

> They say that Dianah Darden would attack all that
> had to be done with the energy of a whirlwind.
> And there were so many things to be done for a
> family the size of hers—curing the meat in the
> smokehouse, making the soap, boiling the clothes
> for laundry[,] and baking. But canning and
> preserving were the things that gave her the most
> satisfaction. She felt that the whole process just
> seemed to pull her into the rhythm of the universe.
> She'd plant her seeds in the spring, pick and prepare
> the vegetables and fruits from the earth in summer
> and fall and serve them in the winter.

Clearly, Mama was no slacker.

There is a lovely picture of Mama Dianah Scarborough Darden and a short biography, which includes the possibility that she may have "worked herself into the grave but, perfectionist that she was, she could not be stopped." I'm not sure how that makes me feel, given that I am often worn out and exhausted after completing a mere fraction of her workload. Honestly, I don't know how folks managed all those chores, but I'm sure practice and limited options had a lot to do with it. I am indeed lucky to have some way to lighten the load without totally eliminating the logic of it. That logic was made manifest in the black- and blueberry cobbler I made from the berries Mom and I picked together.

FORTY POUNDS AND A MOM

A few days earlier, Mom and I picked forty pounds of blueberries. The thirty-five pounds I didn't use in my class I ended up putting in the freezer. That quantity certainly supplies my blueberries for the year, but getting them into the freezer took three days of on-and-off activity. First there was the picking, which took a good half day, including going to and from the farm. Picking was followed by washing, air-drying, and freezing the berries on cookie sheets. Once they were frozen, I transferred them into a bag that was then vacuum sealed before being placed into deep-chill storage. I repeated that process twice before declaring my annual blueberry storage complete. Blueberries, as I have suggested, are one of the items to put on the season's food-preservation list, but how was I to know that the day to pick them would creep up so quickly? I had called my favorite blueberry farmer a couple of weeks earlier, and she'd suggested a late-July/early-August date for picking. I knew the day was approaching, but the darn hot weather pushed the season into overdrive. When I called to double-check the date, I was told that picking was already in full swing. If I wanted to get my fill, I needed to go out there that day. So out we went on Friday. I taught my classes on Saturday, and picked blackberries and bought loganberries at the farmers market on Sunday. Trying to juggle the contents of my fridge, I knew that the leftover blueberry compote from the canning class had to give up its space. I was simply running out of room, which brings me back to the black- and blueberry cobbler the compote was destined for.

A DISTINCT RHYTHM

I'm glad that the recipes in *Spoonbread and Strawberry Wine* are a little makeshift. Since no one ever got exact recipes from their mothers or grandmothers, the instructions offered are from memory. Mama Darden's extended family share these recipes, since she herself was long gone by the time the book was put together. These relatives watched Mama cook and passed on her recipes through trial and error. "As children," Nora Jean and Carole write, "we had always been intrigued by the women in our family as they moved about in their kitchens, often preparing meals for large numbers of people. Each one worked in a distinct rhythm, and from the essence of who they were came unique culinary expressions. They rarely measured or even tasted their food but were guided, we guessed, by the aroma, appearance and perhaps some magical instincts unknown to us."

In that same book, Garnett Henderson, of Montclair, New Jersey, says, "My mother had no cookbooks or menus as guides, but her food was delicious." Now, I know her mom had recipes—only she didn't have to write them down, because she went by feel and experience, which is what, I am sure, Garnett means. It confirmed my opinion that recipes are often just the bones of the thing, with the particular this or that coming from the experience of the cook or the nature of the ingredient. I rarely follow recipes myself, preferring, like many cooks, to trust my intuition. And that's what Garnett did when she offered a recipe for blackberry cobbler from memory. Not to quote it exactly, but it goes something like: mix berries, sugar, lemon juice, and flour. Spread in the bottom of a well-greased pan. Mix eggs, melted butter, and sugar. Mix baking powder, flour, and salt together and stir into egg mixture. Spread over berries. Bake, and serve with light cream.

Got it.

In the end, I didn't grease the pan. I figured the berries had enough moisture. And, yeah, adding some flour to the berries could be a good idea, but I was starting with a berry compote that had already been cooked a little with sugar, so it was thicker than raw berries.

There is a fiery twirl to any harvest summer day. Something is always on deck. I'm not complaining, just remarking, and it does little good to complain anyway.

Instead of the oven, I was going to bake it on the outdoor grill with a system I've put together. Besides, what could go wrong with delicious berries and some kind of baked dough on top? And that's what I made (it was delicious), but only after blanching the five pounds of Romano green beans I had in the fridge.

There is a fiery twirl to any harvest summer day. Something is always on deck. I'm not complaining, just remarking, and it does little good to complain anyway. So what if I don't go with friends to the beach today? So what if I have to skip a weekend at some getaway or another? I'll just wait until winter to get my vacation groove on. Today there are beans to put up. I picked them from my garden over the past two or three days, and we need to face off. Big, plump, and meaty, Romano beans are among my favorite pole beans. I try to eat as many as I can during the summer, but these babies are prolific. Every morning Mom and I freak out at the sheer abundance. Picking them just promotes new growth. What a lovely thing it is if you want to put up stores to last the year. What a damning thing if you are trying to get other work done. Before baking the cobbler, Mom and I sat out in the garden to tip, slice, wash, blanch, and chill all the beans, using my backyard kitchen, which, as I have said many times, is a gift from the universe to me. How in the world could you think of boiling five gallons of water in the house kitchen when you know it will be a sauna once the heat of the day finds its way inside?

It is somewhere within the haze of the day that I think of Mama Darden again. Though the amount of work she had to do seems ridiculous, I imagine experience made it easier. I think about all the kids (and anyone under thirty is a kid to me) who take my classes and wonder how they manage. Of course, I know they don't, in most cases. Their lives are too busy. Their commitment is new. But I also know that many of them don't have a lot of skills past basic cooking. Nor do most folks. In place of those skills, they have microwaves and takeout, cereal, peanut butter, pizza, burritos, and ramen. That is surely what keeps most college kids alive, which is too bad, because fast cooking often translates to bad eating. I don't want to be too hard on them; I understand they often don't know any better. I suppose it would be okay, except that at some point they seem to wake up and want to start growing and preserving food—and find themselves out of luck. Besides the particular skills of food preservation, putting up your food requires a modicum of basic cooking knowledge. It's hard to teach food preservation when your students don't even understand what blanching or poaching means. Even I—and I like to think I resemble a cross between Mama Darden, Courtney Love, and Coco Chanel—have a hard time doing it all. I can only imagine how overwhelming it would be if you had to read up on blanching before you even got to the canning or freezing. Like so many other

MY BARBECUE OVEN

Place a few bricks on the grill to create a platform for your baking pan (you may want to put a grate across them to create a shelf). Turn the flame to a low heat, close the lid, keep any vents closed, and let the "oven" heat up. If you do not have a temperature gauge, don't worry. Just wait fifteen minutes or so. Put a casserole (or some other oven-safe dish) on the bricks and close the lid. Use the vents to regulate temperature. You will grow comfortable with your own grill after a while. Without worrying too much about it, I know the temperature will hover somewhere around three hundred to four hundred degrees. This sort of laissez-faire attitude will work with something like a cobbler. It is, after all, a rugged dessert.

aspects of cooking, these skills are lost to our youth. I always wonder how they will take on the challenge of putting up the harvest without some basic cooking education. If there is no one left in the household to pass on those skills, I vote for teaching them in schools. Not as home economics used to be taught, but as the radical and empowering subject it could be. Learning how to cook, preserve, and work with the farmers of your world is nothing short of revolution in its tastiest form.

The expression "Mad dogs and Englishmen go out in the midday sun" comes from Noel Coward's description of the delirium produced by the heat in India.

MAD DOGS AND ENGLISHMEN

By two o'clock I have finished the kitchen chores, put up that day's harvest, completed whatever cleaning up I needed to do in the house, and eaten the lunch Mom prepared for us (bagels and lox, of course, with garden lettuce, tomatoes, and cucumbers). The beans, now waiting in two large colanders for their place in the freezer, will be put off until later in the day. My older son will tend to that chore, since he's all about the vacuum sealer, having used it for his own nefarious purposes in the past (it seems to lock in the pungent, fresh flavor of bud). It's nice when a tool has so many uses. I am always glad when I can pass off a task to a son, or to anyone else for that matter. Remember, we are the new farm family, that eccentric unit derived from the original version of days gone by. I take my help wherever it shows up, which is just one reason why it's so nice that Mom lives with us for the summer. At eighty-three she is a force to be reckoned with, and she takes a certain pride in that. She taught me most of what I know about basic cooking. Like Mama Darden, she offers me a reference for my own memories and creations. But unlike Mama Darden, she knows the value of a good nap, because only mad dogs and Englishmen want to preserve food in the midday sun.

I have grown accustomed to napping in the afternoon. It is a wise thing to do when the heat turns all action into folly. These are the dog-day afternoons of summer, and they invite a siesta. What better payment for all the hard work of the early morning? I like to lie down in the garden house with a good book and rest before the dinner meal. Tonight, I will grill some pattypan squash and a pork loin. We will make a cold green-bean salad with some garden shallots. After dinner, I will serve the cobbler with some homemade ice cream. Then, I will sit in the garden house with my family until exhaustion wins. Then it is off to bed and sleep, before I wake to a new morning with its cup of coffee and the promise of the morning paper. One of these days (after the summer harvest, to be sure), I'm actually going to read it.

COBBLER

The thing I love about cobbler is that it is so easy, so forgiving. Like its cousins the crumbles, buckles, and pandowdies, cobbler is a rustic dessert. It is not meant to be fussed over. In fact, there is an exact correlation between cobbler success and your commitment to making it while you're "in the spirit." Not only will you not worry about how it comes out, but in an hour or two when your sugar level drops and you get the munchies, you will happily shove anything in your face. Cobbler? Oh, hell yeah.

Whether you start with fresh, canned, or frozen fruit is up to you and the season's availability. Canned peaches? Fine. Frozen raspberries?

That will work. Fresh rhubarb—perfect.

Whether you top it with your favorite biscuit dough or a pour-on batter is also your choice. I was taught a recipe by a Southern friend who uses strips of pie dough layered throughout the cobbler. She put some hot peach filling in a pan, layered some strips of pie dough, baked it for a while till the pie crust was getting cooked but not brown, added some more peach mixture, topped this with more pie dough strips, and baked it again. She used store-bought canned peaches and frozen pie dough. Though I shielded my eyes, I devoured the final results. And I assure you she did not start with a recipe.

Do you want nuts and cinnamon in your biscuit dough? Fine. Do it. Do you want to use cornmeal in place of some of the wheat flour? Knock yourself out. Some folks like to add an egg to the mix for a more cakelike texture, which is perfectly okay. Some like to add an additional crumble on top. Also fine. Some want to bake it in a pie pan, others prefer a casserole dish or a heavy cast-iron pot. Fine, fine, fine. Just keep in mind how much fruit is going in. My Southern friend baked hers in a disposable aluminum-foil tray. Though I wanted to fish it out of the trash after the meal, I didn't. She was already getting sick of me. "I tell you what was wrong with your green beans: olive oil. You don't use no olive oil. You put in butta, only butta." I can't even begin to tell you how hard she was laughing at this Yankee.

Whether you want to thicken your fruit with tapioca, flour, or cornstarch is your call, as is the sweetness of the mix. As far as I'm concerned, the only thing to keep in mind is the temperature of your fruit mixture when it goes into the oven. I suggest starting with a hot fruit mix, particularly if you are using a biscuit topping (which is generally my approach). Starting with hot fruit allows you to cut your baking time down to twenty minutes in a four-hundred-degree oven. It also allows you to see how "juicy" the mix is before you bake it. Everyone has experienced the heartbreak of a runny pie filling. While there is a whole lot less to worry about with cobblers (if the fruit stays juicy, who cares?), cooking the fruit mixture on top of the stove before baking it in the oven does make you more confident, especially if you are starting with frozen fruit—which I generally do in winter.

As *The Farm Journal's Complete Pie Cookbook* suggests, "Cobblers are a busy woman's quick and hearty dessert standby." And so they are. In the following recipes, you will note the variations (some I added), but also remember how I did it back when I had extra blueberry compote and blackberries in the fridge—I winged it and baked it in the barbecue "oven."

Adapted from *The Farm Journal*

FRESH FRUIT COBBLER
(BASIC DIRECTIONS)

Mix together in a saucepan ⅔ to 1 cup sugar, depending on natural sweetness of fruit or berries, and 1 tablespoon cornstarch.

Gradually stir in 1 cup of boiling water. Bring to a boil. Boil for 1 minute.

Add prepared fruit and pour into a 10-by-6-inch baking dish or a 1½-quart casserole. Dot with 1 tablespoon butter or margarine. Add spices as desired (cinnamon, nutmeg, clove, vanilla).

Sift together 1 cup sifted flour or ½ cup flour and ½ cup cornmeal, 1 tablespoon sugar, 1½ teaspoons baking powder, and ½ teaspoon of salt.

Blend in ¼ cup shortening until the mixture resembles cornmeal.

Stir in ½ cup milk to make a soft dough.

Drop spoonfuls of dough over the hot fruit filling. Bake in a hot oven (400 degrees) for about 30 minutes. Serve in bowls with cobbler juices, light cream, ice cream, or whipped cream, or whatever your heart desires.

VARIATIONS:

CANNED FRUITS IN COBBLER: Drain and use liquid in canned fruit for thickening with cornstarch. Add more liquid as needed. Adjust sweetness based on sweetness of canned liquid.

FROZEN FRUIT IN COBBLER: Thaw your frozen fruit before using it. Measure collected fruit juice and use in place of the water as suggested in the basic directions. Add more water if necessary.

AUGUST

The Home

The New Barn Building

I'm always moved when I read about pioneer women going crazy from the isolation of their lives. Sometimes, when I am walking around the backyard talking to the squirrels, I tell myself it is time to make some householding friends. Though I am busy during the harvest, it is not constant. There are moments that would be suitable for a shared cup of coffee or a conversation, but most of my friends are working in offices. I could call them up at work, but that would miss the point. I would rather meet them in their gardens or in their homes, to have a quick exchange in between the chores of a busy day. That's when I get to wondering how exactly it could work. Will there ever be a neighbor I can talk to over the clothesline, or who is home in the middle of the day when I need a cup of sugar? Where have all the neighbors gone, long time passing?

VIRTUAL ABSTRACTIONS

There are all sorts of virtual communities springing up as a way for people to connect with others who have similar interests, but virtual connections are a little abstract for me. I'm looking for face time, particularly with those who are similarly aligned with the house-holding program. Not that I haven't tried. I have reached out more than once to create new networks, but somehow it always comes across as forced. Folks are simply too busy. Where do we find the time to make a life in here if we are always out there? And being out there is still the majority of everyone's life. Frankly, I don't care too much about out there anymore, which seems to worry my family. Coming home to find me in the same clothes I have worn for a week (and sometimes I sleep in them) can be disconcerting, I suppose. But why go out? After stocking the pantry, I have little need to shop at the grocery (praise the Lord—I hate to do it). Hanging out in coffee shops is nice on occasion, but with everyone plugged into his or her computer, what's the point? I used to forbid the use of computers or cell phones in my coffee shop, insisting that people talk to each other, but I got little response other than pissing folks off. With its great tradition of fomenting revolution, coffee-shop culture deserves more respect than a laptop can offer; at least, that's how it seemed to me. But just try to get someone to talk to you. It's generally not going to happen.

Walking the streets or hanging out on the corner with a cigarette dangling from my lips looking for a passerby willing to talk to me is a funny image, but I do feel like I'm trolling for friends when I sit on my porch. Just try and get past me if you're walking your dog by my house. "Hey, what's your name? Want to know how special I am?" It's just that with so much damn intention crammed into a life, a person needs a little camaraderie. Of course, there is the distinct possibility that I'm annoying as hell, and that even if everyone was home,

> Hanging out in coffee shops is nice on occasion, but with everyone plugged into his or her computer, what's the point?

I'd still be out in the cold. My friend Myo says she loves my "self-obsession," but that's because she's Italian and is used to people talking over each other. I understand I'm looking for a very particular relationship. Me: expat New York Jew, living in the land of hipsterism, growing food and still talking about Woodstock. You: someone who likes listening to me talk. Which is why I'm writing this book, I guess. Wow, a captive audience. But honestly, where do we meet?

CLOWNS WHO DRUM

Over the past couple of years, my husband and I have participated in a series of rotating neighborhood work parties. Six families in all, we move from house to house over the course of the spring and summer months, working on the projects each host has proposed for the day. It's a great way to build fellowship and to knock out projects that could take you years to tackle on your own. The host supplies the breakfast, and the following month's host supplies the lunch. If we are honest with ourselves, we admit that no one really *likes* working on these projects, but everyone is happy, and a bit proud, when the day is done. And so the practice has continued over the past few years. Does it really build community? I'm not sure. Other than these work parties, it has not really forged deep ties between us. Some of it has to do with children. Many of the families have young children and most of their interactions are related to the tasks involved in raising them—sleepovers, T-ball, trips to soccer practice, and such. Some of them were friends before they moved into the neighborhood and have known each other for years, which is an amazing thing to me. My old girlfriends from the Bronx are scattered all over the country, but even if they lived across the street, I don't know how I'd act with them. Which brings me to another point: I'm cranky.

I have often said in jest, though my husband repeats it in public more times than I would like, that I love the idea of community, but I hate people. How funky is that? But there it is. Most people bug me—and, not surprisingly, I bug them. If that's your problem, what is the solution? I suppose you must pick and choose and try to find the right mix. More and more folks are moving to intentional communities with that goal in mind, but my only experience looking into it ended with my husband and me fleeing the meeting. Well, not exactly fleeing . . . but, as I admitted, I'm a crank. After hearing about one woman's sideline interest in being a clown, I shut down. Heck, clowns are creepy. I've been scared of them ever since I went to Rockefeller Center to see Emmett Kelly, the clown of a million children's nightmares. Not only was this woman at the meeting into being a clown, she also dressed in purple. Every-thing was purple—even the home she lived in, where she and her husband held a monthly drumming circle. Yikes! What was I getting myself into? I could just see her knocking on my door to ask for some sugar before she set out for the annual "Clowns Who Drum Celebra-tion." Would I be nice to her? I can't say for sure, but I know I'd be muttering something under my breath.

During house parties, hoedowns, harvest, and "happenings," we are trying to resurrect a world that will be both joyous and confounding.

Sometimes I think I need to join a collective with a big garden, an outdoor kitchen, a storage shed where I could smoke cigarettes when the husband's not around, and Sunday *New York Times* delivery service. I'd need a collective with at least a few expat New York Jews who like gardening and talking about the glory days of the sixties, and who, for all their self-proclaimed brilliance, can occasionally enjoy the company of others, and who, when the spirit moves them, will partake in a certain decadent generational pastime as long as someone, preferably a young disciple, is there to walk them back to their apartments. And herein lies the irony of it all. We Americans, as a people and a culture, carry the oddest assortment of amalgamated instincts. We are hopeful and outreaching, sullen and complex. We are building new futures and breaking down old conventions. We are living in cities and on farms. We are young and old. We are dyed-in-the-wool activists and women who dress like clowns. We are cranky, or hopeful, or just a little unsure, but together we are raising the barn of the future, either virtually or on solid ground. During house parties, hoedowns, harvest, and "happenings," we are trying to resurrect a world that will be both joyous and confounding. All I ask is that you keep the drumming circle out back—and completely out of earshot.

The Garden

Sowing Carrots—Again • Troubleshooting Cucumbers • Taking Stock of the Harvest

With the blazing days of July behind me, I can now begin to think about my winter garden. I hate to admit it, but my carrots did meet their end—and for exactly the reason I mentioned. I overlooked them for a couple of hours during the high-noon heat. I can't tell you how crestfallen I was, since their tops had made it up through the ground and were trying to give it a go. I uncovered them in the early morning to give them some daylight and then forgot about them. No good. When I finally remembered, they were fried. There you have it—the sentry left her post. I replanted yet again during the second week in August, despite the fact that many "professionals" do not suggest planting carrots in early August. Oh, some do and some don't. Some suggest waiting till September to plant varieties that will winter over. Some folks say you can plant carrots every two weeks if you shield them properly. Some of this, I know, has to do with soil temperature and variety, but I cannot worry about it now, sorry to say. I am so obsessed with having carrots in my garden during fall and early winter—and longer if there is not too heavy a ground freeze—that I am giving it a go. The carrots, along with the turnips I planted in July, as well as rutabagas and beets, have been sown in a bed that I turned over with some compost. The package of rutabaga seeds stated, "Too much nitrogen-rich compost will cause hairy roots." Well, I don't know how rich my compost is or what "too much" really means; I just threw some in my bed. Actually, I put more thought into it than that. Once again, I tried to think like a plant.

I thought about the green leaves my spinach and lettuce would put out and how it made sense that they would need more nitrogen. Nitrogen, after all, encourages green growth. I thought about the soil my carrots and other root vegetables needed and how what they needed, more than nitrogen, was loose and arable soil to move their long or wide roots through. It would make sense that they'd appreciate a little extra compost to lighten the soil, so I added some and hoped the nitrogen content was not too high. Phosphorus is another nutrient root vegetables need, and I knew mine would have plenty, since I had applied rock phosphate to all of my beds a few years back. Rock phosphate decomposes over a long time, offering its nutrients in a slow, organic drip. And since it was still a little hot out, and I knew my spinach, lettuce, turnips, and rutabagas like cooler soils (75 degrees for turnips and 60 degrees for rutabagas), I thought a canopy would be appreciated. Once again, I covered the kitty defense system with screening.

At the same time that I want the sun to be at bay for my fall seedlings, I long for its furious rays to cast heat on my tomatoes. These are the days when you hope to beat the clock, since, as I mentioned, a successful tomato harvest is not always guaranteed in the Pacific Northwest.

This year, given the serious sun and heat of July, most of the tomatoes are well on their way, but the late-ripening varieties are still green on the vine. And as luck would have it, those are the varieties I like the most, for my paste tomatoes and my slicers alike. This year I have grown early- and late-ripening varieties for both purposes, and the early-ripening varieties of each are up and running. But it is the Brandywines, for slicing, and the San Marzanos, for paste, that are still tempting me with only the slightest pink hue. But it's mid-August, and there is plenty of time for them to flourish. When they do, I will be ready with my fork and knife or canning jar, as the variety demands. The few peppers and eggplants I planted from starts back in early June are equally enamored of the sun, as is the one pattypan squash I planted, which is now putting out one or two lovely golden orbs a day with no sign of giving up soon. The same can be said for my pickling cucumbers, even though I have had a certain amount of bad luck with them.

TROUBLESHOOTING CUKES

I'm not sure why my pickling cucumbers turned hollow when I put them up in brine (which I do to get old-fashioned crock pickles), but this year, when I fished some out of the brine and sliced them to demonstrate to my students the stages of fermentation (early on they are not dark green all the way through), I noticed they were hollow inside. That hadn't happened in past years. The "trouble-shooting guide" in my preserving book

It is too late to start worrying about what people think of you once you have made it into the club in a leopard-skin jumpsuit—it's best to just go with it.

said the problem lay in how they were grown and that "there is no solution." A while later, when I was buying a twenty-five-pound bag of them at the farmers market, I asked the farmer if he knew why it had happened. Now, it is true that you rarely see a farmer, even at the farmers market. Most of the time, it's the young kids (under thirty) helping out, and while they're cute, they're not much help when you ask about specific varieties or gardening problems. Which is why I turned to Frank at Big B's, even though he and I had gone through a little rough patch a few years ago.

A FRANK COMMENT

It was during a Market Halloween party, when he suggested that in my chosen costume I looked like Julia Roberts in *Pretty Woman* (and I'm not talking about her outfit at the races). I guess it was the skin-tight black velvet leggings, purple cowboy boots, cropped jean jacket, blond wig, black sunglasses, and cowboy hat that did it, but still, I was insulted. I think I went off on some odd defensive trip about not being a streetwalker. He just looked at me like I was crazy, and he was probably half right about that. I don't know why I was so worried about what he thought—and besides, looking back at those pictures, I think he was right. Like I said to a dear and now-departed friend, it is too late to start worrying about what people think of you once you have made it into the club in a leopard-skin jumpsuit—it's best to just go with it. Since then, I have come to rely on Frank for growing advice and concrete information about vegetable varieties. Goodness knows what I will do for the sake of my garden—even overlook an imagined slight to my virtue.

According to Frank, the cucumber bloat was due to a lack of water. He said that if cucumbers don't receive enough moisture, they will be hollow inside. "But mine are only hollow when I pickle them," I told him. "That's strange," he said. "I've never heard of that." He probably thought I was lying, just looking for attention like someone inflicted with vegetal Münchausen syndrome (okay, that's not funny—but, then again, it sorta is).

But it was true, my pickling cucumbers were not hollow when picked—they became hollow during fermentation. Despite his years of experience and clear knowledge base, Frank was stumped, which I guess serves him right for that *Pretty Woman* comment (which I am *totally* over). I have yet to speak to the county extension agent about the problem. Unfortunately, regardless of the reason, I was stuck with a bunch of homegrown pickling cucumbers that would not stand up to fermentation, and that just made me sad, and mad. Sometime during the winter I will call the seed grower to ask about this. But that will have to wait. I have other things to fret about now—for example, my delicata squash.

After transplanting two of my delicata squash from their original space under the nectarine tree, I began to be concerned about how the late move would affect them. I had originally planted them in the plot by my back door, but two years ago I planted a nectarine tree in the same spot. I had not taken into consideration the canopy of leaves that would shade that formerly sunny spot. This oversight resulted in squash plants that withered from lack of sunlight and an insect invasion. Remember, choosing the right spot for your vegetable plants is vitally important. And since delicata squash was one of the few requests my husband had made (that and the Brandywine tomatoes), I was determined to set things right. So I transplanted them to a sunny spot. After the initial shock (they were withered and weak for a while, until they established a new root system), they came on strong and full. But their fruit are still green and only three inches long and one inch thick, so I am wondering how they will do. I have four plants scattered throughout the garden, so even if the two I have transplanted do not produce, I'm sure the others will, but that would be quite a loss to the side-dish garden I like to plan. Along with my butternut squash (which I have also planted and which are doing their job), delicatas are favorites for my "root cellar." Once they are cured and their skins have hardened for winter storage, they will do nicely for fetching into the kitchen throughout fall and early winter. Delicatas will not last as long in storage as butternuts, but they still provide plenty of good eating until early December. After that, they begin to soften and need to be eaten all at once or stored in the fridge. If the fridge doesn't stop them from softening, I bake, blanch, or sauté them and then freeze them. Yippee—a side dish! Right now, however, my concern is whether this year's crop will ripen before the frosts. Allowing your winter squash to be exposed to one or two slight frosts will most likely be fine, but a serious frost will turn their skin glassy (you will notice a "wet"-looking discoloration) and negatively affect their storability. A winter squash that has suffered from frost should be eaten right away or processed for the freezer. We'll see. With any luck, the growing gods will reward me for my anxiety and dedication and give me a full crop before the onset of the winter chill.

TAKING STOCK OF THE HARVEST

By early to mid-August I have harvested most of my volunteer fingerling potatoes. If you ever plant potatoes, you will notice volunteers popping up the next spring. That's because the potatoes you do not harvest, or overlook, become the seeds for next year's crop. This year I left the volunteer patch to its own devices, and since the potatoes were setting green growth early in the season, I figured I would be able to dig them up early. Any potatoes I got out of that bed would be a bonus, since I was not planning on them. On the other hand, they were taking up a bed in which I'd planned to grow squash. I'm not sure I should have obliged them, but I did. This year I'll be more aggressive in digging up my loot or, if I miss some, will uproot the volunteers as they emerge next spring. The bed of potatoes I planted intentionally still has some green growth, which is a signal to leave it be. You stop watering potato plants once they start flowering, to encourage them to put their energy into forming tubers. Not watering them also encourages their curing process, as their skins begin to toughen. New potatoes, as they are called in the market, are the spuds that you root out early in the season. Generally no more than an inch or two in diameter, early potatoes are often just the same as the ones you will pick later in the season, but smaller and with a more tender skin. Letting your potatoes grow for the full season gives you larger potatoes or, at least, they get as large they are meant to be. Russets (traditional bakers) are larger and starchier than fingerling or red potatoes, and each is suited to different cooking methods. This year I have thrown at least three different varieties in one bed, and if you think I know which is which, you're wrong. I also planted way too early, which means the soil was not only a little too wet but also very dense. I knew when I was doing it that I shouldn't. Over and over, I fall victim to my own impatience. In March, as you may recall, I suggested that prudence is a major virtue. Did I listen? Not really. Am I—or rather, are my potatoes—paying for it? Yep.

FORCING MOTHER NATURE

Chalk it up to being human, but it does bug me when I force the season. The consequence for my potatoes is that the ground around them is rock hard. The bed never received the compost it required and as a result is

August is the everything month—a whirlwind of production. It is the month that shows me what I am made of in the preserving kitchen.

suffering with a solid mass of impenetrable soil. Conditions such as these will not make potatoes happy or prolific, because they like to set out their roots a bit. Potatoes grow underground, in case you didn't know (and some folks don't), and the little nodules that form on their roots grow up to be the big fat tubers we love to eat. Even in poor soil, they will produce a respectable crop, but nothing like the bounty you'd receive if you are good to them. I guess if you are to neglect any particular vegetable, potatoes are the one you can get away with neglecting. But why bother growing them if you don't take the time to give them what they need? This is a self-directed question and the answer is, because I was impatient. Silly me, silly March. I have yet to see the consequences of my handiwork, since I have not yet dug them up. I will wait until September or later to do that. Actually, I have heard many people suggest that you can leave them in the ground all winter and dig them up as you need them, but that too would require a virtue I don't have—patience. I want to see how bad I was or, rather, how obliging my potatoes were in spite of my badness. On the one hand, I hope I am made to pay for my folly—it would teach me a lesson. On the other, I hope I get away with it and have a bumper crop. If the latter is the case, I won't learn anything except that sometimes you are given a second chance. What I will do with it is to be seen. We'll see next March, when I am given to madness again.

My Romano green beans have given up the ghost. Having shot up and yielded like madmen in July, they are tired now, and the bean pods they create are tough and full of seeds. I am letting them dry on the vine and will pull them up by late August in preparation for sowing winter vegetables. The beans were planted from seeds I collected last year and yielded about ten to fifteen pounds of beans over the season. They are done for the year. I have to admit, I was ready for it to happen—there was a lot of green-bean eating going on for a while.

With chard, collards, and kale still to be planted in August, I think I'll spend the rest of this month putting up the harvest. August is the everything month—a whirlwind of production. It is the month that shows me what I am made of in the preserving kitchen. Over and over, I tell myself I am a squirrel, and to be patient, and that it will soon be winter, when I can rest. Oh, but not now. There are miles and miles of jars, crocks, and drying racks to go before I sleep. Lordy, Lordy. August is no joke.

The Kitchen

The Pears of Epiphany • My Temperamental Peaches •
Walking the Rows • The Godfather of Ferments •
Loving Me Some Plums

Writing about my kitchen tasks in August while doing all the kitchen tasks in August is an exercise in the absurd, though I guess the challenge is not so different from the one that faces those who work full- or part-time jobs while growing and putting up their stores. Dealing with this both keeps me honest and makes me empathize with those who are struggling to manage two sets of interests or obligations. But I have a choice. I can forgo a day or two of writing and respond to the endless barrage of Bartlett pears raining down around me. I could ignore the pears, but they're what got me started on all of this. Besides, ignoring them will result in a bigger mess of rotting fruit, fruit flies, and the sweet/sour scent of fermenting pears wafting through the yard. I juggle my commitments in an endless round of tasks. Had I only my pears to deal with, things might be reasonable, but August falls in the season of our disconnect— the season when we lose all rational connection with the modern world.

Sure, I am making this sound a little desperate, but you would never forgive me if I didn't. You'd be standing knee-deep in tomatoes or peaches, wearing that cute little apron you thought was *sooooo* darling and appropriate for your new life as a householder, and you'd be putting a pox on my family. I'm not going to leave myself open to that. When I say August will try your patience, I mean it. This will be the month when you finally understand my suggestion for developing a Food Preservation Game Plan. This is the month when you will understand my call for prudence and reasoned systems. Of course, as with all my other calls for prudence, I tend to ignore it myself. How can I help myself, when friends call to say they have a special lead on some crab apples and wild blackberries and would I like to go picking? Of course I would, even though it will lead to a three-day marathon of apple and blackberry picking; chopping, cooking, draining, cooling, testing, recooking, and canning one gallon of pectin stock; and making crab-apple jelly (really yummy) and a blackberry cobbler on a ninety-five-degree day while coping with the tender garden starts (which are going through hell under that sun) and the nonstop cascade of pears.

> Sure, I am making this sound a little desperate, but you would never forgive me if I didn't.

THE PEARS OF MY EPIPHANY

I've already told you how my Bartlett pears fell on my head like Newton's apple. I'm glad they did, and I'm glad about everything that has happened since—but that tree is thirty feet tall, and it must yield two hundred pounds of pears each year. I don't take any credit for its size, since it came with our home. It's massive and proud and as productive as all get out. There has not been a year in which it has not bombarded us with pears. Most of the ones that fall are mottled babies, the wormed and spotted ones at the bottom of the branches, while the nearly unblemished, enormous fruits are at the very top, where I cannot reach them. All of them, however, make their way to the ground in torrents if I don't harvest them with my fruit picker. But even with the best fruit-picking intentions, a good third of the crop will fall to the ground. Every day, I fill another grocery sack half full with pears and set it out on the porch for them to ripen. Pears, as you may know, will not ripen on the tree, which is definitely a good thing, since having ripe pears hurtling to the ground would be so, so sad. It's even sad that they bruise when they land, but I can cut out most of those blemishes when I peel and slice them. Pears seem to be forgiving that way. I already have some fifteen bags waiting on the porch in various stages of ripeness. I go through them daily, picking out the few from each bag that are ready for me to peel, slice, and cook up in a sauce; then I put them in the fridge until I have a large enough quantity to justify heating up the water in the canning pot.

A small-batch mentality seems to work in early spring, when I contentedly make jam a jar or two at a time as the strawberries are coming on in my garden. But August offers no such story. It is all sultry mornings and nights, and if it weren't for my outside kitchen, there would be no food preservation going on at all. After the first cup of coffee in the morning, I forbid anyone to turn on the stove. Poor Mom. In Florida, she lives a life of air-conditioned indifference to the weather, so this obsession with keeping unnecessary heat out of the kitchen bugs her. She is used to having her way, and I recognize she makes an effort to respect my desires, which is not to say I don't annoy the crap out of her sometimes. Although she has warmed up to my "lifestyle" somewhat, I believe she is waiting for me to outgrow it and go clothes shopping with her. I can't really blame her. At eighty-three she is generally sold on the virtues of ease and convenience. That's what retirees of her generation are all about, and I suppose I should say no more on that subject until I am her age. Still, there is a bit of a tussle at times between our conflicting agendas. Mine—put up as much of the harvest as humanly possible. Hers—dress up and eat good Chinese food. But I can't think about it too much in August. In August I have to crack the whip—if not on her, then definitely on my own householding ass.

GOING FOR THE GOLD

By mid-August I have finished freezing my beans and blueberries for the year. They, at least, have been checked off the list. I have made all the jam I am going to make, and with this last addition of crab-apple jelly, the sweet-spread section of the store is full. I might make a few apple butters, but that will be it. Maybe some pear butter, but then I am done. I finished making my supply of apple pectin for the season, and the tomatoes are beginning to show themselves proudly. I have already put up twelve pints, but I'm going for the gold. Lord forgive me if I don't manage to make forty-five quarts by the time all is tallied, but we'll see. I have a five-gallon crock of fermenting pickles in the basement, which I will put up sometime in the next few weeks. They will give me some thirteen quarts of pickles, at least. That's definitely enough to get us through the year. I'm working on the pear sauce right now. By the time the pears are done taunting me, I should have twenty quarts of sauce, another fifteen pints of sliced pears (the ones that turn into upside-down gingerbread cake), and I don't know how much pear leather and dried pears.

That's okay, because I really like dried pears, and once they're peeled and sliced, all you have to do is put them in the food dryer. When all is said and done, I should end up with at least ten pounds of dried pears in the basement. Most of the fruit drying will be finished in September, when my food dryer is working overtime, steadily humming away. My neighbors just built a solar dryer, and I'm excited to see how that works. I don't think they have it up and going yet, though, since they keep borrowing mine. They took full advantage of the cherry harvest this year, which is a good thing because it was madly productive. Unfortunately, that was a very bad thing for the growers.

THE CURSE OF THE GLUT

There were many articles in the local paper about how the glut of cherries was hurting our farmers—too much supply of any one fruit, and the price plummets. I always feel bad for folks who grow single crops; too much of their livelihood depends on it. I understand the dilemma, since modern farming encourages a mono-crop mind-set. I understand the demands of fruit brokers, big-chain grocery stores, and international markets and how, depending on your given business model, you might be forced to adopt the single-crop production model. Still, it always appears risky, and I wonder how they must feel about the line of reasoning they've been sold on. But this is something I can't think about in August. My mind is too engaged in the practical to wade into conjecture. It just won't do, particularly when I must confront the folly of my harvesting ways. Even after telling myself I would pick only—and I mean only—twenty pounds of peaches this year, I lost control. When will I learn?

MY TEMPERAMENTAL PEACHES

Sitting on the table in my garden house are forty pounds of summer's aromatic beauties, whose golden, fragrant orbs speak of the season's good graces as almost no other fruit can. There is something particularly intoxicating about the fragrance of a perfectly ripe peach whose sugars have been allowed to ripen on the tree. You cannot replicate that experience in a farmers market. You must walk the orchard to breathe in the scent and then, ever so carefully, pick the lovely babies blushed by the summer sun and swaddle them in paper to get them home unbruised. I am not kidding here.

Veteran is the variety that makes it onto my preserving game plan each year, but Veteran peaches are temperamental children. They will bruise and blemish if you merely look at them, let alone lug them to market. In fact, you will generally not see Veterans in the market for just that reason, which only makes them dearer to me. They, too, resist the system. They are rogue players who will not be hybridized into submission. You have to respect them for it, but peaches do not hold up for long in fresh storage, so unless you want to process them, you must pick them in small quantities. I like fresh peaches a whole lot more than canned ones, which is why I told myself that I would show moderation this year. But as is the case with most things, I ignored good counsel. The consequence is the additional labor I face as I blanch, slice, can, and freeze all forty pounds of these fabulously fragrant fruits. Of course, lots are eaten fresh—made into pies, sliced with berries and cream, or simply on their own. What a treat! It used to be that my favorite dessert was peach melba—layers of peaches alternating with raspberry sauce and ice cream or whipped cream. It's still a contender, but you have to make it right. There is a marked difference in the results when all the ingredients are just as the season intended—ripe off the tree and in peak flavor. That it's possible to eat it that way at only a few times of the year makes it oh so much better. Digging down into a peach melba parfait for the perfect peach, cream, and raspberry bite offers the kind of delight that makes me feel like a kid again. My toes curl. These are the moments of summer that should not be missed. Canned and frozen peaches don't produce the same effect, but work well in lots of other desserts, so I'm not really complaining; I'm just saying I wanted to go slow on them. It was a good idea, given all the rest of the work I have to do. Like the harvesting of summer's corn, which I hunger for when winter comes.

KNEE-HIGH BY THE FOURTH OF JULY

I love walking through a cornfield. I can only imagine the great hideouts that have been built there. What adult doesn't have memories of childhood fort-making? I know that if I'd grown up anywhere near a corn patch, I would have hidden out in it with all my imaginary friends, having tea and reading racy magazines. I love the way the cornstalks tower overhead, creating muted green walls around you as you snap off the full, heavy cobs from the stalks. I love being completely hidden from the world and how, in a short amount of time, I can emerge into it again with a brimming armful of corn. Over and over, I am reminded how the natural world wants to offer its abundance to you, if you give it a chance. In fact, as Michael Pollan told us in his book *The Botany of Desire*, our agricultural brethren need us. They need us to spread their seed far and wide. It's good both for me and the bounty that we can meet to our mutual benefit like we do in the cornfields every year. The corn is full, tall, and ready to reseed, and I am hungry, able, and willing to oblige. Year after year, we play out this dance. This year will be no different, but I must wait to find time in September, since I have enough on my hands with the twenty-five pounds of cucumbers

> Over and over, I am reminded how the natural world wants to offer its abundance to you, if you give it a chance.

fermenting slowly in a crock and waiting to be canned.

I start my cucumber fermentation sometime in July, when the pickling cucumbers start showing up. It would be nice if I had enough space to grow the quantities I need (or the quantities I need at one specific time, at least), but I don't. To make a full batch of crock pickles, I need a ten-pound load, which is difficult to harvest at any one time unless you are growing quite a few cucumber plants. Even if I had the space, I'm not sure I would dig it. Too much of a good thing. I thought my four plants would offer me a nice starting supply— and they did, until I got that cucumber bloat problem I mentioned. Having replenished my cucumber supply from Frank at the farmers market back in July, I now have cucumbers that have been sitting patiently in their brine solution for about six weeks and are ready for canning.

THE GODFATHER OF FERMENTS

You don't really need to can your fermented pickles. They could just sit in a crock submerged in brine all year, and you could trot down to the cool basement to fetch a sour pickle whenever the mood struck you. That is a fine approach, and many people eschew the entire notion of canning due to the "pasteurization" involved in the process. I can relate. There are a number of fermented products I keep on hand to help me provide my body with active cultures. Yogurt is something I make all the time, and it is a wonderful source of healthful cultures. Kombucha, kefir, and other wild ferments that I have around tend to die from lack of attention. As with all living creatures, wild ferments need to be fed from time to time to keep their bubbling, fermenting selves alive. As with everything in this householding movement, you need to be honest about what you can do and what you will eat. Yogurt matches my natural

As with everything in this householding movement, you need to be honest about what you can do and what you will eat.

cravings, and I don't need to force myself to make it. Kefir makes me happy, as does the occasional glass of kombucha on a hot summer's day, but kombucha wants more than that. It appreciates the regular addition of food (in my recipe, some form of sugar and black tea), because that's how it stays alive. A white gelatinous culture forms on the surface of the beverage and feeds off the sugars. Over time, it will grow thick as more and more layers form on top of one other. Each of these layers, submerged in a solution of sweetened black tea, will serve as the starter culture for a new batch of kombucha. You can get away with ignoring that buildup of layers in your kombucha for only so long. If you don't separate out the gelatinous layers and give each of them its own home, they will compete with each other for food and finally die from starvation. That will make you sad. This subject deserves much more space than I can devote to it here; for those who want to know more, I suggest you read Sandor Katz—he's the godfather of ferments. As for me, I resist reason and good advice and do just what the live-culture folks reject—I can my fermented pickles. I have enough wild things in my home and would rather put these babies up. I love the way they taste. And they are one of my husband's favorite things in the pantry. I found this recipe in Linda Ziedrich's *The Joy of Pickling* and reprint it here with her permission, along with her amazingly good recipe for plums soaked in wine and red wine vinegar (see page 277).

A PLUM MEMORY

I was first introduced to Italian plums when I was a child; Mom would have them in bowls on the table for snacking and on top of one of my favorite cakes. The cake was a simple creation—a butter-and-egg-rich dough with a little baking powder to help it rise. Patted into any pan of a suitable size, it was topped with halved plums and baked until the dough rose around the cooked, juicy fruit. Mom would wait until the cake was baked before sprinkling the plums with sugar, which made good sense—doing so before baking would pull out too much juice from the plums and make the cake a little wetter than either of us liked. Along with the scores of dried plums (prunes, to you) I make each year, this cake always makes an appearance in late summer. But this year, after tasting Ziedrich's recipe for plums, I was hooked. I am not joking here—they are really good. I sent both my boys up a tree to fetch me as many plums as they could. My neighbor had given permission, so it was legit. I find this is the case in Portland. Even with all the gleaning going on, in a year with a bumper crop there is plenty to go around. In the past, I've received calls from exasperated friends asking for help with the bounty of one fruit or another. When I arrive, big harvesting bag in hand, they are ever so relieved. And while I usually have more than enough of my own to keep me busy, I almost always take more. I hate to see things go to waste, and there are always other neighbors with whom I can share. Not that many of the plums made it their way, because I was happy to put them up. Fresh plums, plum cake, dried plums, and plums pickled in wine. Sounds good, doesn't it? Oh yes, we will be rewarded throughout the year when the jewels of the pantry come forth with all the goodness that went into them. But what am I saying? It is only August. With September staring me in the face, it is silly of me to think of rest quite yet. Nope, September and October offer their fair share of bounty. If only I can make it through to the other side of autumn, I'll be home free. After the crazy-making month of August, you cannot imagine such a state of grace, but with the first whiff of September's cooling mornings you know that rest is soon to come. Just not yet. Not when the last of everything is waiting for your attention.

> Oh yes, we will be rewarded throughout the year when the jewels of the pantry come forth with all the goodness that went into them.

QUICK PICKLES vs. BRINED

What distinguishes brined pickles (which these are) from quick pickles is the active ingredient in the recipe. Quick pickles are "pickled" by the acetic acid in vinegar. You do not need to let them ferment, merely allow them to sit in the vinegar for a week or so (preferably longer) before you eat them. They are easy and quick, hence the name. Brined pickles, on the other hand, are pickled, or acidified, by the development of lactic acid during the fermentation process itself.

This recipe follows the guidelines for full fermentation and therefore safe canning. As I mentioned, some people choose not to can and either keep a pickle barrel in the basement or store the pickles in the fridge (though this is a hefty amount for refrigerator storage). I choose to ferment and can my pickles by August, so I can check them off my to-do list.

The leaves in this recipe are supposed to keep the cucumber firm. But even though I use them, I find that long brining takes a little of the crunch out of the pickle, no matter what you do. That's okay by me. That's how I remember eating them on Jerome Avenue.

SPICY CROCK PICKLES

This recipe will fill a 3-gallon crock.

2 handfuls grape, sour cherry, or currant leaves
   (not necessary, but nice)
About 12 pounds of 3- to 5-inch pickling cucumbers
2 tablespoons mixed pickling spice
1 garlic bulb, cloves separated and peeled
4 to 8 dill heads (you can find them in some farmers
   markets during pickling time)
6 quarts water
1 cup cider vinegar
1-1/4 cups pickling salt (do not use less)

Line the bottom of a 3-gallon crock with half of the leaves. (I use one of my food-safe plastic containers; using ceramic would be nice but heavy.) Wash the cucumbers gently so as not to remove the live bacteria and yeast that live on cucumbers and participate in the fermentation. Remove the blossom end (as opposed to the stem end). Hopefully, you will get cucumbers at the market that are young and fresh, not shriveled, and still have a fading blossom attached to them. The blossom end is said to contain enzymes that impede fermentation, hence the need to snip it off.

Layer the cucumbers, spice, garlic cloves, and salt in the crock. Combine the water and vinegar, and dissolve the salt in the liquid (this is your brine). Pour the brine over the cucumbers and lay the remaining leaves on top. Keep the leaves and cucumbers submerged by weighing them down with a plate topped with a clean rock or a water-filled jar, or with a large food-grade plastic bag filled with additional brine (in case it breaks—you don't want to be adding straight water into the mix) and sealed. You want to make sure all the cucumbers are safely under the brine and not exposed to air. I like the plate-and-filled-jar system best. Cover the crock and the weight with a pillowcase or towel sufficient to cover them completely and store the crock at room temperature. I keep the crock in my kitchen for the first few days, unless it is crazy hot, and then I transfer it to the basement.

Within 3 days you should see tiny bubbles in the brine, but don't freak out if you don't—it might take a little longer. The bubbles mean that fermentation has begun. If a white scum forms on top of the brine (which it almost always does; it looks a bit like baby powder sprinkled on water), skim it off daily and rinse off and replace the plate and weight or brine bag. Doing this cuts down the yeast load that is developing in the brine, which can affect fermentation.

The pickles should be ready in 2 to 3 weeks (though the process can take up to 6 weeks in cooler weather), when the tiny bubbles stop rising and the pickles are sour and olive green all the way through. (Cut one open earlier in the process; you'll see that it is still somewhat white inside. A fully green pickle means that the fermentation has reached the center of the cucumber. This is important if you are going to can them.) Skim off any scum.

Pour the pickles and brine into a colander resting in a nonreactive pot (to catch the brine). Discard the leaves and spices. Remove the colander from the pot and transfer the pot to the stove top. Bring the brine (not the pickles!) to a boil, reduce the heat to low, and simmer the brine for 5 minutes. Skim off the scum that forms. Rinse the pickles with cold water and drain them well.

For refrigerator storage, let the brine cool to room temperature. Pack the pickles into 2-quart or gallon jars. (This will be a hell of a lot of pickles in your fridge. If you give some of them away, remember to tell folks to store them in the fridge as well). If you like (which I do), add fresh dill and garlic to each jar (maybe a sprig and 2 cloves to each quart jar). Pour enough cooled brine over the pickles to cover them. Cap the jar and store in the refrigerator for as long as 6 months (and I think it can be longer).

For pantry storage, pack the pickles into pint or quart mason jars, adding fresh dill and garlic, if you like. Pour hot brine over the pickles, leaving a ½-inch space at the top of the jar. Close the jars with hot 2-piece caps. In a boiling water bath, process pint jars for 10 minutes, quart jars for 15 minutes. Or pasteurize the jars for 30 minutes in water heated from 180 to 185 degrees (a process I agree with but some extension offices do not). When the jars have cooled, store them in a cool, dry, dark place.

PICKLED PLUMS WITH RED WINE

6 pounds firm Italian or other prune plums

1 teaspoon whole cloves

Two 3-inch cinnamon sticks, broken

4 thin slices fresh ginger

4-2/3 cups sugar

3 cups red wine vinegar

3 cups red wine

To prevent bursting, prick each plum three times with a large needle. Tie the dry spices and ginger in a spice bag or scrap of cheesecloth. Put the spices into a large nonreactive pot with the sugar, vinegar, and wine. Bring the contents to a boil, stirring to dissolve the sugar. Reduce the heat and simmer the mixture for 5 minutes. Remove the pot from the heat and let the syrup cool for 20 minutes or more.

Put the plums into a bowl. Pour the cooled syrup over them, and let them rest at room temperature for 8–12 hours.

Drain off the syrup into a nonreactive pot, add the spice bag, and bring the syrup to a boil. Remove the pot from the heat and let the syrup cool again. Pour the cooled syrup over the plums. Again, let the plums rest in the syrup at room temperature for 8–12 hours.

Put the plums, their syrup, and the spice bag into a large nonreactive pot. Heat the plums over low heat, stirring gently, until their skins begin to crack. Using a slotted spoon, transfer the plums to quart or pint mason jars.

Boil the syrup until it is slightly thickened, and then pour it over the plums (which will have sunk in the jars somewhat), leaving a ½-inch headspace. Close the jars with two-piece caps and process the jars for 25 minutes in a boiling-water bath.

Store the cooled jars in a cool, dry, dark place for at least a month before eating the plums.

Makes 3½ to 4 quarts

SONJA'S PLUM KUCHEN

I grew up eating this cake (*Kuchen* in German) made with a type of European plum, which, it turns out, grows wild all over Portland. Lucky us. But even if you don't find them growing on the street, these plums have become ubiquitous in most regions of the United States and are often available at local markets. If you can't find plums or you just don't like them, this dough will stand up to many of the season's fresh fruits. It serves as the base for a very simple open-face tart that just can't go wrong. The trick here is to follow my mother's instructions. In deference to the oral tradition, I will give it to you in her words.

Preheat oven to 350 degrees.

Lightly grease a 9-by-11-inch pan ("not too much because the dough has nice butter").

KUCHEN DOUGH

> 2 cups unbleached white flour
> 3/4–1 cup sugar
> 2 teaspoons baking powder
> 1/4 teaspoon salt
> 1/2 cup unsalted butter at room temperature
>   (1 stick cut into small chunks)
> 2 large eggs
> 1 teaspoon vanilla

Mom says: "I put the flour on a board or in a very large bowl. I add the salt and baking powder and mix. I add the butter to the flour, but just enough to cover the butter with the flour—don't rub the butter into the flour, just mix the small pieces of butter into it enough to cover them. I make a well in the flour, put the sugar around the inside of the circle, add the 2 eggs and vanilla in the middle and then I mix the eggs and vanilla a little with my hand and slowly add the sugar and flour in until it comes together—not too much, because you don't want to overwork this dough. I knead it very lightly and let it rest at least 20 minutes in the fridge before rolling out."

Anyone who has ever made pasta by hand will get what she is saying. You may be a little unnerved the first time you try this process, since using your hand will probably be a little unfamiliar. Don't be afraid. Even though the dough may be tacky at first, that is part of the process. Just add a little more flour and continue kneading. Eventually, it will reach a texture that will be suitable for rolling out. There is no way to understand the varying texture and quality of your ingredients unless you work with them on a regular basis. If you are using farm-fresh eggs, for example, you know no chicken lays the same size egg every time. This I why I say over and over that you must follow your ingredients, and not a static recipe.

Roll out the dough to a ¼-inch thickness to match the approximate size of your pan, or alternatively just pat the dough into the pan, patching up the pieces if they fall apart. If the dough has become a bit overworked, chill it for at least 15 minutes to allow the gluten in the dough to relax.

PLUM TOPPING

Okay, the dough is now in a 9-by-11-inch pan, or two pie pans, or whatever suits you. Mom has taught me to butterfly the plums, which means cutting them almost in half (leave them attached at one end), removing the pit, and then slicing each of the halves in half again but not down to the end. In essence you will have splayed or butterflied plum. This allows for more of the fruit juice to cook off during cooking, which you want. Of course, if you slice through the plums, don't worry. Mom's process is mostly for looks, but it does look nice.

Stagger the layers so the plums overlap one another in long rows (or in circles, if you are using pie pans). Once completed, pop the cake in the oven.

Bake for about 50 to 60 minutes. After removing from the oven, sprinkle the hot plums with a little sugar to bring out their juices. Doing this after the baking keeps the fruit from getting too "juicy" while baking. Cool before eating.

SEPTEMBER

SEPTEMBER

The Home

Taking In the Stranger

In Leviticus 19:34, the Torah offers the following command-ment: "The stranger who resides with you shall be to you as one of your citizens; you shall love him yourself, for you were strangers in the Land of Egypt." And Exodus 22:20 states: "You shall not wrong a stranger or oppress him for you were strangers in the Land of Egypt." In the New Testament, Jesus tells us to welcome the stranger (see Matthew 25:35), for "what you do to the least of my brethren, you do unto me" (Matthew 25:40). The Qur'an tells us that we should "serve God . . . and do good to . . . orphans, those in need, neighbors who are near, neighbors who are strangers, the companion by your side, the wayfarer that you meet, [and those who have nothing]" (4:36). The Hindu scripture Taittiriya Upani-shad tells us: "The guest is a representative of God" (1.11.2).

Alright already, I hear you say. Love the stranger, love the stranger. Yada, yada, yada. But what about actually giving stranger-love a go? Easier said than done, particularly when the stranger comes with the kind of baggage you would rather not deal with. But, as I am wont to tell my husband, anyone can offer charity when it is easy, or at least when it is not needed by someone staring you in the face and calling you Mom.

AN UNUSUAL PORTRAIT

This is when all the pretty pictures of family go tangential. Not that anything I have told you heretofore about my family would make you wish for the same. That's okay. My mom always says that if you could throw your worries in the river but had to fish out someone else's, you would probably choose your own again. At least they are familiar. I'm not sure if that is my sentiment exactly, but I do know life is not always easy; you get what you get. It is not whether you are dealt easy things that matters, but how easily you can deal with the hard stuff. Of course, some folks get a much bigger bag of hard than others, so it must be said, there is hard and then there is *hard*. My own particular variety of nuttiness is, on most days, very manageable. I have seen lots of folks who could not manage their worlds, and I try not to judge them. I understand, in a deep way, that "There but for the grace of God go I." This is how I approach the issue of my son's girlfriend, Diane, moving in with us one fine, sunny September morning.

At the time, my mom was still staying with us, so for the last few weeks of her visit we enjoyed a full house. There was an excitement in having Diane there, because both Mom and I were happy to see how happy she was making my son Wyatt. After so many years of drama, a full smile on his face lifted our spirits (nothing like a Jewish mom and grandmother to hope beyond all hope). But as time went on, and the contents of Diane's baggage revealed themselves with ever greater clarity, her status as our housemate took a little getting used

It is not whether you are dealt easy things that matters, but how easily you can deal with the hard stuff.

to. Forget about the fact that Wyatt and Diane met at the methadone clinic. I was way over getting flustered about that. As far as I'm concerned, medication is medication, and if it keeps my son off the streets, I'm happy. After living through that hell and coming back, I cannot get caught in a conversation about enablers (am I one?) with anyone who, as a parent, has not lived through the same thing. So I realize I am more open to all the possibilities than most. How else, upon hearing of their meeting, star-crossed and bedazzled, across a crowded methadone clinic, did I not freak out? Actually, it sounded sweet in the way those streetwise stories can be. To see the two of them together lifted my spirits. According to Diane, the first thing I did when I met her was ask if she was hungry. Go figure. Momma is as Momma does. She said I gave her some peach cobbler.

FARM RAISED

The fact that Diane was born and raised on a farm in Tennessee worked, more or less, to her advantage. The fact that "Nanna," her grandmother, still canned and her family still worked the land on which they raised cattle and "crops" was a sort of wet dream for me. And, as I came to find out, the land they owned was only a few miles from where Sandor Katz and his merry band of fermenters lived. That only seemed to complete my vision of having my own farm family. There we'd all be, Sandor, Sonja, Nanna, Slim (my husband's nickname), the kids, and me, cooling off on the back porch after a hot summer day in the hemp fields, drinking iced Everclear with kombucha and snacking on boiled peanuts, pig's ears, and tempeh. Unfortunately, my mother and long-suffering husband did not share my vision. They were terrified, and honestly, I could hardly fault them. Imagine the scene. It is my birthday, and we are eating at Higgins, Portland's premier and fabulous upscale local-food haunt. I had asked for that dinner out as my only gift, because I wanted to enjoy my meal with complete abandon. Great cooking, as you know, can come with a hefty price tag. Being the gal that she is, however, Mom had invited Diane along.

GOING MARTYR

First came the cocktails. I ordered a martini; Slim, a beer; Mom and Miles, water. Wyatt, a gin and tonic, and Diane ordered a shot of bourbon with a Coke back. Oh, now we're talking. Gently, I whisper to her, "You don't have to chug that down." "Oh, you think I can't?" was her response. From that moment on, the dinner turned into something a little less tony than Higgins—or even my family—is used to. I surrendered to the back-road barroom spirit and decided to get drunk. Discarding the pretension I usually adopt for such occasions, I walked around the restaurant, slapping on the back everyone else who was there to celebrate his or her birthday. I whooped and hollered when a birthday song was sung, something I would have heartily condemned if I'd been in a less festive mood. I think I was martyring myself. I felt bad, and somewhat responsible for the discomfort at our table. I knew Diane was out of sorts. Higgins was not within her comfort zone. I watched Wyatt rub her back, offering loving support, all the while keeping his own anxiety in check. I watched Miles, Mom, and my husband attempt to enjoy their meals as the psychodrama of our odd, makeshift family played out. Had this really been my birthday wish? Did my continuing delusions blind me to the flawed reality? Of course not. But this was not the time for self-reflection. At that moment, all I wanted was to shift the focus away from the young stranger and onto me. Like a rodeo clown, I hoped the bulls of civilized society would focus their attention on me instead. So what if I was making a fool of myself? It would not be the first time.

It has been many months since that birthday outing. Mom has gone home and only occasionally asks me how the kids are doing. The husband, well, he just sits tight, hoping something good will emerge from all of this. God love him. He is getting a lesson in accepting things that are not within his comfort zone. What can he do? Wyatt has almost no money and Diane has less. They do some work, as I mentioned, within our family farm system and try to keep their heads above water. I shuttle them to meetings and doctor's visits, settle medical bills they could never afford to pay, and sort out the missing pieces of two lives that seem too ravaged for the short time they have been in the world. And all the time I am thinking, "There but for the grace of God go I." It is then that I realize why this experience can be a blessing: I have not shut down. I have not forgotten. I have not decided to forget where I came from and how difficult it can be. I am, in fact, blessed to be able to rise above the pettiness of a life that is perfect for me and feel the struggle in someone else's.

Who knows, maybe the two of them will be able to build a life together. I listen at times when she talks about what their children will look like and wonder if she understands how much is in front of them. I listen to them laugh and want to feel warmed, but I worry just the same. I think about how they will support themselves, how they will ever pay their bills, and then I quiet myself down. *One day at a time. At least we have the farm,* is what I tend to think. Besides, nowhere in the edict to "remember the stranger" does it say you will always know what to do when they arrive. If you're like me, you'll keep baking peach cobbler and feel moderately enchanted as your son's girlfriend continues to call you Mom.

Nowhere in the edict to "remember the stranger" does it say you will always know what to do when they arrive.

The Garden

Pulling Up Potatoes • Planting Cover Crops •
The Winter Garden

In the generally mild climate of the Pacific Northwest, you can usually plan on September being a month of sun and growing glory. A month that can start out hot and fiery will end with days that hint at the winter ahead. This is the month when I feel my intentions shifting, as if synchronized with my garden's process of decline. You may not notice the decline during the first part of the month, but you will anticipate its arrival with both grief and lust, knowing the days of summer's furious production are coming to a close. September is a bittersweet month that foreshadows the long winter's sleep and requires that you start preparing for it already. The process will not be complete before the end of October, but happens in fits and starts, which is why I've pulled up my potatoes already, even though it was a little earlier than I would have liked.

THE ANNUAL POTATO PULL

As I mentioned, I planted my potatoes too early, in soil that was heavy and compacted with clay. The result was a disappointing crop. I like being scolded in this way. It was not a heavy-handed diatribe, but rather a dispassionate explanation of the consequences of not listening, watching, and responding to the conditions of the soil. Taking the time to consider the cause of my folly offered the possibility of potato bounties in years to come. But it was too late for this year. The extra growing days offered by a sunny September would do little to increase my crop, so I turned my attention to repairing the soil for next year. I dug up, cured, and stored my meager potato crop, then ladled a generous six-inch layer of compost over the bed, and broadcast a liberal quantity of crimson clover seeds, so they can take root before the winter months cast their chill. I wanted to give the bed a fighting chance for next spring, when I approach the prospect of growing food again. Growing cover crops is an interesting endeavor. It took me a while to understand it in a deep, experiential way. I needed to see, firsthand, how a bed left bare in winter would respond to the onslaught of our Northwest winter rains, how it would inevitably lose its structure and nutrient composition to the runoff. Of course, I had read about the importance of cover crops, but that was very different from seeing the results firsthand. Luckily, I had two beds—one with and one without a proper fall planting—so I could compare the results.

PROVIDING COVER

Planting a bed with a cover crop (or green manure, as it is often called) in the fall will improve the quality of your garden soil in three significant ways. First, there is the growth of the cover crop, which, depending on the variety, will present itself as a low mass of green vegetation over your bed, or as the tall, near-succulent growth of a legume, its stalks standing like soldiers in the soil. Either way, I like to think of the growth as a kind of umbrella for the soil, protecting it from the harsh, crushing rain that would otherwise fall directly on it. The second benefit of a cover crop comes from its root growth. In spring, turning over a bed planted with a fall cover crop—in this case crimson clover—will expose a multitude of thin white roots woven into the soil. Resembling the fine tines of a comb, these lacy fingers spread themselves throughout the soil, at once breaking up and protecting an otherwise compacted soil. Turning the tines of my pitchfork into this spring's earth revealed soil that was both fluffy and dark with the rich earthy fragrance of humus. You will know what I mean by good soil when you see, smell, and feel it. Actually, as you go along in this process, healthy soil will make you swoon. And why shouldn't it? It is the mark of your garden's health. Once you have converted your entire garden to good tilth (and I think this can take a good five years or more, given how sick most of our soils are), it will make you weak at the knees to see it. I do love a good-smelling bed. The third improvement derived from planting a cover crop is that it brings nutrients to the soil. Exactly which nutrients and how much of them depends on what you plant, but each, in its own way, will bring something. Each variety (your regional and local nurseries can help you choose which one, and when to sow it) will improve the quality of your soil. Considering what you want will affect what you plant, but one way or another, even if you don't want to get that analytical about it, make sure you plant something into a bare bed before the winter rains come.

I'm not saying your garden will die if you forget to plant a cover crop or if you just run out of steam by fall, but the soil I left exposed was, by the following spring, dense and pale, reminiscent of red clay. If it had a fragrance, it was not noticeable or in any way particularly

NUTRIENT ENHANCEMENT

CROP	HAIRY VETCH	CRIMSON CLOVER	AUSTRIAN WINTER PEAS	RYE
	LBS./ACRE	LBS./ACRE	LBS./ACRE	LBS./ACRE
BIOMASS*	3,260	4,243	4,114	5,608
NITROGEN	141	115	144	89
POTASSIUM	133	143	159	108
PHOSPHORUS	18	16	19	17
MAGNESIUM	18	11	13	8
CALCIUM	52	62	45	22

*Dry weight of above-ground plant material

sweet to me. Whatever nutrients it had were undoubtedly watered down by the long winter's rains. Whereas the soil in the bed that had been protected by a cover crop was healthy, fragrant, and friable—the difference was like night and day, as they say. If I became convinced of the value of cover crops, it was, once again, because I took to watching and feeling the soil. This will always be your best guide. Watch, feel, and smell the world around you (a much nicer prospect in a garden than in a subway station). But it also took a bit of timing, since cover crops (and crimson clover is not alone in this) require particular planting times. Crimson clover likes to be planted in September, which is why I dug up my potatoes then to make way for it. In any case, I had had enough of the potatoes' sad progress and was more than ready to set that bed right with the world.

It takes very little time to sow crimson clover, and it will sprout in a heartbeat (generally no longer than a week). I broadcast the small seeds and rake them into the bed so they have a little soil covering them. The seed doesn't need more than a quarter inch of soil over it, and, since I am fairly generous in my seeding, I figure that if one in every ten seeds sprouts, I'm good. Within days, green sprouts emerge. By the first frost the plants should be strong enough to make it through the winter and have sufficient root mass to keep the soil from running off. Think about how an aggressively felled forest responds to heavy rains. Without a forest canopy to dissipate the downfall or tree roots to keep the soil in place, mud slides occur and nutrients are leached out of the otherwise fertile soil. Or imagine yourself standing naked in the rain, with no cover, no food, no warmth to protect you. You would not last very long.

Not every bed will need a cover crop, since some will be planted with vegetables and bulbs in September. Remember, timing is everything, but I am more inclined to follow the weather than the guides. If, for example, a guide suggests I can transplant (not seed) my winter brassicas by September but the weather is still blazing hot, I wait until the sun will be kinder on the tender starts. Other times, when I don't want to wait, I plant them in the heat but shield them with screening (as I do at other times of the year), giving their roots time to develop while protecting their tops from the sun. There is competition for space between the plants you hope to harvest by fall and those you need to plant in fall because you want them to grow through the winter so you can harvest them in early spring. You don't want to rush things, but you also don't want to wait. Confusing, isn't it?

THE FALL, WINTER, OR EARLY-SPRING GARDEN

It has taken me a long time to understand the cycle of fall and winter sowing and harvesting. If you are planting seeds for a fall harvest, you might sow in early to late June. But depending on the variety you choose, you could also transplant a start anywhere from July till August and still get a fall harvest. When you're thinking about growing a garden for a fall or winter harvest, the issue is what size you want the plant to be by the time the first frost comes.

Vegetables intended for a fall harvest want to be fully matured by October or November. Though some of them might make it through the winter's frost, they are not intended to do so. You will be harvesting them in fall, which is why a late June and July planting is suggested. Vegetables intended for an early-spring harvest are generally planted in late summer or early fall (August–September) since they want to be only half-way through their growing cycle by the onset of winter. Thanks to their genetic coding, these early-spring harvest plants will shut down in winter but not perish. If all things go according to plan (a big "if"), they will resume their growth cycle in the earliest days of spring and give you good eating by March and April. For those vegetables you hope to eat throughout the winter (the hearty greens like collards or kale and some of the root vegetables), I suggest planting seeds around late July, early August—later than the fall harvest vegetables but earlier than the spring harvest varieties. You want them to be near full maturity by November but not entirely so, since they will, and do, continue growing well into December and January. Having said that, the only thing separating a fall garden from a

Cozy up with a good gardening book over the winter (many winters, in fact) so that you are continually expanding your knowledge of seasonal gardening.

winter or spring one (besides appropriate varieties and luck) is a few weeks on either side of the calendar. But as I mentioned before, all this theory can be shot to hell if the weather does not oblige you.

Finally, if you are choosing transplants for your fall, winter, or early-spring garden, remember to add twenty or thirty days to your date of maturation calculations. In other words, a variety of broccoli that suggests a maturation date of ninety days will, if planted as a transplant in August, be ready for harvest by late October or early November—the equivalent of approximately ninety days from seed to harvest.

KEEP READING

The best way to understand the logic and requirements of fall and winter gardening is to keep reading. Cozy up with a good gardening book over the winter (many winters, in fact) so that you are continually expanding your knowledge of seasonal gardening. Each year you will learn a few more things, until you get to the level of competent novice. Each year you will have a new goal. This year I was determined to have some root vegetables in the ground for fall soups and winter stews, which meant things like carrots, turnips, rutabagas, and celery were high on my list. I planted the celery starts (which are not suited for overwintering) in spring (darn, those things grow slowly) and set my mind to seeding the root vegetables in July (my carrots needed a double sowing due to the sun tragedy). By late September my garden was well on its way to soup. Hopefully, all the ingredients will be in place for at least a few good winter stews. But even though I am thinking about winter, September is still very much about the summer harvest.

LATE-SUMMER SENTINEL

September is when I continue harvesting the rest of the tomatoes, eggplants, summer squash, peppers, and basil. It is the beginning of my serious grape harvest, autumn raspberries, and the new spurt of rhubarb growth that September seems to invite. Early September encourages the continual deadheading of late-summer flowering annuals—snapdragons, chrysanthemums, dahlias, and cosmos. It is also the time to start considering fall plantings of garlic and shallots and overwintering crops of leeks, overwintering onions, and any fruiting perennials you want to get in place before winter comes on strong. It is the time to decide, once and for all, if you will take on the responsibility of a winter garden. But before you decide, you will spend time in your preserving kitchen, because September, like August, is not for the faint of heart.

The Kitchen

Canning Tomatoes • Drying Fruit • Tuna •
The New Benevolent Overseers • The
University of Grandmothers

In a word, the September kitchen is about tomatoes. Whether the tomatoes are sauced, diced, pureed, made into ketchup or barbecue sauce, or cooked with other end-of-summer vegetables to form the endless stews of summer, September is a furious world of red. In the universe of food preservation, canning tomatoes is one of the things I am most interested in, and my game plan entails forty-five quarts of them. Putting up that many tomatoes means getting my hands on over one hundred pounds, which is far more than I grow in my garden. I suppose if I combined varieties—slicers (early and late) and plums—I could do it, but they don't all ripen at the same time. For example, my big, beefy Brandywines do not deliver until late August and early September. They also come on slowly—a tomato here, a tomato there—which is not what you want for canning.

My favorite canning tomatoes are San Marzanos, but, as with Brandywines, I do not rely on them entirely. They, too, are a late-ripening variety. Some years they yield incomparably long, red, and meaty tomatoes; other years they taunt me by staying green on the vine. I cannot bear such disappointment, so I grow varieties that come on early and, as the seed packet suggests, will produce tomatoes all at once. Simultaneous ripening is a quality canners appreciate. It means you can get your work done at one time instead of canning a jar here and there as your tomatoes ripen. Sorry, but the Heinz tomatoes I grew (for just such a characteristic) didn't exactly live up to their promise. Not to mention that I felt a tad squirrelly growing any tomatoes with the name Heinz on them. It smacked of world domination.

Were it not for Teresa Heinz (yeah, that Albert Schweitzer Gold Medal for Humanitarianism was pretty cool), I could not have brought myself to buy tomatoes called Heinz—which is just plain silly, since I'm sure she has no say in anything that corporation does (although she is the chair of the Heinz Family Philanthropies). Still, I'm feeling a little guilty about growing them; it reminds me of how organic seed companies, like every other industry, are being bought up by corporations trying to profit from this movement. For example, I wouldn't have known that Seeds of Change is owned by Mars Inc. if my husband hadn't mentioned it. They are not the only company to go that route. Lots of big companies have their hands in the world of groovy, even when groovy doesn't want it. Small companies face a serious conundrum when the larger corporations come a-calling. It is not always a matter of selling out for greed.

THE HEINZ REPORT
The H.J. Heinz Company had annual sales of over $10 billion in 2009 (according to its annual report) and manufactures thousands of food products in production sites on six continents, with some 150 top- or second-ranked brands worldwide.

PRODUCTS OF THE REVOLUTION

During the first wave of the "back to the land" movement, hardworking and honest hippies tried their hand at developing products for the market. They did so because living off the land is hard, and because Strider (every commune has someone named Strider, at least they used to) would not stop smoking the bud, and someone, for God's sake, had to make ends meet. Together they worked to develop some kind of beverage, potato chip, peanut butter, granola mix, yogurt, ice cream, or organic/open-pollinated seed stock to provide them with a source of income. For a long time, the kids worked hard to simply get by. Slowly, if they were lucky, they started making a living and defined a market for themselves. That's when the big boys showed up.

The R.W. Knudsen "family" of juices is now owned by Smuckers. Kettle Chips is now owned by Diamond Brands. Deaf Smith Peanut Butter was bought by Arrowhead Mills. Ben and Jerry's is owned by Unilever. Seeds of Change is owned by Mars.

This, as I have been told by insiders, is how it goes down. The big guys say to the little guys, "Thanks for defining a market, thanks for creating a market share, thanks for building up your little business to the point that we can take it seriously. Really, we salute you. Now we want to buy you out. And if you don't sell out to us, we will simply compete with you. We will create a similar product, design it better, market it better, get better product placement, and sell it for less. Oh, you know we can do that. If, on the other hand, you sell your company to us, we promise (wink, wink) to keep you on as CEO and we will never (wink, wink) change the fundamental principles of your company. We will also pay you a bazillion dollars for all your hard work."

Faced with that situation, I really don't know what I would do. After standing knee-deep in peanut butter or over hot frying oil (potato chips) for years, would I let them compete with me and, most likely, destroy the business I had built up? Honestly, I think not. And mostly because I would think the buying public would not care, or even know. Oh, some might, but it would amount to a minority. Do you know, in fact? I bet at least 75 percent of the products you buy in the groovy grocery stores are owned by corporations you more than likely do not want to do business with, but you do. I do, too (though less and less every day). Even if corporations promote sustainable values, there is absolutely no way that they will deny their commitment to capturing market share. This can mean that they own a staggering number of products on the shelves of your local grocery. Yes, you think they are all unique little companies, and maybe some are (or were at one time), but be assured, the empire is as comfortable in the health food industry as it is in any other. In some cases, even more so.

THE HAIN CELESTIAL GROUP

The Hain Celestial Group (NASDAQ: HAIN), a leading producer of natural and organic products in North America and Europe, is quite a behemoth. Though you would not know this (well, I didn't), it owns most of the products you are buying in the groovy store. In particular: Celestial Seasonings®, Terra®, Garden of Eatin'®, Health Valley®, WestSoy®, Earth's Best®, Arrowhead Mills®, MaraNatha®, SunSpire®, DeBoles®, Gluten Free Café™, Hain Pure Foods®, Hollywood®, Spectrum Naturals®, Spectrum Essentials®, Walnut Acres Organic®, Imagine®, Rice Dream®, Soy Dream®, Rosetto®, Ethnic Gourmet®, Yves Veggie Cuisine®, Gronse®, Realeat®, Linda McCartney®, Daily Bread™, Lima®, Alba Botanica®, Queen Helene®, Tushies®, TenderCare®, and Martha Stewart Clean™.

Hain Celestial has been providing "A Healthy Way of Life™" since 1993.

Believe me when I tell you, even funky or relatively enlightened corporations are in it for profit, and their survival is contingent on constant brand acquisition. If corporations today do not grow, they perish. In this game of product Pac-Man, companies gobble up or merge with one another until only the very largest corporation remains. These corporations do not stay within any particular market niche, which brings me back to my discomfort with buying Heinz seeds. I felt squirrelly about my participation in this maneuvering for market share, because clearly Heinz, like all other corporations, is in it to win it. If it wasn't, you'd hear its stockholders squawking, big time.

Though the Heinz plum tomatoes promised a big one-time harvest, like most varieties they came on in a trickle. My response was to blanch, seed, and dice them as they ripened and leave them in the refrigerator until I had a five-gallon bucket filled. Since I would be bringing the entire mess to a boil before ladling them into the jars, I knew that would be fine. Even so, there was no way these homegrown tomatoes would yield forty-five quarts. Honestly, I don't know if I cared. That's something you notice by September—you start losing steam.

WHAT WOULD MAMA DARDEN DO?

By September, I'm just too stinking tired to imagine canning that many more tomatoes. A sort of hysteria sets in. My effort to return to the good earth and all its glory becomes thwarted by dreams of vacations on sunny beaches. In September, I learn what I am really made of. I wonder to myself, *What would Mama Darden do?* I take a moment to rally. I feel determined to get to the other side. Even if my leisure-loving mind is balking, I know I have to forge on. Here is the test: do I run to the beckoning mai tai or do I welcome the box of begging-to-be-canned free tomatoes offered by a friend? After a slight breakdown, of course I go for the box. I can focus my greed on that now. I have been turned over to a new god. My eyes have seen the glory of the coming of the cans. Full pantries or bust. What a freak I have become.

Even though I am frazzled and dazed, I am determined to meet my tomato quota. Though canning is my chosen method, some days I toss them whole into the freezer. Freezing them grants me breathing room during the frantic days of abundance. I can pull them out later in the year to do whatever I want with them. I would consign them all to the deep freeze if it weren't for the cow, the blueberries, strawberries, blackberries, peaches, beans, and corn already taking up space, and the apple cider, grape juice, walnuts, and pig that are soon to come. By September, the freezer section of my store is getting a little overloaded. I think it may soon be time to get a new freezer, which would bring the total number of deep chest freezers to three—preposterous, isn't it? Where will it end? But I'd better not go there. Better to stick to canning, since there is nothing to it.

With so many books out today to assist you with the canning process, you will be amazed at your lingering resistance. You will not poison yourself; you will not blow yourself up; you will not make mistakes. Honestly, if you can open a can of tomatoes you can can a can of tomatoes. You don't need to peel or cut or seed them if you don't want to. Many an old-time cook just jammed them into very clean jars (no need to boil the tomatoes first) with a little salt and lemon juice (one tablespoon for a pint and two for a quart), and set them in a pot with a rack inside it (to keep the jars from sitting on the bottom of the pot) and covered the jars with a good inch of water. Putting your tomatoes in whole and unheated will require a very long processing time (depending on elevation, at least eighty-five minutes for a quart), but I cut down the processing time by chopping and heating my tomatoes before adding them to the jar. So how you choose to put your tomatoes in

I have been turned over to a new god. My eyes have seen the glory of the coming of the cans. Full pantries or bust. What a freak I have become.

the jar (whole, diced, sauced, heated, or unheated) and what size jar you use (pint or quart), will affect both your processing style (boiling-water canning or pressure canning) and your canning time.

I suggest you buy one of the many reliable canning guides for illustrations and the specifics of canning. Your local county extension office will offer a great selection of booklets on individual topics for a nominal fee. Though many still offer classes throughout the summer, not everyone is lucky enough to have an extension office nearby. Small businesses are popping up to take their place. When Marge and I first started teaching canning in Portland, Oregon, we were the only ones doing so in our county. Now there are quite a few. Just know who is teaching and where they learned. Though there are only a few steps you need to know in order to can safely, you do need to know them. Other than that, there is no reason not to try your hand at food preservation. And while most people like hands-on experience, getting a good book on the subject will suffice.

DRY UP

Boiling-water canning is just one of the food-preservation tools I use on tomatoes. I often dry them to eat as snacks or to use, reconstituted, in spreads, soups, and stews. I like the way I can store dried tomatoes almost anywhere—on a shelf or under the bed in containers, if need be. I also like the versatility and ease of drying foods. Almost no process is easier. It is one of the oldest systems around and in hot, arid climates has happened naturally for centuries just by making use of the heat of the sun. Here in the Northwest, the effort requires a little more machinery. Even our solar ovens have backup power in case the sun decides to take a hike. Foods that are interrupted in their drying process can mold if left unattended, due to the moisture in them. Along with

natural enzymes in food, mold will break food down. When drying foods, you are essentially removing the water content and creating foods that will be "shelf stable." Some, like pasta or bread, will air-dry happily on their own. Others, like the grapes I have hanging heavy on the vine in September, require a little help if they are to become the raisins I will use for baking and in my granola.

Over the years my raisin supply has increased with the productivity of the vines. By luck and circumstance (because I didn't really research it), I have a tasty seedless variety called Venus, which makes for delicious eating, both fresh and dried. During the first few years, I did not wait long enough before picking them, which resulted in somewhat tart raisins. Now I wait until mid-September for the harvest, then dry them night and day in the dehydrator. They can take as much as two to three full days of drying and, after the first day, will require constant checking, since not all grapes are the

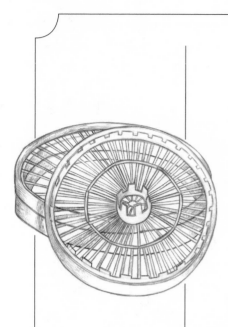

same size. Failure to pay attention during the last six hours of drying can result in some pretty hard pellets. Not that those don't get used—almost anything can be brought back to life with a little reconstitution. I just cover the pellets with boiling water and let them sit until they are softened. Sometimes that takes no more than fifteen minutes, sometimes longer. I don't use these softened raisins in my granola, since they would be too wet for dry storage, but they are great in muffins, cookies, cakes, or oatmeal. I also like them in a summer-vegetable stew mixture called caponata—fabulous really, particularly when made with the poor man's capers I make by pickling nasturtium seeds.

FUNCTION OVER FORM

Caponata is an Italian-style mixture made with end-of-the-season summer squash, peppers, tomatoes, house-made raisins, and pickled nasturtium seeds (poor man's capers), and it is a delicious thing to eat. It is a perfect way to use those foods, which are all coming to fruition at the same time. It is a meal that embodies both the goodness and the logic of summer. But here is the thing: imagining a lovely plate of caponata and making it are two different things. I am trying to warn you, once again, against harboring the fanciful notion of me gracefully making caponata for my family to dine on in the garden house on a hot summer's eve. It's a lovely image, I know, but it would be more accurate for you to picture me picking nasturtium seeds off the ground in despair, knowing they would reseed themselves high and low if I didn't. Just as I was about to toss the seeds into the takeaway pile of garden refuse (throw them in the compost pile and you will find them all over the yard), I thought, *Hey, I can pickle these.* That was it, an act of transference—the seeds were out of my garden and into the cupboard. To date, they have been brined and pickled in white-wine vinegar with juniper berries and shallots, for use in the caponata. But honestly, they don't really deserve the glorified revisionist account that a fancy photo or romantic narration would offer, not really. This is more a story of necessity than whimsy.

LIDIA'S STEW

I remember my mother buying caponata in small cans when I was a child. I don't know why I liked it—it must have had something to do with its intense, unctuous texture and flavor—qualities usually unappealing to a child. I have since discovered the real thing, and that's even better. It is a lovely blend of summer flavors that only improves after a few days in the fridge.

I gleaned one of my favorite caponata recipes from Lidia Matticchio Bastianich's book *Lidia's Italy.* I like watching her on TV. She occasionally has her mother, who is in her eighties, on the show and shows her such lovely deference that I can't help but be charmed. Besides, she is one of those cooks who simply make food look good. My mom is one of those people, too. She can be eating almost anything and you will want some. It must have something to do with her enjoyment of food and cooking, but it translates to everyone around her—you want what she is eating. In both Yiddish and German, we call that eating with *geschmack*, meaning

EATING WITH "GESCHMACK"

My mother eats, and enjoys, something called *Handkäse mit Musik* (literally: hand cheese with music)—so called because this sour-milk cheese was originally formed by hand, while the "music" comes from the sound of the flatulence brought on by the onions that top it (lovely). The cheese has a painfully pungent fragrance and is one of those regional dishes (it hails from Frankfurt, Germany, where it is enjoyed with the local apple wine) that you have to grow up with to enjoy. Watching her eat *that* with *geschmack* convinced me to take the plunge, but only once. I do have some limits.

In tribute to Lidia and her mom, Mom and I made caponata together and called it way good. As a matter of fact, our eyes rolled back in our heads and we shook with delight. My husband wasn't too impressed, but we cared little about that. We kept repeating one of my father's favorite phrases: "Good, you don't get none of my good stuff." Of course, he used to say that about the herring and rye bread he would eat over every meal or the cold cow's foot jelly he would eat lathered with horseradish— two dishes we kids very rarely cottoned to. These days? Oh yeah, give me some herring or some *pecha* (cow's foot jelly— made from the gelatin in the foot, don't you know) any day. And I will eat it with *geschmack*.

"hearty appetite" or "enjoyment," though it doesn't really translate. It's hard to describe, but when you meet someone who *esses mit geschmack*, you will know it. You might find yourself digging into some kind of food that you would otherwise avoid.

According to *Lidia's Italy*, "Caponata is a dense condiment of chunky fried eggplant and other vegetables and seasonings, jam-packed with flavor—sweet, sour, and salty all at once. Sicilians make caponata in many variations and enjoy it in countless ways. Use it as a condiment on grilled meats and steamed fish, as a sauce for pasta, or as a topping for bruschetta."

Note: I add summer squash, red peppers, or whatever else I want. It all cooks down to something good. I also like to include a cup or so of my raisins. I find they enhance the sweet-sour flavor Lidia refers to, particularly since my Venus raisins have a little extra-tart punch.

A FISH STORY

Another lovely use for capers is as briny accents in a Niçoise salad. I am crazy for a good Niçoise, and none is as delicious as one made with Oregon's albacore—a gift from the September sea. Oregon's hook-and-line-caught young albacore are considered a responsible (sustainable) choice; they also have nutrient qualities that older tuna does not. The fish are caught one at a time on barb-free, single-line fishing boats, are frozen almost immediately, and do not have to be shipped far. These albacore are less bruised than fish caught on multiple-line boats or in nets, and because they are young, they contain fairly low levels of mercury. But all fish, as we now know, are in trouble, and some a little more so than others. While eating albacore is a lesser evil, it is still somewhat problematic. I have weighed the issues and come down on the side of putting up your own albacore, and supporting a local

Continued on page 308

CAPONATA

1 lb. eggplant

1 lb. summer squash (cut into 1-inch pieces)

2-1/2 teaspoons coarse sea salt or kosher salt to taste

1/2 cup red wine vinegar

2 tablespoons sugar

2 medium onions (1 pound)

2–3 celery ribs

2 red peppers

1 pound fresh plum tomatoes

1 cup Cerignola or other large, green, brine-cured olives

1/2 cup raisins

1 cup vegetable oil (for frying)

6 tablespoons extra-virgin olive oil

1/3 cup small capers, drained (I use my pickled
  nasturtium seeds instead)

10 large, fresh basil leaves

Trim the eggplants, and slice them (leaving the skin on) into chunks about 2 inches long and 1 inch thick. Toss the chunks with 2 teaspoons of salt and drain in a colander for 30 minutes to an hour. Rinse and pat them dry with paper towels.

Meanwhile, pour the red wine vinegar and ½ cup water into a small pan, stir in the sugar and bring to the boil. Cook until reduced by half and syrupy, then remove from the heat.

Slice the onions into 1½-inch pieces—you should have about 4 cups. Trim the celery stalks (peel them, too, if they're tough and stringy), then chop into 1-inch chunks. Slice the plum tomatoes lengthwise into 1½-inch-thick wedges; scrape out the seeds and put the wedges in a sieve to drain off the juices. Roughly chop the pitted olives into ¼-inch pieces.

To fry the eggplant, pour the cup of vegetable oil into a heavy-bottomed skillet or sauté pan (at least 12-inch diameter), and set over medium heat. Spread out all the eggplant chunks in the hot oil and fry for 10 to 15 minutes, tossing and stirring frequently, until the eggplant is soft and cooked through and nicely browned on all sides. Turn off the heat, lift the chunks out of the oil with a slotted spoon, and spread them on paper towels to drain. Discard the frying oil and wipe out the skillet.

Pour ¼ cup of the olive oil into the skillet and set over medium heat. Stir in the onion, red pepper, summer squash, and celery chunks, season with ¼ teaspoon salt, and cook, tossing often, until they are wilted and lightly colored, 8 minutes or so. Toss in the olives, raisins, and capers, heat quickly until sizzling, then scatter in the tomato wedges and fold them in with the other vegetables. Season with another ¼ teaspoon salt and cook until the tomatoes are hot and softened but still holding their shape, about 5 minutes.

Spread the eggplant chunks on top of the onions and tomatoes, still over medium heat, and turn them gently with a big spoon or spatula. When everything is sizzling, pour the vinegar syrup all over and stir it in. Cook a bit longer, then drizzle the remaining 2 tablespoons of olive oil over everything and stir.

Cook the vegetables together for about 10 minutes, then turn off the heat. Tear the basil leaves into shreds and stir them into the caponata. Taste and adjust the seasonings; let cool to room temperature and serve.

Makes 8 cups; serves 6 or more

industry that seeks to promote responsible practices. But if you do go for it, do it right—canning tuna requires a little patience. Some years I have been very careful to fillet the tuna to remove the darker meat and bloody veins. Other years it has been cram and can. The difference is between having tasty white-meat tuna in your cupboards or something a little more . . . well, muddy in flavor. So take the time to prepare what is going into the jar. It makes a difference. And make sure to can it properly, because tuna, like lots of other low-acid foods, needs to be pressure canned to be put up safely.

GETTING OUR GROOVY ON

The crusty raisins I mentioned earlier were the result of leaving the grape-drying responsibility to the kids while my husband and I went on a four-day trip to Applegate Valley, in southern Oregon. Man, was it pretty there. The Siskiyou mountain range, organic farms, and young hippies—what else could a middle-aged, right-of-return boomer want? We went down there to look for land, thinking we would become today's kinder, gentler overseers. We would buy the land and let the kids (the ones with heart but no cash) work it. We would live up in the big house and let them buy back the land after paying off their debt to the company store. Funky, but oddly true. Six months earlier, I had met a young woman who talked to me about the lack of affordable land for young farmers. To get banks to loan money to them is impossible. Evidently, the business model of small organic farming does not cut the mustard with banks. Other than borrowing from a bank, what model is there? Perhaps, if you were lucky, you might inherit the land, or manage to work out some lease arrangement with a benevolent landlord. But the hills are alive with stories of benevolence gone bad, so I was not surprised that, when it came down to it, we did not find the right match. This is not to say it can't be

The world's oceans are in crisis, with more than 40 percent heavily degraded and over three-quarters of fish stocks either overfished or severely depleted.

SOURCE: "WHILE STOCKS LAST," A MARCH 2010 SUMMARY OF RECOMMENDATION BY GREENPEACE FOR CITES (CONVENTION ON INTERNATIONAL TRADE IN ENDANGERED SPECIES OF WILD FLORA AND FAUNA).

done, or that the instinct to create such opportunities is entirely suspect. No, it's just that it is difficult and, with regard to me and my husband, somewhat confused.

The truth is, we only half wanted to move back to the land. As we get older, we notice the limitations of what our bodies can now do. Today I can barely turn my neck. And for my husband—well, not to be disrespectful, but raking the leaves on a city lawn can, if he's in the wrong mood, represent hard labor. So as much as we love the idea of merging fully into rural

THE CANNERY

The distinction between boiling-water canning and pressure canning depends on the temperature. Boiling-water canning requires a water temperature of 212 degrees. Pressure canning requires the water to reach 240 degrees, which can be done only by increasing pressure, hence the name. Most people are a little wary of pressure canning because they've heard stories of pots exploding, but today's pressure canners have release valves, so that pressure cannot build up to the point of explosion. Your pressure canner, not to be confused with a pressure cooker, comes with all the instructions you need. Again, you can take classes from a reliable teacher if you prefer. Just know that low-acid foods (vegetables, meats, fish, soups, stews, and much more) must be pressure canned. The length of time required varies for each item. Canning tuna, for example, takes some time. Between the prepping of the fish and putting it into jars and the heating up, canning, and cooling down of the pressure canner, your efforts will take the better part of a day. But I really like home-canned tuna, so for me, it is well worth my time.

Seasonal changes are the foundations of most of our holidays, though we can barely recognize them as that anymore.

life, we don't have the chops to make it happen, which is why I am grateful that householding is entirely within the scale of our universe. Even in its greatly reduced form, this lifestyle keeps me busy. I think that is why householding is so well-suited to urban life. It is manageable within limits, and it allows for the expression of a range of needs, some of which are related to rural life, some of which lie beyond it. Yes, we must think like farmers and take our cues from the land and the history of natural systems, but we can also get our groovy on, at least occasionally and in moderation. We can engage in the opportunities a city life offers—fine art, food, design, and the expression of urban sensibilities. It's not that rural life offers none of that. Clearly, much art is to be found where it has always been—in the spirits and souls of a people, regardless of place. But city life has a different appeal, which is why coming home was so sweet, despite the raisins having been turned to toast.

Goodness knows, it could have been worse. The raisins could have been dried to oblivion, but really they were just a tad crisp. Sometimes it's a little hard to tell how dry is too dry with fruit. What seems pliable and soft when still warm in the dehydrator hardens a bit on cooling. So maybe that was the problem. Another possibility is that the kids were distracted by other interests. But I had no proof. Besides, how was placing the blame going to change things? Instead, I used the raisins in caponata and turned a bad situation into a great meal. We ate caponata on crackers, or mixed with pasta with a little of the tuna on top. Delicious in every way. And why did I tell you that story? Well, because I wanted to spare you the silliness of imagining that lives (especially mine) and recipes are governed by anything much more than chance. Besides, turning those raisins into celebrities for the "fancy pantry" wouldn't be fair to the other dried fruit in my cupboard. Like the characters in this story, the fruit in my stores grew up on the streets.

THESE FRUITING STREETS

I'm not sure how it is in other cities, but in Portland, Oregon, the practice of urban fruit-gleaning is alive and well. Generally, people are happy to share, since ripe fruit on city pavement is a mess. Gleaned fruit is good not only for eating fresh, for canning, or for making sauce—it's also perfect for drying. I have earmarked my supply for backyard fruitcake, which has become a tradition of sorts. Seasonal changes are the foundations of most of our holidays, though we can barely recognize them as that anymore. What was an honest celebration of the seasons has been co-opted by shopping malls and catalogs. I'm just happy to participate in holiday traditions that are a hell of a lot groovier. Like making backyard fruitcake, and the annual September cider-pressing party on the mountainside where my friend Sarah Deumling lives.

DESPERATELY SEEKING SARAH

I first met Sarah Deumling during a radio show I was hosting. Actually, both Sarah and my mentor Virginia Yoder were on this show, paying tribute to women who were living as householders way before anyone thought to define this lifestyle. Certainly they were not alone. There are probably millions of men and women out there who remember, and still pursue, a life that is in keeping with the notions of householding. Even though householding as I define it (and particularly as it translates to city life) is a modern response to the challenges of our modern world, those who have long practiced the lifestyle need no convincing. I have been lucky to meet many of these folks. In fact, Virginia (who is now in her eighties) continues to be a role model, and if I ever feel punky about the work I have taken on, I visit her farm and pantry to see how it is really done. So it was only logical that I would invite her on the show to talk about "the life," as it were. Sarah is the mother of a friend of mine. Twenty years earlier, together with her husband and young children, Sarah had built the family home on a cleared mountain ridge in the 1,400-acre forest she now managed for sustainable harvesting, habitat restoration, and education. With Sarah's support, her son Ben built a timber-frame mill on the property to supply local builders with sustainably grown and harvested wood. According to friends and family, it is only the latest expression of Sarah's commitment to a world she hopes to preserve. I wanted to know her better.

BRING IT WITH YOU WHEN YOU COME

I have to say, on the day of the radio show, the ladies brought it with them. Virginia expressed the motivation of her lifestyle in terms of a matter-of-fact commitment to raising a family within the rural ethic of 4-H, family, community, and church. It was a life everyone lived, and she took no particular pride in her efforts. This is Virginia's charm—the charm of a culture that understands utility, thrift, and stewardship as a way of life that needs no special recognition. Sarah's lifestyle derives from more politicized thinking (her awareness of the environmental, social, and political consequences of society's inaction), but it is equally rooted in the understanding that is a respectful and ethical way to live on the land.

Both women are committed food preservers and food gardeners, growing nearly their entire annual food supply. In her younger years, Virginia and her now-departed husband, Emerson, raised cattle; they processed one cow each year for their meat, and kept a dairy cow (yes, they drank the milk raw, and, Virginia says, "I don't think I ever knew anyone who got sick"). Virginia still raises chickens and sells eggs to the occasional person who drives along her country road. Rolling a lawnmower to the edge of her driveway, Virginia balances a hand-printed sign on the mower's battered frame that reads, "Eggs for sale—$2.00 a dozen." I have to force her to take more than two dollars from me. She says, "Today they're still two dollars, but tomorrow could be different." Fair enough, Virginia.

I feel blessed to know women like Sarah and Virginia, but I realize there are many more of them out there. We young kids (and here, I mean anyone under sixty) should not imagine ourselves as mavericks; rather, we should look to our elders and absorb their knowledge. Vandana Shiva suggests we glean knowledge from our elders at "the University of Grandmothers." I heard her mention this phrase at a Slow Food Symposium in San Francisco a few years back. It is a fitting and brilliant reference to the knowledge the older generations can offer. We need to talk to our mothers and fathers, talk to our neighbors and the old guy on the street who still keeps the type of garden that would put you to shame. If we are lucky, they will be happy to pass on their knowledge, to share their stories and teach us their trades. And maybe, if you are lucky, you will be invited to a really great party.

SARAH'S WORLD

By luck and the grace of friendship, my husband and I found ourselves in the bucolic setting that is Sarah's world. Amid new friends, old hearts, and the turning colors of autumn, fifty or so of us washed, cut, and pressed some one thousand pounds (at least) of apples. By the end of the day, we had gallons of cider to take home, along with the promise of a new yearly tradition, the one that the Deumling family has observed for the past twenty years. Of course, I couldn't get my own kids to come up to the mountain with me. They are too old now, and it is hard to convince them that they need such down-home conviviality. But I still try. Who would you be if you didn't even try?

Rolling a lawnmower to the edge of her driveway, Virginia balances a hand-printed sign on the mower's battered frame that reads, "Eggs for sale—$2.00 a dozen." I have to force her to take more than two dollars from me.

OCTOBER

Home

Miles

Originally, I was intending to write about turning back indoors at this point, and how, as the year rolls back around to winter, I return to the comforts of four walls and a blanket. But then I realized that all of these chapters on the home have, in one way or another, centered around the family members that reside within it, and I would be remiss to overlook my stepson, particularly since he is so dear.

Every parent loves their child, and I am no different. But as a stepparent, I am always impressed by how deep an affection you can have for a child you did not bear. Many other stepparents will know what I am talking about; it is a lovely thing to discover. After raising my own child in often turbulent circumstances, I was given the chance to help raise another. It is a generous gift to be allowed to raise a child when you are old and wise enough to do it well (and without the stretch marks).

Miles (which is not his real name, because he wanted anonymity—fat chance) was eight when I met him, and ten when his father and I married. According to

I understood how perceiving yourself as awkward or an "outsider" can hobble you, keep you from participating in the world or going where you otherwise could go.

the books I've read, it takes at least five years before most stepfamilies fall into a comfortable relationship. And though I wasn't counting on it happening immediately, before too long Miles and I became friends. He was tentative at first, and always diffident, but in his own way Miles warmed up. In the beginning I think it was resignation; there was no getting rid of me. Later, the draw became the cool factor of my café and the fact that he had the right to go behind the counter to make his after-school snack. He liked the vote of confidence and the feeling of being an insider. At home we would talk (or I would talk and he would listen) about the workings of the world. I told him stories about flowers and how, when the sun is warm, they spread their petals to the sun. I explained that without water or light, without caring and love, no plant can grow strong. I think he understood what I was saying to him, but he was silent as I spoke. We talked about his feeling "abnormal" and how he felt he was different from other kids, how he didn't like hanging out with most kids because he couldn't relate to them. I listened. I worried. I understood how perceiving yourself as awkward or an "outsider" can hobble you, keep you from participating in the world or going where you otherwise could go. And that was something I would not wish on anyone. I had seen how hurt and confusion had silenced others I loved.

In time there were the birthday parties, the sleepovers, and the summer trips with friends. Once I had sold my café, there were the gardens, the talks, and always, always the meals. In the beginning he hated my obsession with family dinners. He hated sitting down. But in the ten-plus years we have known each other, he has come to enjoy them and regularly sets the table. He has endured the books I have given him as gifts ("Don't tell me, it's a book"), and he has patiently listened as I have told him over and over that he can be whatever he dreams. I don't mean to suggest that things were always sunny between us. He was, after all, still a kid, and I was, after all, still on a mission. There were bound to be times when our agendas did not overlap. Like the afternoon he came home from school and I was in the garden.

Perhaps kids, or at least adolescent boys, are prone to indifference. Without a doubt, Miles is more prone than most; he is not given to expansive emotions. So when I asked, semi-rhetorically, "Isn't the garden just so beautiful?" I was surprised by both his answer and my response. "To be honest," he said, "I really don't notice it." I suppose I could have just shrugged off his answer as a normal teenage response, but the dismissiveness in the sentiment was jarring. "Really? I said, "You don't see anything? You can't see the beauty? You don't notice anything in this setting that would translate as lovely?" At that moment, trapped like a spider in a web, Miles understood the consequences of his words. Yes, he knew he was going to get a lecture, but more importantly, he knew that his words had betrayed not only the moment but also himself, because more than any other child I have known, Miles loves the small things.

Dotted throughout our yard are memorials to frogs long gone and trinkets that preserve old memories. When, after closing my café, I found a spoon taped to his wall, I understood that he wanted something to remember it by. When we bought a new couch, Miles grieved for the one that was lost. If you change the room around, he claims he liked it better before. I take it as a sort of sentimentality, the sign of a soft heart and a loyalty to whatever was in his world. And when, as he could do for hours, he swung in the backyard hammock to look at the sky, I knew the boy was dreaming and watching the birds. Attention to detail is not his problem. The boy is witness to it all. That's why I have such hopes for him.

We had a moment that afternoon. What started as a conversation about the natural flora and fauna evolved into a rant. I told him, "There are those who care and look around, and those who cannot be bothered. There are those who act, and those who dismiss the world around them because it is easier not to be involved." I'm not exactly sure why I had to take it there, but I know it was, in part, out of love. Of course, he would not be the first child to have to live under the glare of a parent's unrelenting visions, but I pray he sees it differently. Actually, I know he does.

I don't know if it was because of that fateful afternoon, or our many talks, or reading Michael Pollan's *The Omnivore's Dilemma* (a summer reading assignment) or the workings of his natural personality, but when his friends stopped spending the night because I would make them work in the garden, he did not get angry. He never asked me why I was a freak or why we did not have video games or an entertainment center like his friends had (which might also be why they don't hang out at our house anymore). Not only were such things not my style or his father's style, they were not Miles's style, either. As I mentioned, he feels what is happening to the small things—the flora, the fauna. He knows the price they pay for industry's onslaught. I sometimes wonder how he will sort it out. In truth, I am still the only one who talks about it in our home, but I know he is listening—always, always listening. And when I am out in the garden he offers to help, not because he has to, but because he knows what it is worth. I doubt he'd say it so clearly, and he certainly wouldn't say it to his friends, but I would bet my bottom dollar that he will never forget the gardens, our talks, or the need to witness the beauty in all things great and small. I think I've taught him that much, or perhaps we taught each other.

The Garden

Sowing Garlic and Shallots • Cleaning Up the Garden • Lurching toward Darkness

In September I spoke of cover crops, particularly crimson clover. Its growth creates a tight mound of green foliage with a fine yet densely matted root system. I like to throw these seeds amid my winter crop of collards and kale and see where they sprout. If, for some reason, my winter vegetables bite the dust, at least there is something to keep the soil in place. But clover is for September, while fava beans and field peas are great to plant as cover crops in October.

GETTING A SOIL FIX

Fava beans and Austrian field peas will fix nitrogen in your soil. What exactly does that mean? Through a biological process the foliage of the plant pulls gaseous nitrogen from the air, and beneficial bacteria "fix it" in nodules on the plant's roots. When it comes time to turn the cover crop into the garden bed the following spring, you are "adding" the nitrogen from the plant into the soil. For many gardeners, growing cover crops is one of the most important things you can do to increase soil fertility, particularly in an organic garden. So the way I see it, what could it hurt? I make a point of sowing crimson clover, fava beans, and Austrian field peas and wait to see what sprouts. What I have discovered over the years is that both crimson clover and field peas will stand up to a hard frost, whereas the luscious, near-succulent fava bean will not. I still try planting favas every year, though it is a little heartbreaking to watch the sprightly spring-green shade of fava turn limp and olive-drab. That's what a hard frost will do.

Besides cover crops, October (and even September) is the time to sow your garlic and shallots for next year. Now *that* is cause for celebration. I am endlessly amazed at how easy it is to grow these alliums, and how abundantly they yield. You plant one little clove out of the bulb you harvested earlier in the summer (or from one you buy in October at the nursery), and you get a whole head of garlic the following year. In the case of shallots, one clove will yield a cluster of bulbs—sometimes as many as eight or nine. I cannot fathom why shallots are so darn expensive at the market. Growing them is child's play. The same with garlic, so do not miss the opportunity. You will be proud as punch when you harvest, cure, and, in the case of garlic, braid them in strands to hang in your pantry. Really, it is very easy, and aside from my storage onions and tomatoes I doubt I make more consistent use of anything I grow. What, really, does not benefit from the addition of garlic? It can make a meal from the most meager of ingredients—pasta, olive oil or butter (or both if you are so inclined), and garlic (roasted, sautéed, or fried). Yum. So rejoice when the time comes to plant garlic, because, quite frankly, it is one of the few things in the garden you will be rejoicing about at this time of year.

TOO MUCH OF A GOOD THING

Now, that isn't a good attitude, is it? I know. There are those people who love every last little minute they can spend in the garden. Honestly, I'm not one of them. I am over, over, over working in the garden by the end of October—which means I'm kinda over, over, over it at the beginning of the month, too, if not completely so. This is too bad, since there is lots to be done before I can safely ignore it. I must harvest the last of my tomatoes (or rather, green tomatoes—more on them in our kitchen section), eggplants, and peppers, and also make a last-ditch effort to eat all the lovely salad greens that have obliged me so abundantly again. (When will I learn about moderation?) All through October I am harvesting the spinach and turnips I sowed in August, as well as the celery that has finally amounted to something. Wow, now there's a plant that needs some time. I think I planted starts around May or June and they're getting bushy only now. I can harvest a stalk every now and again as I need to. I think with a little cover they should stand up to the earliest frosts, though I've never tried that before. We'll see. In addition to the last of the summer and early-fall harvests, I am pruning my raspberry canes, gathering up the now decayed runners from my winter squash, and generally cleaning up and straightening all the lingering flower stalks and vegetable growth that have hung around for the last hurrah. All of this goes into my compost pile to undergo its long winter decomposition. We just load it all in and wait to see what good comes of it the following spring, when I need to ladle it onto the beds.

COMPOST HAPPENS

Making (or rather encouraging) compost is a bit of a trick. The professionals can make it seem pretty complicated for us newbies, but I generally ignore most rules in favor of what's easy. I know that might be a bad thing, but I don't care. I just throw in most of my garden waste (excluding diseased plants) and see what comes out. There is certainly tons of information out there about just the right formulas, how and when to mix it, different layers, etc., and maybe one of these years I'll get scientific about it. But for now my general composting process involves two bins; at any given time the contents of one of them is in a more advanced state of decomposition than what's in the other. The one I start in fall is ready in early summer. The one I get going in early summer is ready by fall. That's only a general approximation, but somehow it seems to work.

The crux of the matter is heat. A compost pile with no heat will decompose really slowly, over the course of a full year or two. A compost pile that is hot will break down pretty quickly, sometimes in as little as a month. So heat is the goal, but I don't worry too much about that either. Sometimes the pile is hot and sometimes it's not.

I guess my only rule is that once I deem a bin off-limits for any new garden waste, then it is officially off-limits. I let the family know not to put any more stuff in it, because I'm letting that baby cook. Apart from turning the pile every so often (mixing it with a garden fork) and adding moisture when it gets too dry, we let it be. Somehow this has worked for me, but it is far from a science. I salute you if you are more systematic. Coming up with a formal composting system just hasn't made it to my frontal lobes yet. Besides, like I said, I'm really over it all about now, so it's all I can do to load up the fall compost pile. I know I should take advantage of the remaining sunny days October offers, but sometimes—well, I just don't, at least not as enthusiastically as I should. But then again, I know that the day will come when I wake up and take care of business. As in early spring, when you have to all but hog-tie me to keep me out of my garden, I will awake one October morning and be out like a flash before the sun has fully risen, overalls over my pajamas, to do my garden's bidding. I wait for those days, because experience has taught me that I can get more done in an hour fueled by full-speed conviction than I can in four hours of a drag-my-ass kind of day. I guess we'll call it the miracle of biorhythms.

I AIN'T NOTHING BUT A CHICKEN

I should not be too hard on myself. I think I'm doing what the rest of the natural world is about to do. Like the chickens my friend wrote to me about the other day. She told me her chickens stop laying in October, when the days begin to shorten. She could do what industrial egg farmers do and keep her chickens in a constant state of production by using artificial light, but that would make them little more than egg-laying machines, rather than the lovely little participants in the larger farm ecology that they are. Well, just like the chickens, I'm feeling a little egg-shy. The days are getting shorter, and I don't feeling like producing all that much. I'm getting ready to batten down the hatches, turn inward, and go quiet. At least, I'm getting ready to put the garden to bed and myself into the kitchen. I suppose that makes sense; there seems to be a logical rhythm to the process—sun out, I'm out; sun in, I'm cooking.

Well, just like the chickens, I'm feeling a little egg-shy. The days are getting shorter, and I don't feeling like producing all that much.

OCTOBER

The Kitchen

Green Tomatoes • The Root Cellar • Apples •
Romancing the Squeezo

October is to green tomatoes what September is to red. Whether they're slicers, plum, or cherry varieties, October tomatoes are green in a way that St. Patrick could have only dreamed of. They were once the bane of my existence, but they are slowly finding their place in my kitchen. Were it not for the fact that they come at the end of the season, when I am tired, I would actually like them. It is a kind of tribute to this life that I don't pitch them into the compost as many a less-committed preserver might do.

Green tomatoes can be tasty things. Cut, floured, and fried, they become the stuff of Southern legend. I pile platters high and offer them to the neighbors. Talk about home cooking. Give a Southerner a fried green tomato and you have a friend for life. I also fry and layer them in a casserole between slices of provolone and a white sauce to make a zesty parmigiana of sorts. The white sauce acts as a foil for the tart green tomatoes, and the entire thing is surprisingly good. Frozen to serve later, this casserole has become our happy meal on days when I don't want to cook. At other times, my green tomatoes are made into a sauce with prosciutto, onions, oregano, spices, white wine, and pickled peppers to be ladled, like a pizza sauce, onto a dough topped with goat cheese. Sometimes they are the thing I add to pork and hominy to make a stew. Actually, at this point in my cooking career, they become whatever I can imagine when I squint my eyes. But while green tomatoes are a newfound friend, in October I have other (and generally better) fruits to fry—or to store in the "root cellar," as the case may be.

DOWN TO THE ROOT

A few years back, I started considering varieties of apples that would store well. I had read and spoken to root cellar expert Mike Bubel, who, many years earlier, when living in Pennsylvania with his wife, Nancy, wrote the book *Root Cellaring*. Many of you may be familiar with the book, because it has recently enjoyed a resurgence—and with good reason. In the introduction, written by Mara Cary, I read the following:

> Slowly we are carving a new lifestyle. To some it
> might seem to be one that is looking backward, for it
> cherishes the homely, the rude, the unpackaged, the
> unmechanized, the careful. We do not think of it as
> a blind shutting out of any visions of the future, but
> rather, for us, the right way to face the future. The
> carving is not easy. It is often painful. But in it are
> the seeds of sanity, of joy.

Written during the first (second? third?) wave of the "back to the land" movement, this sentiment embodies a logic that we are moving toward again today. To the extent that we want to apply it, we must find ways to adjust it to the realities of city life—which is exactly why I spoke with Mike, who is now an extension agent in Oregon. I asked him how root cellaring might work in the soggy Pacific Northwest, so I could relate that information to my backyard urban homestead.

The first thing to understand about root cellaring is its underlying logic. It makes use of the natural refrigeration of the earth. In cold, dry regions, root cellaring requires digging a hole in the ground, securing it from seepage, creating a means of access to it, and topping it with a weather-resistant covering. When properly constructed, root cellars offer a dry storage space for fruits and vegetables that do well at underground temperatures and humidity levels. But what makes sense in cold and dry regions makes less sense in the wet and occasionally balmy winters of Oregon. Each area is different, and climate should be considered before you dig. I have heard of folks constructing the most elaborate spaces only to have them flooded during an unusually wet winter. You must make adjustments for the climate of your region, because it will affect which foods can be stored, how they can be stored, and for how long. Some of this I learned the hard way, by experimenting with the fruits of the harvest in my shed.

After speaking with Mike, I understood that those of us west of the Cascades have winters with higher temperatures and moisture levels than those who live east of that mountain range. What might be well suited for storage in eastern Oregon stands a greater chance of sprouting or rotting in the western part of the state. Mike explained that while weather conditions in other regions might not permit winter gardening, ours are well suited to it, and this in many ways removes the need for a root cellar. Hearty greens are perfect choices for a winter garden, as are the brassicas that, if you select the right variety, are often genetically predisposed to make it through the winter. In certain years, root vegetables like carrots, beets, turnips, and parsnips will, if covered properly, survive in the ground through the winter, and even be made sweeter by the freeze. That is the concept behind winter gardening, which is an entirely different practice from root cellaring.

THE BIG CHILL

Root cellaring (or cold storage) is a perfect choice for certain varieties of produce that are not suited to growing in winter gardens. It makes a difference, however, whether you are attempting to store a sweet, moist onion like the Walla Walla or a yellowy, paper-skinned variety like the Copra. The former would rot in storage, while the latter is destined for greatness in soups and stews throughout the year. This is why it is important to read the label with the pack of starts or on the seed packet you buy to know if you are growing a storage variety. With certain vegetables, the difference between ones that store well and ones that don't involves the amount of water or sugar. Walla Wallas are known for their moist, sweet flavor, and should not be stored but eaten fresh. Copras—as I mentioned—are quite different. With other varieties of produce, their ability to store well has to do with when their seasons end. Winter squash, for example, is quite different from summer squash. Winter squash has a hard skin and comes on later in the season than summer squash, which, with its delicate skin and soft interior, is more commonly destined . . . for giving away to neighbors (hence all the knock-and-run zucchini jokes).

Even within the winter squash category, some varieties store better than others. Butternuts and the huge, warty, heirloom varieties of winter squash stand up beautifully to cold storage once they've been cured (curing allows the skin either to dry or to harden—specifics vary according to the crop). Some of the biggest

BENEFITS OF A HEALTHY FOODWEB

A healthy foodweb occurs when the correct ratio of fungi to bacteria, and predator to prey, exists, so that soil pH, structure and nutrient cycling produce the right forms of nutrient, at the right time, for plants to thrive.

SOURCE: SOIL FOODWEB OREGON.
WWW.OREGONFOODWEB.COM

brutes will even allow you to slice them into little sections over time, the surface creating a new, sealing skin over each successive cut. Safely protected from the elements, the rest of the monster squash will wait in good condition until you want more. What a brilliant system for reliable, no-fuss eating. If you do get a little darkening or mold on the outer skin, just cut it off. As long as the entire squash isn't soft and clearly decayed, the firm squash meat can be enjoyed. I would grow those big behemoths in my garden except that, as a rule of thumb, the bigger the squash, the bigger the plant and vine. Anyone who has grown winter squash knows those plants can wander, which is why I smile or shake my head when a new young gardener with a small backyard chooses (or is advised to choose) a big jack-o'-lantern pumpkin. Yes, it will delight the kids, but it will put their parents in shock. Wait until they see the wild growth and the white blooming mold that winter squash can't seem to avoid getting on its leaves way before harvest time. It makes for a Kodak moment, but not the one you might have been dreaming of.

THE CRANKY LADY'S PUMPKIN PATCH

I must admit that for the first year after taking up my concrete driveway (before the laying of the stone pathway that took its place), I turned over a long run of space there to pumpkins. I wanted to see if anything would grow in that sickly soil, so I let the jolly orange brutes be my guinea pigs. I planted two big carving pumpkins (not their true varietal name) and a few sugar pie pumpkins (smaller, for baking). For a while it was a wild, glorious mess out there. But my garden and I could handle it. I had space to spare. I laid down straw around the plants and invited the kids of the neighborhood in. When the time was right, each of them got a pumpkin from the cranky woman who gardens. I did not let the kids pick their own, despite my inclination to let them do so, because, well, those kids can be wild. I have seen some of them hammer the bodies of bees with a croquet mallet just because they thought it was funny, or steal the few fruits off my friends' espaliered fruit trees just for spite. Yes, kids will be kids, but I was taking no chances. Besides, an improperly harvested winter squash (stems must be intact) will rot quickly. Not that those pumpkins were going to the root cellar. I knew I would be seeing the decayed sweethearts (pumpkins, not kids) all over town soon. Pity the poor pumpkin that lives such a short and disrespected life. But then again, I suppose it is happy for the assistance it receives in doing its pumpkin end-of-life job—spreading its seeds all over the place. Let that be the rule then. Next year, when you are carving pumpkins, throw a few seeds to the ground (preferably in your neighbor's yard) in deference to the pumpkin. Like my Irish friends used to do before drinking their beer, spill a little in memory of the dead.

> Pity the poor pumpkin that lives such a short and disrespected life.

THE BLUE CORRAL

Apart from that one year of growing big pumpkins, I buy the biggest of the winter squash for my dry storage supply; the ones I grow myself are a little more manageable in size. This coming year I am going to grow lots of butternut squash in a little fenced-in garden space my husband built. It is very cute. It sits near the garden house and looks like the world's smallest corral. For a while we used to joke that we were keeping the grass in, and we were not always sure we hadn't built a monument to silly city gardening. We painted it a groovy in-vogue blue. You know the color, that muted violet blue that is just a little off from what you were hoping for when you first saw it in the gardening books (yes, I have fallen victim to that faux-vintage cottage-garden aesthetic). My husband built the picket-fence garden corral, complete with a swinging gate; folks made fun of us for it. Of course, none of them were gardeners, so who were they to talk, but nevertheless, until the day I started growing winter squash in there, I did not truly understand its brilliance. Besides keeping the fat cat entirely off its sacred ground, the fence holds the wandering vines in place. If I could do the same with every one of my beds, I would. Wouldn't that be something? Little picket fences with swinging gates around each four-foot-by-eight-foot bed. It sounds a little ridiculous, but the idea is not without merit, given kitty. I suppose I will end up sticking with the kitty defense system I have already described, though. Besides, even if I keep my little wandering darling out of the garden, I have the neighbors' nocturnal prowlers to fend off. It is a hassle—that I must admit. But when Kuddoo comes to bed at night—and she often finds her place between my husband and me—I can't help loving the fatass (as if I'm one to talk).

WINTER FRUIT

Unlike winter squash, fruit stored over winter does not need curing. What it does need is a late ripening date. In our region, apples and pears are the choice for winter storage, though pears are a whole lot fussier. They need a more controlled temperature and moisture level to permit decent ripening once they're removed from cold storage. Remember, pears ripen off the tree. Producers put them in the chill box right after harvest and only pull them out to ship them to market. That's why they're still hard when you buy them at the grocery store and you have to ripen them at home. Those pears could well have come off the tree in August, September, or October but have been held in cold storage containers until needed. Most Oregon pears are shipped overseas in temperature-controlled cargo containers. All this is a long way of saying that pears can be a little fussy to store at home. I've never tried, which seems silly when I think of all the pears I have, but for whatever reason I limit my fruit storage to apples. Today I know how to deal with apples, but it did not start out that way. Oh, no. I had to go through some pretty funny adventures to get to the logic of the thing.

POMMES OF PEDIGREE

It was pretty cool to meet Susan Christopherson, whom I call the Heritage Apple Lady. On a bluff above a now developed cul de sac, we walked the orchards of her Old World Apples. Susan has been growing, or the trees have been bearing, "apples of legend and distinction" for many years. Some are heirloom varieties, while others are fairly new. Some, as the chefs and food enthusiasts suggest, are the traditional kinds used to make the very French tarts of Normandy, while others are just the good old keepers of yore. These were the ones I was after, the keepers. After a bit of conversation and a piece of apple pie, she explained that among the last of her apples to ripen were the Arkansas Black Twig, the Calville Blanc, and the Ashmead Kernel. Like the willing student I am, I ordered some of each of them, to be picked up when harvest time arrived.

My initial plan was to store them in the shed and enjoy them through the winter months, eating them fresh or in pies till April. Part of that plan was to feel pretty darn proud of myself for scoring so precious a booty and having the foresight to plan ahead. But my plan was just a plan. The reality was quite different. I have since learned a lot about apples. With regard to growing them, I wish I had understood the highly disease-prone varieties I have before I planted them. Know this: folks in the business of selling trees will not always tell you what you need to know. Like everything, it behooves you to do a little research. But whereas I know a little more than I used to about growing apples, I know a lot more about storing them, particularly in the Northwest.

YOU HAVE A FRIEND IN REFRIGERATION

To cut to the chase, I will say that refrigerators aren't a bad choice for your storage apples, particularly if you want them to keep. Today I still look out for the late-ripening varieties, but I put them in my fridge, the one I have bought specifically for such things. It is not that I do not store any foods in my shed (or garden house); I do. I keep my long-storing butternut squash, onions, and potatoes there for as long as they will last (generally the issue is quantity rather than quality). But apples are another matter. When buying them in the quantity I do (and that first year I bought a bushel of each variety), I find I don't go through them quickly enough for an outside storage environment to be up to the task. At least not at the temperatures we got during my first year's experiment. Some years, the growing season will be absolutely perfect and deliver apples that will go the distance. But sometimes they may also have been picked too soon or too late, although a layperson may not be able to detect the difference. Harvesters can measure the ripeness of a fruit (this applies to pears, in particular) with a tool that suggests the best time for picking (I suppose old-timers can do this by sight). I am convinced that well-timed harvesting matters, but whether all growers and marketers can afford such specific timing is unclear. More likely, they are bringing fruit to market at *about* the right time, which translates to *about* the right conditions for storage. Unfortunately for me, while everything has a role in successful winter storage, everything is much more than the sum of what I know.

What *is* clear to me is that until I know more, I will not risk storing apples in my shed. My first experiment ended with most of the heritage darlings turning into dark, rotten fruit destined for the compost. Not all of them, mind you, and not without some of them being eaten fresh and baked into the occasional pie, but that experiment was designed to see how long they would last, so I sat back and waited. I did not want to use them up too quickly, in case I lost track of the experiment. Unfortunately, even though I'd hoped for pies in April, by February I was casting apples to the wind, or rather, to the compost. I do not hold it against them. Mike was right. Some things work in the Pacific Northwest, and some things don't. Which is why I think an extra storage refrigerator is not a bad investment. Not everyone will be able to stomach the additional energy usage, which I understand. But with all my storage fruit and the big-vat cooking I do, I could not manage without it. Today, along with my two freezers, I have two fridges: one upstairs for everyday supplies, and one in the basement for the stuff that I store or that is waiting to be stored— not just apples or pears, but everything else that needs more space than my upstairs fridge will allow. Please, let me sing its praises. I love my second fridge.

SECOND TO ONE

It is in my second fridge that I store all the big birds and brine pots for the holidays, and my bottles of raw milk to haul upstairs as needed. It is my second fridge that holds the delicata squash when it is close to losing its staying power in the root cellar and the potatoes that are close to sprouting. It is my second fridge that holds the big pots of applesauce and pear sauce that are waiting to be canned. Having a second fridge is a very good system for me, because whenever a free load of fruit comes my way in late October (or earlier in the season), I turn it into sauce. And one thing is for sure, I love me some applesauce.

A SAUCE FOR ALL SEASONS

I love making applesauce because my family loves eating it. I bake with applesauce and serve it as a side dish with potato pancakes or pork chops. It is a nice companion to most fowl, and, when topped with the creamy uppermost layer of my yogurt, it is nothing short of heaven, a down-home heaven at that. In fact, applesauce takes a prominent role in my Preserving Game Plan. I love making applesauce because it generally costs very little (most of the apples are given to me or gleaned) and requires little or no sweetening or spices—it is good all on its own. It is also so very easy to make. Most times, I just cut the apples in half and throw them in a pot with the barest amount of water. I let them come to a boil and then lower the heat to cook them slowly until they are broken down into a mash. Once it has cooled, I put that mash through my Squeezo—my lovely, lovely Squeezo, the warrior of food mills.

ROMANCING THE SQUEEZO

Included in the box with my Squeezo was an instruction manual. I can't find it now, but I remember being amused by a passage entitled "Romancing the

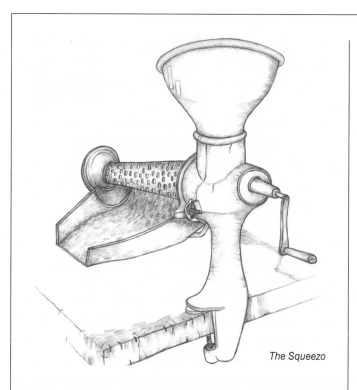

The Squeezo

Squeezo," an ode to the machine. Invented by a man who was inspired by a glut of tomatoes, the Squeezo is nothing more than a really large food mill made to cope with the harvest. It can process the pounds of fruit that would turn me into a babbling idiot if I had to put them through my small conical food mill. Those pretty V-shaped tools with their accompanying wooden mallets are a lovely addition to the everyday cook's kitchen, but for big-vat sauce cooking, I suggest you take a different approach. If you peel and seed your apples ahead of time, of course, you do not need to mess with any mill. A few stabs with the potato masher after the apples have been cooked and you should be good to go. I turn to the Squeezo when I have done nothing more than halve the apples and toss them in a pot. This late in the season, I get lazy like that. I'd rather do the work of putting them through the mill than have to peel and seed them at the start of the project. I guess you just pick your battles. Either way, I end up with many pots of sauce, which is where the second fridge comes in; the sauce can rest in

We of the householding profession do not care about the outer appearance of an apple. We'll leave that for little schoolboys and big-chain grocery stores.

it unattended until I'm ready to can it. I have to admit, however, that not removing the seeds from the apples before you cook them can lead to a slight bitterness in the resulting sauce. You may not always notice it, but it can be annoying. If you are interested in a particular variety of apple, that bitter overtone might offend your purist sensibility. Some varieties are legendary saucing apples, not only because of their taste but also for the way they easily break down when cooked (though any older apple will generally turn to mash quickly). Some, like Gravensteins, are not only great saucing apples; they also come early in the season—in July or August. If you find them in October, it probably means they've been in storage somewhere, and their texture will have started to change. I have made Gravenstein applesauce in October but only because I missed them when they were first ripe and the farmer sold me some from storage for cheap.

Which brings me back to the Preserving Game Plan. It is important (or will be, over time) to know not only what you want to make with your apples (or any produce), but also what varieties you want to make it with. Making applesauce with Gravensteins will be a July affair in the Northwest. If you decide to make applesauce with Kings you can wait until late October, if not later. And don't worry about apples being pretty when you're using them in sauce. We of the householding profession do not care about the outer appearance of an apple. We'll leave that for little schoolboys and big-chain grocery stores. We know that a few spots (even a wormhole or two) will matter very little to the final product. So go for the ones that others refuse. It matters little to the jar.

Certain fruits lend themselves to drying, and apples are one of them. You may peel them or not, dip them in lemon juice to prevent discoloration or not, cut them thick or thin, but one way or another, dried apples are a great addition to the pantry. Just make sure you start

HARRIET'S APPLESAUCE COFFEE CAKE

Preheat oven to 350 degrees.

Grease a 9-inch-square cake pan.

Make streusel topping and set aside:

> 1/3 cup flour
>
> 1/3 cup brown sugar
>
> 3 tablespoons soft butter

Mix together first until thick crumbs form, then add:

> 1/2 teaspoon cinnamon
>
> 1/2–1 cup chopped walnuts (as you like—
>
> you could add other nuts, or oats, or omit entirely)

In another bowl combine:

> 1 cup unbleached white flour
>
> 1 cup white whole-wheat flour
>
> 2 teaspoons baking powder
>
> 1/2 teaspoon baking soda
>
> 1/2 teaspoon salt

In a separate bowl mix together:

> 1 cup applesauce
>
> 1/3 cup buttermilk
>
> 1/4 cup real maple syrup
>
> 2 egg yolks (beaten lightly)
>
> Rind of one lemon

Whip 2 egg whites until stiff.

Mix dry ingredients with wet. Add half the egg whites. Incorporate. Add second half. Do not over-mix.

Pour into greased 9-inch-square pan (1½ inches tall). Top with streusel topping.

Bake in preheated 350-degree oven for 30 minutes. Inside of cake should be dry when a toothpick is inserted.

with apples that are in their prime and not mushy, and if you will be leaving the peel on, always go organic. No one wants to eat the concentrated chemicals that have dried on the surface of a conventional apple skin. Choosing organic fruits and vegetables is a decision I always endorse. It is the one I employ in my gardens. But growing a healthy organic apple takes work. Knowing the varieties that are less prone to disease is very important for organic growers. I was saddened to learn that my own apple varieties are prone to a certain degree of nastiness. As they are still young trees, I cannot yet gauge the full extent of the threat, but I am prepared to go to considerable lengths to keep the darlings unscathed. My friend Glen covers each of his apples with a paper bag early in the season to prevent bugs from laying their eggs on his crop. And it is the eggs that you need to be concerned about, particularly if you are growing your own crop. But we are in the kitchen now, and at the other end of the cycle. We have taken the harvest home to turn it into pots of gold. We can cut away what we must and love what we are given. Besides, we can put apples to a million good uses. Sauced (and spiced in many different ways), dried, baked in a pie, made into butters, turned into cake, eaten with yogurt, layered in parfaits, served as a side dish or eaten fresh throughout the year, the options for using them are endless and endlessly divine. In addition to apples, there is a bounty of fall fruits that can be transferred to your shelves to brighten up your days and meals as only chutney can.

A CHUTNEY FOR ALL SEASONS

Who among even the most occasional preservers has not tried his or her hand at chutney? We turn to it because it is exotic and because it tastes unique. We turn to it because it is forgiving and makes a nice gift.

But honestly, I often turn to chutney because it enables me to use up the last of the harvest in the nick of time. Chutney is the final escape route. It turns the world of excess into something I can eat. I can throw in the last of my green tomatoes, apples, or straggling ripe pears, together with brown sugar, spices, onions, and vinegar (in one combination or another), and make something wonderful out of them. Chutney is technically considered a kind of pickle, because the vinegar is the substantive preserving agent in the process. This is where I tell my students to follow a recipe if they intend to can the chutney, because the exact pH level can make all the difference. Whereas fruits, on their own, may be safely canned in a boiling-water canner, vegetables require a pressure canner. Combining the two ingredients (fruits and vegetables in chutney) changes the pH formula and requires a careful attention to balance, which, for chutney, is controlled by the addition of vinegar in the proper proportion. Vinegar makes it possible to can chutney using a boiling-water bath (as opposed to a pressure canner), but you cannot just rush into canning chutney without a tested recipe—unless, of course, you plan to keep it in the fridge, rather than sealed and stored safely in shelf-stable jars.

I always caution those who are unwilling to follow instructions to turn to something other than chutney for creative expression. It's important to follow a "tested" recipe, one whose combination of vegetables, fruits, sugars, spices and vinegar constitutes a safe mixture for sealing and storing. Don't worry, there are lots of recipes. My own students start with recipes from the *Ball Blue Book® Guide to Preserving*, published annually and available in most canning supply and hardware stores. Those recipes offer a tried-and-true formula for safe canning. Linda Ziedrich's *The Joy of Pickling* is also a good source. By now, though, I have a formula in my head for making chutney. I know which ingredient I can or cannot substitute for another, and otherwise I do as I

> Chutney is the final escape route. It turns the world of excess into something I can eat.

GREEN AND RED
SWEET TOMATO CHUTNEY

Warm a very large saucepan over medium heat. (If you are not canning your recipe, you can add 1 cup canola oil to the pan to fry the seed mixture in.)

Throw in the following spice mixture:

> 2 teaspoons fennel seeds
>
> 2 teaspoons nigella seeds (available at Indian and
>   Middle Eastern groceries)
>
> 2 teaspoons cumin seeds
>
> 2 teaspoons black mustard seeds

When the black mustard seeds start to "pop," add:

> 3 bay leaves
>
> 6 dried red chili pods

After 5 seconds or so add:

> 4 cups chopped green tomatoes (skins on)
>
> 6 cups blanched, skinned, and diced red tomatoes
>
> 1/4 cup apple cider vinegar

Stir and cook for about 10 minutes.

Then add:

> 2 cups brown sugar
>
> 2 cups raisins
>
> 2 teaspoons turmeric
>
> 3 teaspoons salt

Cook for about 20 minutes until the chutney is glazed and fairly thick.

please. But I put in many years of chutney-making first, and I strongly suggest you do as well.

I started making Green and Red Sweet Tomato Chutney (recipe on previous page) some fifteen years ago, back when I was living in Georgia. I made it first for an Indian buffet I was catering and have been making it ever since. We used to serve it in a sandwich at one of my restaurants with sliced turkey and basil leaves and it was very good. Served with turkey at Thanksgiving, I think it makes a nice alternative to cranberry sauce.

In this version, revised from *The Art of Indian Vegetarian Cooking* by Yamuna Devi, it is made with both green and red tomatoes and does not use oil for toasting the spices, as the original recipe instructs. But if I am not planning on canning it, I make it exactly as Ms. Devi suggests, because it is darn tooting good.

A complete list of food preservation rules would require an entire book—as always, I encourage you to do your own research. But there are techniques—like those used in Italy, such as preserving in oil—that are not approved of by our American food preservation standards. I cannot tell you one way or the other what is right for you, especially since I'm somewhat erratic myself about which rules I choose to follow. Remember, I'm the one who makes her own pectin and happily drinks raw milk. My world of food preservation is a mixture of investigation, intuition, and willingness to go a little further than the norm. I am part traditionalist and part rebel. I cannot always decide where, in the long history of traditions and techniques, one system trumped another. Do we have the rules and procedures we have as a result of sound research and safety issues, or do we subscribe to systems because of industry's agenda and the absence of readily available farm-family instruction? I do not know, for example, if boxed pectin has become standard because of industry marketing campaigns or because it really is easier for the busy cook. I suspect, in that case, it's a bit of both.

> My world of food preservation is a mixture of investigation, intuition, and willingness to go a little further than the norm.

I do what makes sense for me, and you should do what makes sense for you. If you don't want to figure it out for yourself, then go the mainstream route. Don't take my word for it, because I don't want the responsibility. This is the message I give my students. I show them the mainstream systems and I explain my own. In the end, your systems should always make sense to you. It will be you, and your family, who eat the fruits of your labor.

So that is October in my householding kitchen. Green tomatoes fried, sauced, and casseroled. Foods cured, stored, and refrigerated. Apples sauced and dried, and the last of the season's bounty turned into chutney. All in all, it is a busy time of year and just a little bit closer to its end. But close does not mean we're there yet. With a few notable additions, November can still be quite a bit of work. Keep the faith. You will be rewarded with a long, quiet winter of good eating, I promise.

GREEN TOMATO SAUCE

Increased to make use of the large quantities of green tomatoes that many folks have on hand at the end of the year, the original version of this recipe—taken from the *Oregonian*, our local daily—called for bacon. It was suggested that this sauce be used as a topping for pizza, but I have used it in lots of different ways. Served in lasagna between layers of mashed butternut squash, pasta, ricotta cheese, and a basic béchamel sauce, it makes for some good eating. Added to a pork and hominy stew, it takes the place of tomatillos. Though I've altered this recipe to suit vegetarian tastes, you can easily throw in some bacon or pancetta as your taste buds instruct; in fact, I encourage it.

DIRECTIONS:

Heat a large sauté pan. Put in ½ cup olive oil and add to it:

> 1 whole bulb of garlic (about 10 cloves, peeled)

Sauté quickly so it does not burn and add:

> 5 pounds diced green tomatoes (skins on)

Mix well and add:

> 1–2 teaspoons crushed red pepper (or more, if you are into it)
> 2-1/2 cups white wine
> 1/2 cup pickled pepperoncini (I use my homemade pickled peppers; you want peppers with a bite, for sure)

Cook all to a nicely reduced, thick sauce. Add salt and pepper to taste.

NOVEMBER

The Home

Repair

Being the child of a Polish Holocaust survivor and his young German bride who met in Frankfurt during the period of post-war "reconstruction," my vision of the world is influenced by particular events in world history. Through the experience of my father, I understand the horror of the concentration camps. Through my mother I know that the Germans, as a people, cannot simply be written off. Most of my relatives on my father's side perished in the camps, but some on my mother's side also died, at the hands of American soldiers roaming the streets of Frankfurt and doing, if we are to be honest, what soldiers will sometimes do—treating the citizens of a defeated country as disposable. During a fight with an American soldier over a *Fräulein*, my mother's beloved cousin was wounded and ultimately died. No one was held responsible. My mother has told me stories of hiding in cellars and bomb shelters as Allied forces destroyed her city. And

If all was well in the world, why did wars and genocide continue? Why were children dying of starvation?

while that city may have needed to be destroyed as a step toward ending the war, its destruction nevertheless led to innocent children having to run for shelter, suffering shell shock, and worse. But then, we all know wars are merciless and have few true winners. Unlike many of my second-generation immigrant friends, whose entirely Jewish background allowed them a certain distance, I could not so easily dismiss anything and everything German. Just as I loved my father, I loved my mother and her extended family, which made it impossible for me to comprehend the notion of absolute good and evil. If I were to take sides, where would I stand, or rather—more deeply—who or what was the enemy? It makes sense that when you are confronted with such huge existential questions, you can spend your life trying to find the answer.

As a child, I was melancholy; some of it no doubt brought on by genetic predisposition, but some by the difficult emotional struggles my parents endured. There was a cloud that hung over our home. It's not that there were no sunny days. There were lots of them, which I attribute to the honor and fortitude of my parents. They gave my brother and me—and each other—love, shelter, and security as best they could. Still, you could not escape the sadness. By the time I was a teenager, I was restless and searching for a new way in the world. My reading leaned toward existential writers and my behavior toward the dysfunctional. I became increasingly reckless and indifferent to the rules. Some of it was typical teenage acting out, but in a specific way, I projected the inconclusive funk of human existence out into the world. It was not only the rules themselves I was bucking, but also the larger assumptions on which those rules were predicated and the way they continued to manifest themselves. If all was well in the world, why did wars and genocide continue? Why were children dying of starvation? Why was there still such social and economic inequality in the world? If, as I believed, there was no absolute good or evil, could there be a clear and absolute enemy? If so, who or what would it be?

My inability to fathom an answer created a deep emotional and moral atrophy in me. What did it matter how I behaved? In fact, in the face of such endless social and political malfeasance, acting badly felt good. I am not being dramatic or disingenuous when I say my foray into hard drugs was a clear and conscious choice. It was the shroud I wore—a rebellious act against the comfortable complacency of middle-class values. If my choices made people uncomfortable, I did not make them without some silent satisfaction and twisted pride. My dysfunction was anything but random, which is why my eldest son's descent was more than a nightmare for me. It was a gut-wrenching sequel and offered, in no small measure, a source of endless self-recrimination regarding my own toxic and indulgent fascination with despair. How could I discount the possibility that I had handed down the same painful legacy of sorrow my parents had given me? Even more frighteningly, had I handed down some vestige of its toxic culture?

They say it takes three generations for the legacy of genocide (or simply the atrocities of war) to work itself free from those who inherit it, and I believe this to be true. I know the history of my parents' lives still plays out in me and that even today I struggle with anything resembling full-on cheerfulness. I know that painful legacies, once recognized and reconciled, can become transformative, while those repressed and denied go toxic. Taken internally or projected out into the world, the poison will be swallowed. Though I have been speaking of a people, the transference of sorrow from

> I know that painful legacies, once recognized and reconciled, can become transformative, while those repressed and denied go toxic.

one generation to the next can happen to a planet as well. Why else would Mother Earth be crying now? Why else would the toxins of her inhabitants be lapping at her shores? Whether she recovers will have everything to do with the stories we pass on to our children. And as I have said, that is the hardest part.

I do not know exactly how all the sorrow of my childhood, my family legacy, the dysfunction of my teenage years, and my life as a mother, wife, business owner, and activist have led to my life as a generalist, but I do know it is all related. I know that somewhere along my death march I decided to lay down my sword, to give up my despair, or, to be more clinical about it, to step away from my second-generation survivor's guilt and toward something a little more aligned with hope. Today, I know (and tell my son over and over) that a fascination with darkness will only bring more darkness, that atrophy is a drag, that success is an inside job, and that pointing fingers alone does not constitute change. I understand that if I want a better world, I have to live as a better citizen. I have to become a better human. But I was lucky. I know there are millions of people like me who, because of circumstance or personal folly, have a painful legacy to endure. Some may be silenced by the burden and not know how to ease it. Some spend a lifetime understanding the sorrow but never knowing how to respond to it. Let me never suggest that happiness and hope is merely a decision. There is hard and then there is *hard*—there but for the grace of God go I. But what I have also learned is that it is not always—or ever—an either/or situation. You are never just all hopeful or all despondent, totally cheery or totally depressed. If anything, my life is more about an effort, a reaching and a gesture toward repair. *Tikkun Olam.*

The Hebrew expression "Tikkun Olam" literally means "to repair the world." Ideologically, it suggests a wholehearted acceptance of the world's brokenness along with our ability to repair it, or at least our ability

> I understand that if I want a better world, I have to live as a better citizen.

to try. It does not point to a particular time or transgression. It does not cast blame. It does not indulge the notion of absolute good or evil. It simply accepts that we live in a broken world and can, or should (if and when we are ready), reach toward its repair. I consider this a reasonable position. Like the sentiment behind the lovely Buddhist saying "Live joyfully in a world of sorrows," Tikkun Olam recognizes the folly of life but never shirks from reaching for the good.

But it must be said that the practice of Tikkun Olam has emerged from a culture and people that make room for cranks like me. They get me. When, and if, I need to get all "What about the Holocaust?" on them, they will not leave the room. Their eyes will not glaze over. They will understand the message that lies there. Furthermore, though I know it can happen in some of the new-age celebrations of the faith, for the most part this leaning toward repair does not include a drum circle. Ram's horn—maybe. Drum circle—not so much. When, and if, it does, I'll take my leave and head to the back forty to smoke cigarettes and stuff with Strider Kowalski and talk about the glory days. Some things never change.

The Garden

Raking Leaves • Prissiness • The Final Reckoning

November is a perfect time for transplanting. Consider this part of the straightening out that this time of the season is all about. Now is the time for you to reevaluate the bare bones of your garden. Do you want to add an extra bed? Do you want to replace any beds? Which perennials do you need to divide?

This process will never stop. After four or five years, your perennial wonders might need a little more space and must be divided to give each clump its own stomping ground. Sometimes, as was the case in my garden, the shade of that little apple tree becomes the shade of a big apple tree and the rhubarb planted beneath it requires a sunnier spot. These are the things you watch for. Moving or repositioning your plants to happier ground is important, and these last few days of early November are the prime time for doing that. Of course, I am writing from a Pacific Northwest garden. In November, the soil here is still workable, still dry enough to move things. I shiver when I think of the early snows of an East Coast or Midwest October. No one's transplanting anything there. So pay attention to the weather. What I can do in my backyard will be different from what you can do in yours.

RAKING IT UP

As in October, the greatest part of my garden activity in November involves battening down the hatches. This is the time when I set my family to raking up leaves, not just in our yard, but in our neighbors' yards, and to bringing the booty home. It is important to recognize fallen leaves as the friends they are. They are perfect in compost piles or on garden beds as protection through the winter. The value of autumn leaves should not be discounted, which is why it is odd, or revealing, to see all those bags of leaves on the side of the street. Most likely they have been raked up by folks who don't have a vegetable garden; otherwise they would have been happy to pile them up somewhere, anywhere, and let them "cook" down in a compost pile into a fine, loamy mulch. It takes a while for a big pile to get all mushy (to use a technical term), but just throwing a few inches of leaves on every one of your beds in fall is a valuable thing to do. For one thing, it will keep rain from washing away soil nutrients and will keep the soil from getting too compacted. It will also provide a lovely lift to your soil in spring when you turn the leaves into the beds. I go out in early spring (March, perhaps) with my garden fork and lightly turn over the soil, ground cover, and leaves.

I don't do it too aggressively, because I don't want to disturb the underground microbes. In spring, the microbes, too, are beginning to stretch their limbs. I just let the loosened mass sit there for a couple of weeks and wait for the soil to dry. By April I might go at it again. Sometimes I just make a little clearing in the middle of the mayhem and plop my starts right there in the midst of it all. But wait a minute, I'm talking spring again and we're in fall. You can see how it all just merges together. One thing leads to another. What you do in fall will be related to what you do in spring. I love that.

LAST CALL FOR COVER

There is still time to sow cover crops; if you didn't sow your favas and field peas in October, do it now—but do it fast. I don't like waiting past the earliest days of November because I want the plants to make a little growth before the world turns chilly. Try it out. Just get them in and see how they work for you. Make a mental note of it, or better yet write it in your journal, so you can track whether an early November sowing worked. November is also the time I start staring at my beds to imagine where I will sow next year's seeds. There is something called a rotation plan that suggests no plant (no plant family, in fact) should be grown in the same bed as it was the year before. The theory has to do with immune systems and the idea that different nutrients are used by different plant families. As plants become adapted to a particular area, so do their natural predators. Plants have their own inbuilt resistance to microbial, viral, and fungal invasions, but after a year or so in the same location, a plant's natural predators will develop ever more powerful strains of funk to overwhelm this defense system, and you don't want that to happen. That's why you practice rotational planting—following one plant or variety of plant with another from a completely different family. You try and confuse the natural system. In theory, by year three, you can bring back the first variety of plant species again and restart the cycle. As for the soil nutrients, each plant wants something special, and if it keeps drinking from the same well, it might drink it dry. Of course, adding a yearly dose of compost and amendments compensates for any nutrient deficiencies, but rotating your plantings provides an added safety measure and is just as good for the garden beds as it is for the plants.

ROUND AND ROUND WE GO

The rotation cycle goes something like this: root vegetables (carrots, beets, turnips, etc.); leaf vegetables (broccoli, spinach, lettuce); fruiting vegetables (eggplant, tomatoes, squash); and then back around. But here's the deal: some folks say it matters and others say, not so much. What are we to think? Generally, I go for the rotation cycle, which is why drawing a map and updating it each season helps. Right there in black and white (or in multiple colors, as is often the case), I see what I grew where. If you are doing it all from memory, with no visual cues to remind you, then you'd better start thinking about next year's plan in November, when you can still remember what was growing there this year. That's what I mean by looking at my beds in November. Even though I have my guide, I start thinking about next year with this year still fresh in my memory. I know, for example, where I will grow my tomatoes next year, and where I will grow more potatoes, if I decide to do so. Actually, it's amazing to me that I start thinking about this at all now, because I always swear, after the hoo-ha of the harvest, that I will never grow another thing again. But give me a few quiet weeks and I'm at it again. It appears that I am a lifer.

> I start thinking about next year with this year still fresh in my memory.

A FAREWELL TO PRISSY

Besides being a time for thinking about what you will grow and where next year (and remember, if you are into it, succession gardening means you can get a couple of cycles out of each of your beds in one season), November is a good time to consider where you might like to build new beds or revive old ones. This too will evolve as you do. My small three-foot-by-three-foot-square raised beds, which sit in the middle of the garden, made sense when I was just starting out, but they seem a little prissy to me now. All that wasted space between the squares is kind of senseless. I have been staring the beds down for the past few years, and I'm thinking pretty soon they will be replaced with one large bed. So that's on my mental list. Whether I ask the husband to whack it out in November or wait till March or April depends on what I want to grow there. Shelling peas like to be in the ground by March; storage onions can wait till May. You can see the logic. You either get your beds built and soil readied in fall for an early-spring planting, or wait to do that until early spring for late-spring or summer plantings.

THE FINAL RECKONING

November is also the time when I make note of what was really successful for me in the garden, what I used up, and what I want to grow more of. It is also when I cross things off my growing list. With a few years of harvests behind you, you learn what works in your garden and what you and your family will really eat. By then you will figure out what is a good use of your space and what it would be better to buy from a farm. By year five this will be almost second nature; all the fretting and learning-curve dramas of the early years will be behind you. You will be able to survey your gardens and think, organically, what, where, and when work needs to be done. And somewhere in the midst of it all, the frantic noise of the unknown will be replaced with the calm of the seasoned backyard gardener. Not that you will ever stop learning, but you will have taken your shots, made your mistakes, and watched, listened, and observed all that is required in the life cycle of a garden. You will slowly and miraculously feel a natural pace and system developing. And only then—at least, this is how it has been for me—can you put all your maps and journals to bed, because by then you will have transferred it all into your mind. You will have successfully taken in each of those many bits and pieces of advice and instruction and woven them together in an action plan that is more second nature than intention. You will still need to consult reference works—to know when and how to prune, or to get help with this or that unwelcome invader—but nothing will be too daunting. You will become one of those in the know, the ones who show up with mud on their boots at the farm store or nursery early in the year to listen to the sweet start-up questions of the newbies. You will smile and you will shudder knowing what lies before them. You will want to speak out and encourage them to go slow, but you know they will not listen. And sometime later in the season you will see them leave with a jack-o'-lantern pumpkin start for their small backyard garden, and you will silently wish them all the best.

Somewhere in the midst of it all, the frantic noise of the unknown will be replaced with the calm of the seasoned backyard gardener.

The Kitchen

Walnuts • Pantry Cooking • Pork •
Holiday Hoo-Ha

November marks the beginning of my pantry cooking. It is when I begin to pull things off the shelf for meals, even though I am still clinging to the last of the fresh harvest. I am loath to use any of my stored goods until the last of the season's fresh bounty has been eaten. If I am a good steward, this will not happen before the beginning of November. Even before then, it is nice to be able to accent our meals with the occasional representative of months gone by (peach cobbler is always a treat once fresh peaches are gone), but in early November I still have plenty to keep me current. I generally have green tomatoes ripening (they will ripen in your home; they just won't be as sweet and juicy as those that ripened on the vine) and plenty of hearty greens, turnips, parsnips, onions, garlic, shallots, potatoes, and winter squash to play with. There are fresh apples and pears, plus the occasional haul of rhubarb and late berries. Which means that my stores of dried, canned, and pickled foods are generally still off-limits to the family. It is too soon. I am still in the packing mode. Eating from the stored bounty will have to wait until later in the month. For now, like it or not, it is still preserving time.

Even though by this time of year I am all too ready to quit, I cannot. I am still in hot pursuit of the season's offerings—walnuts, quince, and the last of the season's apples. Each will be obtained from a farmer and fitted, one way or another, into my pantry. The walnuts will come from the same farmer I buy my peaches from, the quinces come from my neighbor in exchange for whatever good things I make with them— either quince liqueur (*ratafia de coings*) or paste (*dulce de membrillo*)—and whatever apples I find will be put in cold storage in the downstairs fridge. But the most spectacular event in November's kitchen is the arrival, processing, and storage of the annual pig. Holy cow (or pig) if that does not blow my mind.

STATS FOR BACKYARD GARDENERS
Nationwide, 31 million households participated in vegetable gardening in 2009, compared with 24 million households in 2004.

SOURCE: THE NATIONAL GARDENING ASSOCIATION

THE AUDACITY OF DOPES

I am endlessly amazed at my audacity. Who orders a whole pig, from snout to tail, for the freezer? With two and a half freezers (the half being the freezer section of the fridge) already stocked with a half cow, corn, beans, berries, and walnuts, how was I going to make room for the two startlingly enormous pig legs (among other things) I was to receive? How would I turn back fat into lard for baking, or strips for larding and saddling lean (as in grass-fed) beef? How would I turn pork belly into

MEMBRILLO
(QUINCE PASTE)

Preheat oven to 300 degrees. Bake 4 pounds of whole quinces (or whatever you've got) until fork tender. Depending on the variety, that should take 1–2 hours. Baking gives you the benefit of getting the pectin that is in the skins and seeds into your puree. The pectin plays a role in thickening the paste. Remember, quinces are very high in pectin.

Cool, then peel, remove cores, and mash (use a processor, if you like).

Measure quantity, then place in a pot on top of the stove and add an equal quantity of sugar, plus 3 tablespoons lemon juice (more or less, to taste), and enough water to prevent scorching (depending on the consistency of your quinces, anywhere between ½ to 1 cup water).

Bring to a boil slowly, then lower the heat and cook over medium-low heat until very thick. The mixture will turn a deep umber color over time. As when you're making apple butter, you should stir often during cooking to prevent burning. The entire process could take 2–3 hours. The mixture will become very, very thick.

Scoop the mixture into a container to chill. It will congeal into a very thick "brick," which folks usually serve in slices. Membrillo is usually served with a good aged sheep's milk cheese, but if the paste doesn't set entirely I slather it on toast, biscuits, or scones with very good results. I'm sure it would be fabulous on the bottom of a fruit tart, too.

Note: Some people find cooking membrillo in a 200-degree oven for an additional hour or so after the stove-top cooking helps to ensure the end product sets solidly enough to be sliced. If you do this, I would suggest using the container you intend to cool it in, as the hot mixture can be a little tricky to transfer.

bacon or pancetta, jowls into *guanciale*, and pork shoulder and trim into sausages of every kind? How many folks are willing to eat tongue (as I do, sliced on rye bread with mustard) or head cheese? At some point in my life I intend to work through a book on the basics of charcuterie. Some parts of the pig I will deliver to other shops, hoping they will transform the parts that I have neither the space nor the skills to process. Sometimes I get lucky with the results; sometimes not so much. My lovely bone-in hams, for example, were transformed into oversalted, boneless, netted babies. I did not know that would happen when I delivered them to be cured. I was just happy, if the truth be told, to drop them off somewhere, because everything about buying, storing, and curing pig was a mystery to me. It filled me with joy and anxiety, pride and confusion. What the hell was I doing?

I SPIED PIG

I'm not sure if it was the thought of pig that woke me early the day after the pig's arrival, but I was up at 2:30 a.m. Like a kid at Christmas, I jumped out of bed to unravel the mysteries of my big pork present. I opened the seal on my big bag of miscellaneous pork trim (one of the many, many sealed parcels I received), and with a blend of excitement and trepidation, I looked at the contents. Slowly, I removed the parts. *Hmmm, pieces of fat and trim to make sausage*, I thought. Good, that goes in the bowl (I had set a couple out for the process of separation). More fat. Okay, not exactly the makings of leaf lard (the fat surrounding the kidneys that is legendary for its contribution to great pie crust), but it would do. I was not going to toss it out, that was for sure. Chop, chop, chop in little one-inch pieces with a little water in the pot to get it going. Low, low heat so it does not burn. Done. On to the next adventure. Okay, what's this? Eweeeeee, a gnarly pig's ear? Sorry, sorry, sorry. I

Like a kid at Christmas, I jumped out of bed to unravel the mysteries of my big pork present.

know how good you (whoever you may be) think they are, but I'm not doing it. I thought maybe I would give it to my neighbor, but it was a tad chewed up and, well, I just couldn't. Into the waste bucket for the trash. Maybe next year. Now what's this? A tail? I dropped that baby on the counter as quick as I removed it from the bag. I had read some delightful story about a cook who kept a pig's tail by the stove top to grease her pans with. I can tell you, that account is more delightful in theory than in reality. No stinking way I'm keeping a pig's tail by the stove. Yeah, maybe next year, but this year—oh no. Out you go. Next, what's this? Oh goodness gracious, I know, it's the tongue. Now you'd think if the ears and tails were being tossed to the heap, the tongue would definitely follow suit, but I was raised on beef-tongue sandwiches and I thought, if I can just get it in a pot with the pork bones I have for stock, I can cook it up and think about eating it later. So into the pot it went to cook, on a slow simmer, lest it be tough. I have since come to realize I should have brined it first. That would have given the tongue the flavor I was looking for, but only after cooking, cooling, peeling (I'll spare you that part), and tasting—yes, tasting—did I realize the errors of my ways. No problem. I decided to slice it and soak it in saltwater and try it again later in the day. And just in case I got brave enough to eat the entire thing (it's really not that big), I would buy a loaf of rye bread with caraway seeds to layer it on. The mustard was already in the pantry.

The deeper I dug, the more I realized what I had gotten myself into. Not so much in the sheer quantity of it all (my butcher put nothing but the intestines and organs in the waste bucket), but in my commitment to do something with just about all of it (save the ears and tail, that is). Slowly, over the course of the morning, I removed the contents of the trim bag to reveal pieces of this and that. Just as the fat was rendered for lard and the tongue was set to poaching, the scraps of fatty meat found their way to the grinder in hopes of becoming sausage. I chilled the meat so it would grind nicely and not "melt" with the heat of the grinding wheels. About twenty minutes before grinding them, I set the chunks in the freezer. After removing them from the deep chill, I put the pieces, in two separate batches, through the grinder. I chose one grind for the meat and another, coarser grind for the fat. In no more than five minutes I had a nice bowl of ground pork to transform into sausage. And since I was going to eat this sausage at 4:30 in the morning, it would not only be breakfast sausage, it would be very, very early breakfast sausage.

THE HUNGER OF A HEATHEN

I reached for the sage that was drying on a makeshift hook in my office. I tugged on the rubber band that attached the stems of sage to the pushpin I had shoved into the window frame for just that purpose (my system is less than formal). The bundle would not come loose despite my furious tugging, so I climbed up on the desk to remove it. Then came a walk in the rain with my flashlight to locate some marjoram and parsley. With the hunger of a heathen, I pulled up the sprigs in the dark, damp morning and returned to my invention. In went the herbs, the minced onion, the salt and pepper, and the shot of maple syrup that I thought would make it good. Once the ingredients were mixed, I made a patty—a single, solitary patty—and took it over to the cast-iron pan that was heating on the stove. I thought of fishing out the pig's tail to give the pan a light schmear, but I figured the sausage had enough fat. Besides, this pan was seasoned and ready to rock. In went the patty and out came the sound of sizzle; the smell of divine pork filled the air with goodness and me with lust. On to the plate went the sausage, along with a hefty dollop of applesauce I had made the night before. In the still dark and wet November morning I sat at my dining-room table and consumed the object of my desire and a large side of compote. Surely I had found the fabled hog heaven. The patty was coarse but not too coarse, fatty but not greasy, flavorful and fresh as if I knew exactly what I was doing. Was it worth it? Had all the work required to get the pig here paid off? Wolfing down the patty, I would have to say (between bites), you bet!

THE PORK HORIZON

Like everything else connected with householding, there is a lot of work involved in figuring out how to get hold of a whole pig, and what to do with it once you do. Next year's pig leg will hopefully be cured somewhere else. Next year I will have developed a better understanding of what cuts to order, and maybe I'll even try butchering it myself (though I loved my pig butcher). Those aspects of the process might change. What will not change is the farmer from whom I got my pig, because the folks who raised my pig were everything this urban-house-holding, value-added, culinary-obsessed revolutionary could have wanted. And when you find farmers who are aligned with you in the journey and who, amazingly, are willing to do the work required, you have to support them in the hope that they will survive. Because god and farmers know that growing food within any small-scale setup is a hard life from sunup to sundown. It is not like the sometimes-sort-of farming that we in the city are all about (even though that effort creates its own kind of madness); rather, it is a full-on commitment

Continued on page 366

VERY EARLY BREAKFAST SAUSAGE

The recipe that follows is a composite of recipes from Michael Ruhlman and Brian Polcyn's book *Charcuterie: The Craft of Salting, Smoking, and Curing* as well as from *The Joy of Cooking*. Where the former is very specific about using a pork shoulder butt known for its nice fat-to-meat ratio, the latter simply suggests using two parts lean pork to one part diced fat in the grind. I read up a little here and there, then went with my intuition. With regard to charcuterie in general, however, I suggest you take the time to read the basic information. It will serve you well on your future adventures, particularly if you have any intention of putting your pork to work for you throughout the year.

TO PREPARE:

Wake up really early (alternatively, make the patties the night before and wake up at a sensible hour).

Put your pork through the grinder. I use the attachment on my KitchenAid, which the husband bought one year as a holiday gift (happily, householding permits the buying of home appliances as gifts). If you can separate out the pork from the fat, do so, but try to balance the mix. Too lean a mixture will make for a dry patty; too much fat in the mix will make it, well, fatty. My own intuition calls for 1 part fat to 4 parts meat, but most recipes call for more fat than that.

It is recommended that the meat and (especially) the fat be very cold when grinding. Here is the advice from Ruhlman and Polcyn:

> *It's very important to keep your meat as cold as possible during the sausage-making process. Sausage that gets too warm can "break," meaning the fat and the protein will separate from each other when cooked. You can't always see this happen when you're*

making the sausage but it results in a dry, crumbly texture, rather than a smooth, firm juicy bite. Two tips: Don't leave your meat out at room temperature while you ready your ingredients, and always grind the meat and fat into a bowl set in ice.

I don't find this necessary if I am making a small amount, but if you're making large quantities, or making a batch in a hot kitchen, chilling and/or freezing your meat can be a good idea. As suggested, you should "cut the meat and place it in the freezer until it's thoroughly chilled, for several hours, or overnight. Or place it in the freezer for thirty minutes to an hour until it is very cold. The meat can be on the brink of freezing, almost crunchy as it were, but not frozen through. Fat can be frozen."

Grind the fat (if you have access to a little additional fatback, go for it) using a slightly coarser setting than for the pork meat. Some folks suggest cutting the pork by hand into rough dice rather than grinding it. This allows for different textures and "mouthfeel" but is easier to do when you're making hand-shaped patties rather than case sausage. Actually, the breakfast sausage recipes in my charcuterie books usually call for a casing, which I don't normally use. I'm a patty girl.

Put your ground pork meat and fat in a bowl and add spices to taste. *The Joy of Cooking* suggests thyme, coriander, summer savory, sweet marjoram, bay leaf, salt, and fresh pepper for one of its versions. Other sources suggest minced garlic, sage, ginger, and black or white pepper. Here is my best advice: follow your taste buds and use what you have on hand. You can add some rind from a lemon or orange. You can add gratings of an apple and some bread crumbs. You can add a tiny bit of nutmeg or a splash of maple syrup. Want diced onion, shallots, or grated potato? Why not, I say. Just keep notes and see what works for you.

It is sometimes helpful to add a shot of ice water to the mix. The amount will vary according to the amount of meat, but for a 5-pound hunk of pork the suggested amount is 1 cup of ice water. This allows the mixture to blend nicely.

Form the mixture into patties. I make mine fairly thin (¼ inch thick and 3 inches round) and either store them in the fridge overnight, freeze for future use, or cook immediately.

TO COOK:

The general rule is that cooking sausage requires a medium-low heat to prevent the casings from popping or the exterior of the sausage from browning too quickly, before the interior is cooked. When cooking patty sausage the rules are a little less restrictive, but you do want the interior to cook well. I heat my cast-iron pan over a medium-high flame and give it a once-over with a little oil or pig's tail (oh, yeah). When the pan is hot, I throw in the patty and listen to it sizzle. After no more than 5 minutes on either side, I call it good. The rest is up to you. Serve it with a couple of fried eggs, toast, and apple compote on the side, and you'll know why it's all worth it.

to the insane proposition that working with and on the land can offer you a living. So let me say it again: love and support your small-scale, sustainable farmers because they are the future of the world. I truly believe that.

TALKING TURKEY

Now you'd think, given all the work involved in putting up the quinces (quince paste this year), walnuts (we shelled and froze fifty pounds), and pig (at least the trim bag), that I would be ready for a rest. Silly you. Remember, this is November, and every contemporary cook I know is facing off with the same question: to brine or not to brine? Turkey, that is—Thanksgiving turkey. A Red Bourbon turkey, to be specific. I have to admit that somewhere in this process I begin to feel a little, well, precious. Even I can feel a little overwhelmed by my capacity to separate out the good from the good-ish. Did it matter that I was getting a Red Bourbon turkey at a price few would be willing to pay? Certainly, I understand the importance of raising heritage breeds in an effort to resist the rise of varieties that are bred for one quality or another at the expense of the animal's well-being. Take, for example, those poor big-breasted chickens. Bred to be the buxom babes of Silicon Valley, these girls can barely walk anymore. Talk about back problems. Today's industrial chickens have been selectively hybridized to give Hugh Hefner what he wants—big boobs on a small body. So I get it: heritage breeds are important, and every year I get the Red Bourbon, and every year I brine it, cook it, and add it to the rest of the Thanksgiving feast.

Precious or not, Thanksgiving is my favorite holiday. I can haul out the bounty from my pantry, from the garden, and from my stores, and that connection to the harvest makes this holiday a little less surreal for me than for most folks. Others—most Americans, in fact—approach this day with the madness of sailors lost at sea.

SWIMMING IN A SEA OF SILLY

There's something frantic about preparing for Thanksgiving. Considering this year's recipes, what to order, what to buy, how to set the table, whom to invite, and what to wear can be exhausting. Honestly, though, once you start living as a householder, the focus of your concerns will shift to something less influenced by magazine layouts. Thanksgiving in Householderland is about hauling out the goods from the pantry and paying tribute to the harvest. Not by continuing the oddly nuanced traditions of store-bought pumpkin pie, canned cranberry jelly, and Uncle Aldo's famous Waldorf salad, but in recognition that none of it—not the meal, not the family, not even the roof over our heads—would be there if we did not care for the soil. It was from the soil, the healthy fertile soil, that the foods and opportunities sprang forth for those who came to this land such a long time ago. Only if we remember our responsibility to take care of the soil can we experience the full measure of thankfulness this harvest holiday offers. But even with that understanding—in fact, especially with that understanding—it is not necessary to go overboard. A return to the true foundations of the holiday, to the virtues of common sense and stewardship, will spare you all the hoo-ha of the season.

Today's industrial chickens have been selectively hybridized to give Hugh Hefner what he wants—big boobs on a small body.

HOLIDAY HOO-HA

I think a lot about the fussing around Thanksgiving—why we have gotten so far away from the simple act of cooking what we have, with silent blessings and thanks. Why we do not just *cook*—not in the spectacular fashion of celebrity chefs and fancy recipes—but in our own quiet moments, in our own simple kitchens, and with our own skilled and experienced hands. Why do we resort to a slavish dedication to one ingredient and

November is a great time to give thanks for the work that is behind you (if you are a farmer or householder) and for the peace and joy of the season ahead.

recipe or another (this can apply just as much to the local and sustainable crew, present company included), rather than something that would be a little easier to manage. In the end, what matters is not how well you can follow a recipe, or how many fancy cookbooks you reference, but how inclined you are to cook from the available bounty in the first place. My advice on this matter is to take it easy. Set a simple table and cook a simple meal. Roast a squash and cook some cranberries and a flat-chested chicken if that is more in line with your budget. Then give blessings for the soil and the amazing way it continues to supply our needs, despite our tendency to neglect it. If you can do that honestly, I'm sure your meal will taste great.

These are the promises of a November kitchen. It is the beginning of serious pantry cooking and the start of a holiday season that can lead you to a deeper understanding of what gratitude means. Watch out for your own twisted mythology—it can be subtly influential and weighted with the silliest of notions. November is a great time to give thanks for the work that is behind you (if you are a farmer or householder) and for the peace and joy of the season ahead. Like Thanksgiving, Christmas, Chanukah, Kwanzaa, and the Solstice invite quietness and appreciation. If you are inclined toward traditions, keep them simple and keep them real. Keep them linked to the soil, since everything springs from it. Giving gifts from the pantry is a great thing to do, because they, too, are of and from the earth. My personal favorite is the backyard fruitcake I make each year. It is a creation born of the gleaned fruits of the season and the politics of the movement.

DECEMBER

DECEMBER

The Home

Copenhagen • The Power of "Out There"

I t is December 14, 2009, and I have been watching a report by Amy Goodman on *Democracy Now* about COP15, the UN Climate Change Conference in the Bella Center in Copenhagen, Denmark, and the convergence outside the meeting. Though the official work of this conference is taking place inside the Bella Center, between heads of state and nongovernmental agencies, I am moved by the one hundred thousand people who have come from all over the world to march in the streets and demand greater action on climate change by their governments. Or, in the words of a young activist representing African American communities in New York, action "for systems change, not climate change." Nothing, these activists say, will happen in the Bella Center. They have been closed out, and the negotiations have been reduced to horse trading among insiders, as vested interests do what they have always done—serve the interests of industry over the needs of the environment. The protesters are out there, a heroic mass movement, and it strikes me as odd, after all my talk about being "in here," to realize how important it is to be "out there," on the streets, committing one-self to protest, to action, and to lending a voice to those who are rarely heard. That is what Bill McKibben was saying during the march: "Give the people the armies that they lack." Vandana Shiva was saying: "This is not about charity, but about justice." And Desmond Tutu was saying: "Look in the eyes of your grandchildren." As I watch this broadcast, I know I am witnessing an important moment in history, and it makes me think about where I should go, now that it is increasingly clear that our leaders will not listen to what the people are trying to say.

I used to think that once our children were grown (or at least capable of looking after themselves), my husband and I would move to a community that has not yet been completely dominated by industry. Despite my commitment to place (have I not spoken about it enough?), we might try to find a new place a little more suited to the type of agricultural traditions we lean toward. But now I wonder if we will not all become climate refugees of one kind or another, leaving our homes not only to find a different way of living, or because they have become uninhabitable, but also to engage in protest. Now I believe our move will take me (and more and more, my husband, too) not far from the madding crowd (or not exclusively so), but toward it. Toward the battle that will ensue. We will be in good company. What I saw and heard from the voices of the one hundred thousand who had gathered in the street outside COP15, and from the many other voices of pro-test worldwide, is that they will not give up, and I believe them. This will be a fight. While those of us still sitting

Of the more than 7,600 breeds in FAO's Global Databank for Farm Animal Genetic Resources, 190 are considered "at risk" of extinction.

SOURCE: "FARM ANIMAL BIODIVERSITY." PUBLISHED BY THE FOOD AND AGRICULTRUE ORGANIZIATION OF THE UNITED STATES, SEPTEMBER 2006.

Everything I know about the history, motives, and language of empire suggests that the captains of industry will not change willingly.

in the safety of our homes may express despair and frustration, even come up with small solutions, when it is our land, culture, and family that are dying (as is the case for so many in indigenous communities and for the disregarded citizens of "developing" nations), well, I think we'll start fighting too.

As convinced as I am that by living as householders we can offer the movement a certain allegiance in terms of values—we can live thriftily, and be careful stewards of the resources we've been given; we can live in a way that respects the responsibility that comes with privilege—we need not stop there. It need not be an either/or existence. Just as we are needed "in here," we are needed "out there." Everything I know about the history, motives, and language of empire suggests that the captains of industry will not change willingly. This will be a historic movement, a movement of survival and justice. This is a movement that needs the armies for those who would be otherwise ignored. Which is to say, as "they" become "us," the streets will be full.

A DECADE IN MY MAKING

As synchronicity would have it, this past November was the ten-year anniversary of the protest against the World Trade Organization in Seattle. That protest was the one that turned my world around. It was, as I have mentioned, one of the elements of the change that led to me adopting a householding life in here. It was when I became aware of the connection between my personal life and the subtext of this American life, this industrial life, the life we have all inherited, for good or bad. It was when I came face to face with how the small, unexamined assumptions of my own life were connected to the conditions of the world around me. That was the first time I thought about water and seeds and how the roots of civilization are being privatized. That was my moment of cognitive dissonance, when what I had assumed was my world shifted on its axis. And for the past ten years I have been working on making the connections between the parable of my modern, leisure-loving, post-industrial, über-technological, cranky consumer mind to the story of empire in an effort to construct a narrative that is both instructional and healing. And now, ten years later, it is December, and we are at COP15, and the world is turning again. Who can say what the next decade will look like? But one thing I believe is that there will be no going back to the status quo. Mother Earth will make sure of that.

THE RIGHTS OF MOTHER EARTH

Following the disastrous failure of the COP15 Conference on Climate Change, activists and indigenous people from around the world gathered on April 22 in Cochabamba, Bolivia, for the World People's Conference on Climate Change and the Rights of Mother Earth to discuss the future of the environmental movement. Following a week of events, a proposal for the Universal Declaration of the Rights of Mother Earth was enacted. This is its preamble:

We, the peoples and nations of Earth:

considering that we are all part of Mother Earth, an indivisible, living community of interrelated and interdependent beings with a common destiny;

gratefully acknowledging that Mother Earth is the source of life, nourishment and learning and provides everything we need to live well;

recognizing that the capitalist system and all forms of depredation, exploitation, abuse and contamination have caused great destruction, degradation and disruption of Mother Earth, putting life as we know it today at risk through phenomena such as climate change;

convinced that in an interdependent living community it is not possible to recognize the rights of only human beings without causing an imbalance within Mother Earth;

affirming that to guarantee human rights it is necessary to recognize and defend the rights of Mother Earth and all beings in her and that there are existing cultures, practices and laws that do so;

conscious of the urgency of taking decisive, collective action to transform structures and systems that cause climate change and other threats to Mother Earth;

proclaim this Universal Declaration of the Rights of Mother Earth, and call on the General Assembly of the United Nation to adopt it, as a common standard of achievement for all peoples and all nations of the world, and to the end that every individual and institution takes responsibility for promoting through teaching, education, and consciousness raising, respect for the rights recognized in this Declaration and ensure through prompt and progressive measures and mechanisms, national and international, their universal and effective recognition and observance among all peoples and States in the world.

To read the declaration in its entirety go to pwccc.wordpress.com.

The Garden

Best-Laid Plans • Fancy Talk • Potato Mind

Even when we have done our work, planted our cover crops, laid down our leaf mulch, and shielded our winter crops, nature can strike a blow. Every so often, and without warning, you may find all your good work, or most of it, undone. For me, it was a two-week cold snap that defied the normal pattern of a Pacific Northwest winter. Temperatures dipped into the single digits, and much of what we had hoped to eat from the winter garden went limp in the freeze.

During the first two days of the freeze, I waited it out. I thought, rightly, that the greens and turnips, the carrots and rutabaga would only get sweeter from the cold. By the third day, I realized the frost was a serious threat, and I started digging up the root vegetables and harvesting the greens in the hope of salvaging what I could. I approached the effort as if I were wading through my deep chest freezers, knowing that if I allowed all these now-frozen vegetables to thaw, they would turn to mush. Over the next few days I sautéed all the greens, turned the winter squash and pumpkins into a million pies and casseroles, and, with the help of a few beef bones, turned the carrots, turnips, and rutabaga into many soups and stews.

The sprouted fava beans that were standing strong before the frost gave up the ghost; I was happy to have planted the crimson clover and field peas because they made it through the frost. Next year I will plant all three in each bed as additional insurance. Next year I will be a little more aggressive, knowing that when it comes to setting your beds right for the winter, it is not enough to choose cover crops or leaf mulch. In the case of fava beans, it will be added insurance in leaves *and* cover crops for me.

My garlic and shallots appear to have survived, but a friend suggested they might produce smaller bulbs as a result of having to send out a new set of shoots. Evidently, when the emerging stalks of the garlic bulb take a hit from the freeze, the roots go into shock. Like upstretched arms, those young shoots are all the bulbs have to keep them going. At least they will recover in time, even if it is with reduced vigor and size. I can take that. It was the possibility of losing the whole crop that made me worry.

The garden perennials—the canes, bushes, trees, and herbs—had already shut down for the season. They knew something was afoot and had prepared. Regional perennials are accustomed to the occasional extremes of nature, which is why some folks have taken to growing only native plants. Natives have survived in the same place from one year, decade, and century to the next. They understand a place as only long-time residents do. Mine must have felt the freeze coming and shut up shop in preparation. It will be interesting to see how they emerge in the spring.

In dealing with this attack on my best-laid plans, I was reminded once again of how much more there always is to learn. Being a city slicker, I am able to take this mishap philosophically—I can always go to the greengrocer. But that is not the way to think about it, I now understand. What I experienced during those two frigid weeks is the very thing that makes food preservation such an important tool. When the conditions of the season turn against you, you do not want to be looking at an empty larder. During this unexpected freeze, I was reminded again of who runs the show.

Throughout history, humankind has known it was necessary to put food aside for the hard years. We understood that there will be both fat years and lean years and made adjustments to cope with the inevitable. But it's also the case that when we lived on the land and were familiar with our rural environs, we had a better idea of when bad weather was coming. We knew, for example, that when the birds flew south earlier in the year or the bark on trees grew thicker, the winter would be colder or a freeze was on its way. We knew that insects appearing early or late was a message from the natural world—if only we knew how to read it. We knew by cloud formations and ebbing seas that something was afoot, something that, if we planned for it, we could survive. As a city slicker I marvel at stories of indigenous people who can detect the coming of a tsunami by the look of the ocean around them, and head for high ground long before the flood. I am intrigued by the way farmers can look at the earth's natural vegetation (shrubs or grasses, for example) and understand that pushing it beyond its natural threshold will lead only to trouble. I am reminded of who are the true environmentalists (if that is the word) and wonder why we are so late inviting them to the table.

We are starting to take our lead from small rural farmers and indigenous cultures again, but it is a recent development. Mostly, we have relied on technology and academia to tell us what must be done. We became scientists and specialists, professionals and experts, even though there were always people who were already

We are starting to take our lead from small rural farmers and indigenous cultures again, but it is a recent development. Mostly, we have relied on technology and academia to tell us what must be done.

> Slowly, we are remembering what we have forgotten, which is that only those who are immediately connected to the conditions of the earth learn to read its signs.

experts. We city slickers turned a deaf ear to those experts. Slowly, we are returning to them. Slowly, we are remembering what we have forgotten, which is that only those who are immediately connected to the conditions of the earth learn to read its signs. Only when we are required to survive by its good graces, without the aid of industry and far-flung markets, will we be true stewards and environmentalists. All the rest is just fancy talk.

Honestly, most of the stuff I am writing is fancy talk. I am so much the novice that it is almost embarrassing to be saying anything at all, but there it is. I am writing precisely because I am a novice. Precisely because I have forgotten. Precisely because I know how much I need to learn and because, fitfully, I am learning. This is not an effort of theory alone, but of application. This is not so much the investigation of soil as it appears under a microscope, but a yearning for the moment when I can taste it and know what it is lacking. If I am trying my hand at any of this, it is because I am in love with the teeming fecundity of the world, and I want to live side by side with it. Not, perhaps, as the rural farmer does, but at least as a city slicker who has come to recognize how far she's strayed from the real world. This life is a return to potato mind. Ms. Potato Head with a beret. Why not? Maybe it is the best of all possible worlds.

DECEMBER

The Kitchen

Peas • Luck • Fruitcake • The Future

There have been two times in my life when my cooking has led to a tradition—not creating a new one, but adopting one that was already there. The first happened in late December many years ago and was precipitated by a hankering for black-eyed peas and greens. There was no good reason to crave them; I had grown up in the north. What did a New York Jew know of greens, peas, and ham hocks? Not much, so I opened *The Joy of Cooking*. Page 287, Hoppin' John: "Eaten on New Year's Day, this dish is supposed to bring good luck." Funny, I was reading that on the last day of the year. I took it as an omen. I decided to soak some peas.

For twenty-five years now, I have cooked Hoppin' John on New Year's Day. Whether for big extravaganzas or a quiet gathering of friends, it has become a tradition. The luck part? Well, after moving to the deep South, I learned there was some controversy as to what part of that meal was supposed to bring luck, according to legend. Some said it was the peas, and some said the greens. Some said it was sheer good luck to have anything to eat in the first place, which made sense to me. Gratitude seems to have a surefire connection to luck; it makes what you have into what you love, or at least into something you appreciate—a good policy on New Year's Day, or on any day, for that matter.

The second time, things took a less direct route. I had been thinking about the mess we are in, about the economy, how it works and how it doesn't. I was thinking about equity and wondering how we would ever right the world. I was sitting in my backyard scribbling down my thoughts when the pear dropped. It dropped from the huge old tree in our backyard. It dropped like all the other pears had dropped over the years, one after the other, over and over until each one had found its resting place and fed the frantic orgy of fruit flies lured by the sweet-sour fragrance of rotting fruit, vinegar, and neglect. Oh, we had made use of one or two of those pears in the past, but not many more than that. We ignored them as much as possible. Even though they created a stench, we weren't up for harvesting them. Which is why I wondered, as I sat there writing, how I had taken it all for granted. Why I imagined that solutions started anywhere other than in our own backyards. Which, as it turned out, started the epiphany that started the gleaning that became the spirit behind—and contributed the dried fruit to—my traditional backyard fruitcake.

Throughout the months that followed, I went around picking the neglected fruit of the neighborhood. I found apples to dry in rings and Italian plums to turn into prunes. That year we harvested the backyard pears to dry and store in buckets. When November came around, I cut them into little pieces to mix up for a cake. I thought about Truman Capote and his story "A Christmas Memory," which was first published in *Mademoiselle* in 1956. The story is set in the 1930s, and opens in the kitchen of a rambling house in a small rural town. An elderly woman stands at the kitchen window and proclaims, "It's fruitcake weather!" This delights her seven-year-old cousin and best friend, Buddy, who narrates the tale. Together they collect pecans from a neighbor's orchard to crack by firelight. Together they bake loaves for the people who have been kind to them through the year. It is an endearing tale, and I love the idea of knowing, by the chill in the air, that the time has come for fruitcake.

I too chop nuts—walnuts that we buy from a farmer. I add more than the recipe calls for. It was a good year. Baked in muffin trays, these little cakes emerge from the oven fragrant and dense. Cooled, each cake is wrapped in a piece of cheesecloth soaked with quince-flavored liqueur (traditionally called *ratafia*). I repeat the dousing every few weeks, and by Christmas they are stewed. Now ready to be eaten, each one is wrapped in brown paper cut from grocery sacks and tied off with a ribbon, then the husband and I drop them off on friends' and neighbors' doorsteps. It is lovely that something as mocked as Christmas fruitcake can be snatched from the clutches of a debased holiday tradition and emerge as something perfectly right for the season, steeped in its logic and lusciousness.

What I now know is that preserving fruitcake in liquor will allow it to be stored for years. Like wines, cured meats, or aged cheese, it will keep and be transmuted over time. And when it is made well, with ingredients that are neither green nor Rudolph red, with local fruits that were taken to heart, nuts from the farmer you have supported for years, and quince-infused brandy you made the year before, fruitcake becomes something good enough to share with friends, family, and neighbors.

BACKYARD FRUITCAKE

You already know the story behind this cake, so I will get on with the recipe. It is adapted from one I found in the *King Arthur Flour 200th Anniversary Cookbook*. I like those folks and their cookbook for the down-home and no-frills instructions they offer regarding ingredients and variations. They take a lot of the mystery out of baking, which I appreciate deeply.

As the recipe informs us, "this cake is of the 'light' variety, but light in color only, for it is very dense and meant to be eaten in very thin slices." I concur. Fruitcakes are best when eaten in moderation. I appreciate this recipe's omission of such strong flavors as clove and molasses. I have further moderated the intensity of flavor for which this kind of cake is known by using my own backyard dried fruit in place of the candied fruit called for in the original recipe. That was the point of making this cake in the first place. Form followed function.

As for the alcohol you use, whether rum or brandy or your own fruit-infused vodka (I used my quince *ratafia*), the results are more or less the same. Alcohol was originally used primarily as a way to preserve this cake for extended storage, but my use of it in my traditional holiday fruitcake baking is more about taste than preservation. I have been tempted to set aside one of my small cakes for a year to see how it will fare, but I never make it that far. Either I have too many friends on my gift-giving list, or I can't control myself—the cakes are all gone after one or two months in storage.

LIGHT OLD-FASHIONED FRUITCAKE

4 cups unbleached all-purpose flour
(they suggest King Arthur's flour, as you would expect)

1/2 teaspoon baking powder

1 teaspoon nutmeg

1-1/2 teaspoons cinnamon

1-1/2 teaspoons salt

4 cups (1-1/2 pounds) pecan halves (I use walnuts, because, well, you know)

5 cups mixed dried fruit from the neighborhood, chopped to raisin size (I use dried pears, apples, nectarines, prunes, and raisins, with most of the fruit coming from my backyard)

1 cup (2 sticks or 1/2 pound) butter

2-1/2 cups sugar

6 large eggs

3 tablespoons brandy or rum (or whatever you have around), plus more for the maturing period

Preheat oven to 275 degrees.

In a very large mixing bowl, mix together the flour, baking powder, spices, and salt. Add the nuts and fruit, mixing until they are well coated.

In a second bowl, cream the butter until it is light. Add the sugar, a ¼ cup at a time, beating until the mixture is light and lemon-colored. Add the eggs, one at a time, beating the mixture thoroughly after each addition until it is fluffy. Blend in the brandy or rum.

Stir the wet ingredients into the dry and mix until they are combined.

Lightly grease a 10-inch tube pan, two 9-by-5-inch loaf pans, four 1-pound coffee cans (the wide short kind), or 2 dozen muffin tins (my approach). Fill two-thirds full and bake for about 2½ hours (tube pan or loaf pan), 2 hours (the coffee can), or 45 minutes to 1 hour (the muffin tins).

As soon as you remove the cakes from the oven, sprinkle the brandy or rum over them. After it has soaked in, remove the cakes from their pans and let them cool completely.

Wrap the cakes in muslin or cheesecloth and then aluminum foil. I just load them into my big plastic bucket. Either way, store them in a cool place to mature. Every few days during the maturing period, sprinkle a few drops of alcohol over them. The alcohol will evaporate and leave only flavor. I brush the liquor directly onto the cheesecloth with a pastry brush. I do this once a week or so, since taking out all those little muffins is a drag and their smaller size means they don't require such frequent dosing.

After a month or two of stewing them, I wrap them up in strips of brown paper bags, place one on each of my neighbors' doorsteps, knock on the door, and run. If they don't give me something in return, I take their name off the list for next year (just kidding—not).

HARRIET'S UPSIDE-DOWN PEAR GINGERBREAD CAKE

I have been making this cake for our New Year's Day celebration for some five years now. Sometimes I use fresh ginger, sometimes crystallized, and sometimes ground. For a real blast you can use all three, but go slow—you know how ginger can creep up on you. The pears come from the old pear tree, of course, and I can them specifically for this tradition. There have been years in which I've made over ten cakes to serve our guests. It's not necessary to wait for a holiday, since this is a very nice way to use your canned fruit at any time of the year. Actually, upside-down cake can go through myriad transformations. You can use your favorite butter cake batter, with or without the traditional gingerbread ingredients, and pour it in a pan that has as its base glazed peaches in place of pears. In fact, I'm going to do just that, since I have a lot of peaches in the pantry as well. With a few pecans sprinkled on the bottom (soon to be top) along with the peaches, I think there's some good eating in store for us.

PREPARING THE PAN:

In a 10- to 12-inch round baking pan (or whatever you have—excess batter will do well in a muffin pan) melt ¼ cup butter with ½ cup brown sugar. If you are using the 12-inch pan, you can add a little more butter. I have also added a shot of maple syrup, which makes the whole thing a little "juicier." You can either melt this in the oven or put it on top of the stove on low to melt and mix.

Once the butter has melted and the sugars are as well distributed as possible, I layer my canned and sliced pears in a circular pattern in the pan. Sometimes I am precise, other times not so much. I tend to use up two pint jars of my pears in the process. Don't worry if the pears feel a little mushy. It will work. If you like, you can stud the top with slices of crystallized ginger or whatever nuts you have on hand. Be inventive. When this is done, set it aside and mix your batter.

Preheat oven to 350 degrees.

MAKE THE CAKE:

Mix together dry ingredients:

> 2 cups flour
> 1-1/2 teaspoons baking soda
> 1/2 teaspoon salt
> 2 teaspoons ground ginger
> 1/2 teaspoon cloves
> 2 teaspoons cinnamon

In a separate bowl mix together:

> 3/4 cup molasses (not blackstrap, it is a bit too powerful in flavor)
> 1 cup boiling water

Let cool a little (maybe 5 minutes).

While molasses mixture is cooling, cream together in a mixer:

> 1/2 cup butter
> 1/2 cup brown sugar

Add:

> 2 whole eggs, one at a time, mixing well between additions

Now add in the dry ingredients, alternating with the molasses mixture—
flour, molasses, flour, molasses, and flour.
I like to do it that way, but you can do
just three additions instead of five.
Just start and end with flour.

Pour this mixture into your pan. If you have any leftover mixture, you can cook it in little muffin trays at the same time as the cake. Just pull them out after 20 to 30 minutes. Remember to grease the muffin tins.

Bake cake for approximately 50 to 60 minutes, depending on the size of your pan and the amount of batter it holds. I generally start checking it after 45 minutes, just to be on the safe side.

Even though the base will be moist, the cake should not be. Test it with a toothpick. You know the drill. The toothpick should come out dry. If I start worrying that the sides are baking too much I lightly tent my cake with foil. Actually, I do that with lots of cakes. Anytime I think the sides are cooking too much but the center needs another 5 to 10 minutes, I tent it.

Once you've removed the cake from the oven, let it cool for about 5 to 10 minutes. It will already have begun to pull away from the sides and you will see the butter puddling slightly at the sides. Happy days. Now for the leap of faith—invert that baby onto a plate! Be bold and fearless. If some of the pears stick, just scrape them out of the pan and put them back on top of the cake. It will be fine. What you will have is a lovely, fragrant, moist cake to enjoy.

This cake freezes well and also holds up fresh for a couple of days, if you can keep it around that long. I would just let it cool for at least an hour before slicing, and if you have some on hand, serve with a bit of crème fraîche. La di da.

We, as residents of the planet, still have time to rethink what would make for a true and just economy. We still have time to learn how to manage our households and resources with care.

EARTH'S GRACE

I don't know if it was the black-eyed peas or the fruit-cake that has given me gratitude, but I have found it. I have found gratitude for the soil and the epiphany that all things start there. For the wind and the rain, for the sun and the cool dark nights of winter. Today I have such an immense respect for the earth's grace that I am humbled and ashamed to think of how poorly we have treated it. Even today we do not understand how deeply the history of migrations, displacements, hunger, and longing is connected to our continuing and brutal disregard for the soil. Even today we do not understand what our future will be. This is not the history of a particular people, or a particular tribe, or a specific moment in time. This is the history of us all. Removed from the natural world over time, and convinced of the urban promise, we have all lurched toward and longed for the future that industry was to bring. We were not villains, we were not greedy, we were not fickle. More often than not, we made good use of whatever small and helpful advancements human history offered. But at some point—I am not exactly sure when—we forgot what we should never have forgotten. Somewhere along the line we became deaf to the warnings indigenous cultures are still trying to give us. We forgot there is a balance, and that if we are to survive, we must return our attention to the soil, the seas, the wind, and the rain—or else nothing, absolutely nothing, will save us.

Though we keep turning to them for answers, I do not believe that industry, technology, government regulation, education, or new jobs will be the things to provide them. And it will not be protest, revolution, or the upending of the status quo (at least not exclusively) that solves our problems. I think the solution will come in large measure from the small, grass-roots efforts of individuals. It will come from challenging the odd history we have all inherited and the way the greed of the market has defined prosperity, success, and "the good life." Remember, this is our household, the earth household.

We, as residents of the planet, still have time to rethink what would make for a true and just economy. We still have time to learn how to manage our households and resources with care. We still have time to power down, to rework the assumptions behind our personal goals. And when we can do all that, then, and only then, can we point a sharp and determined finger at "them," whoever they are, and say: we expect better—much, much better. Then, and only then, can we tell them that their refusal to listen to us is no longer an option.

At least, that's when it will happen for me. First by my own efforts, and then beyond. I will effect change

EARTH HOUSEHOLD

The term "Earth Household" simply suggests that we are one with the world. I first heard it mentioned by Fritjof Capra, a physicist who writes, teaches, and speaks about the importance of our cultural unity with the workings of the universe. A founding director of Berkeley's Center for Ecoliteracy and author of the best-selling books *The Tao of Physics* and *The Web of Life*, Capra is best known for his work in systems thinking, a theory that assumes that no one aspect of the physical world can be understood as separate from its environment. Systems thinking offers a way to consider the function and dysfunction of our world. It offers an explanation for why some systems fail, why some systems are contrived, and why some system designers imagine erroneously that their efforts will succeed even when they ignore the workings of the universe.

just like Wendell Berry promised: I began it in myself and in my household as soon as I was ready, by becoming answerable to at least some of my own needs, by acquiring skills and tools, by learning what my real needs are, by refusing what is merely glamorous and frivolous. When I learn to act on my best hopes, I validate them as no government or public policy ever will. And by my actions it becomes more likely that other people will do the same.

INDEX

ACKNOWLEDGMENTS

No idea is new; we just come across them at different times. Among those who led the way to this book, I want to thank, first and foremost, Amy Goodman. I have watched the reports on *Democracy Now* religiously for many years and I can only say . . . thank you, you're one boss babe. The world owes you a great deal of gratitude for reporting the news as if it mattered. And Juan, well, you're pretty suave yourself. In that vein, let me also thank Maude Barlow, Vandana Shiva, Bill McKibben, Evo Morales, Michael Pollan, Naomi Klein, Michael Moore, and the late, great Howard Zinn. All of you have become folk heroes and touchstones to reality for me.

On the local level, thanks to my gardening friend Glen Andresen, who not only had the heart to read over the first draft of the gardening section but who also taught me most of what I know about growing food. Others whose efforts have inspired me are Deb Lippoldt from Growing Gardens, Kim McDodge at Ariadne Gardens, Virginia Yoder, Sarah Deumling, Marge Braker, and Myo Consuelo DeMayo (the Italian one). All of you have been friends and role models.

To every person anywhere who has the heart and spirit to care for the soil, seeds, air, water, and creatures of the earth—thank you. Without a doubt, a mass movement is underfoot. Let those who might underestimate its power think better of it.

To the people at Tin House, thanks for listening to me ramble, for being good friends, and for publishing this book. What a leap of faith.

On the home front, much, much love to "the husband." Thanks for being a devil's advocate and reminding me that it is not always best to preach to the choir. Though you may have questioned the effort, you have never questioned my heart or art. At least you get to eat well.

To my son Wyatt, I love you up to heaven and back. That's forever! Thanks for putting your handiwork to my book and for teaching me how to look backward and forward with humility and hope. And if I have not said it enough, believe in the unbelievable; it allows for the miracles that will yet come. To "Miles," thanks for being one of the grooviest kids I've ever met. I have been blessed to have you in my life. And to all the children whom, in one incarnation or another, I have had in my world, know I think of you all with great fondness.

To my mom and dad I owe the greatest gratitude. Both of them have made me what I am, have taught me, confounded me, and impressed me with the willingness to make sense of no sense. I could not love you more deeply. To my brother for being a few years further along the path, for bringing me potato chips when I wouldn't stop bawling, for suffering the toy pistol whipping I delivered, for having the same two parents, and for keeping track of my ups and downs and even, sometimes, understanding them.

Finally, thanks to Wendell. You have been a clear voice and source of sanity in the world. You have broken down old paradigms and replaced them, lyrically and honestly, with new ones. You are a wisdom keeper. The pages of your books are dog-eared and worn. God love ya.